THE OTHER SIDE OF OREGON

THE OTHER SIDE OF OREGON

by

Ralph Friedman

For Annelisa —

a fellow traveler —

Ralph Friedman

The CAXTON PRINTERS, Ltd.
Caldwell, Idaho
1993

Library of Congress Cataloging-in-Publication Data

Friedman, Ralph.
    The other side of Oregon / by Ralph Friedman.
        p.   cm.
    ISBN 0–87004–352–8 : $11.95
    1. Oregon--History--Anecdotes.   I. Title.
  F876.6.F725   1992
979.5--dc20   92–19731
                                                      CIP

Cover by Kathleen Petersen

Lithographed and bound in the United States of America by
The CAXTON PRINTERS, Ltd.
Caldwell, ID 83605
155016

To Phoebe and Kya

Contents

List of Illustrations

THE OTHER SIDE OF OREGON

Hello Again

Every time a narrative book of mine is published, I am asked if I have not run out of stories on Oregon. The truth is that today I have more to tell than I did before my first book of stories.

Every time I take a trip somewhere in the state I come up with more stories. Readers—I should call them friends—have provided me with more story material than I have given them.

There must be a hundred, or a thousand, old timers in Oregon who have penned tales of their experiences and imagination. There are people like Wilmer Wheeler of Central Point, a timber faller for forty-three years before he bought a gold mine and began working it. In 1985 he advised me that he had written "near a hundred stories and poems over the years" and wondered where he could get them published.

It is a shame that Oregon historical societies and colleges have done so little to encourage the Wilmer Wheelers of the state and that so few resources exist to publish their material, at least as folklore. Sometimes I feel like putting aside my own work to anthologize these writings, but that endeavor belongs to an institution with more muscle than I have.

Everywhere I look, there are people I know I must put into print. One is surely Vera Wagner, who grew up in the sagebrush loneliness of Harney County, where her home-steading mother was the first postmaster (or mistress) of

Wagontire. Mrs. Wagner knew firsthand all the legendary characters out on those surrealistic cubist plains and she has written me some choice tales of their character and adventures.

Roberta Sandy Symons was working behind the counter at a cafe in Southern California when a fresh-faced sailor boy from Jefferson County came in to ask for a milkshake. One smile led to another, the two were married, and the sailor took his bride back to Ashwood, where for decades Sandy Symons ran the store, post office, rock shop, and first aid station, while for years attending with encouragement and love to her diabetic husband. After he died, Sandy carried on alone until she hitched up in matrimony with a sagebrush man she had long known.

One of the most remarkable—and modest—of Oregonians I have known is Sue Morelli of Wasco County. I met her long after her husband, Joe, who had made Shaniko a vivid re-creation of its glory days, was confined to a wheelchair, his back having been broken in a throw from a startled horse. Sue operated the historic Shaniko Hotel, almost all whose tenants were poor, elderly, feeble men. Sue cared for them as cook, nurse, supply clerk, laundress, transportation corps, and friend. In addition, she managed the hotel dining room for tourists as chief cook and bottle washer. As though that were not enough, she was head nurse at the Madras Hospital. And—have I forgotten to say? She was a mother to lovely daughters, ran the gift and book shop at the hotel, and gave succor to all the weary and troubled who came her way.

Joe died after years of failing health. Sue had to close the hotel because she lacked the money to bring it up to fire standards. I wondered what she would do. The answer came in a letter from her a few years after Joe's death. "A cowboy came riding into town and took me off with him." So she became a ranch wife and maybe found time to read (she already had a fantastic knowledge for someone who seemed to be busy twenty hours a day) and to explore some of her world.

Three people in Southern Oregon come readily to mind when I think of stories to write. One was Clarice Nye, a tireless botanist who lived all her life near Prospect, gathering wild flower plants and seeds to grace the great gardens of the varied continents. Another is Ruth Pefferly, whose column, "My Cup of Tea" in the *Illinois Valley News*, captured the rhapsody and rhythm of her backcountry folks. The third is Charlie Skeeters, also of Prospect, a miner, logger, and son of the earth, who climbed the thousand hills of his Rogue River looking for the next view ahead.

I must not close this rustic *dramatis personae* without listing boldly the incredible Vivian Staender, the Thoreau of Wildhaven. Living alone in a stone house she and her husband handbuilt, without electricity, telephone, or plumbing (let alone such a contemporary necessity as television), Mrs. Staender is sister to a porcupine, probation officer to the local wood rats, cousin to all the animals that dwell among the junipers, guardian of trees already ancient when Columbus invaded America, singer with birds, rhymer with the winds, woman gentle, persevering and gifted with almost connate inquisitiveness.

When Vivian and her husband were in their physical prime they spent portions of their lives in the almost absolute pristine Brooks Range of Alaska, on one occasion alone for a year, with the nearest human population an Eskimo village six hundred miles away, and starting with no shelter.

She was well into middle age when, bent and weakened, she climbed Three-Fingered Jack and spent the night on the highest pinnacle, reading until darkness faded the print. Having no road to her house, she piles the groceries she has purchased in town into a wheelbarrow and pushes it a quarter of a mile up a sloping trace.

The first time I saw her she grinned, "Everybody who comes here gives me a hug." I did. My kind of human.

For many years I've written about old timers. This has given me the dubious reputation as "people's historian of Oregon." My obituary will probably begin, "Ralph Friedman, Oregon old timer . . ." I wish that maybe some backcountry weekly would add: "He loved the common folks of Oregon and of the United States and of the whole wide world and the trees and the water and the earth and the animals." And if there is space for one more line: "He never met a good-hearted imaginative liar he didn't enjoy."

The Fabulous Trail

"From this river," wrote the pioneer woman, Mrs. Frizzell, who crossed the plains in 1852, "is time reconed & it matters not how far you have come, this is the point to which they all refer, for the question is never, when did you leave home? but, when did you leave the Mississouri River?"

A starting point of the Oregon Trail at Arrow Rock, Independence, Missouri.

Courtesy State of Missouri

From half a dozen points along the Missouri, the best-known being Independence, the wagon trains rolled west on the Oregon Trail. In the eastern plains the "trail" was sometimes forty miles wide, but as the sky grew big and the country wild the route narrowed. Rivers could be forded only at certain points, and when harsh mountain ranges were reached the wagons had to be agonizingly drawn up sharp hills one at a time, and just as agonizingly lowered down the steep slopes, also one at a time, and all by windlass, or similar technique. It was rugged work.

The caravans started in the spring, in the season of torrential downpours. Along with nocturnal rains came electric storms which panicked the stock and stiff winds that blew down tents and scattered equipment over the Kansas prairie. If some of the men and women who a few months before had cried "Westward Ho!" within the comforts of their homes were now having second thoughts, they could scarcely be blamed. For many, the start was not gentle.

Precious few of the emigrants had any caravan experience. Most of them brought too much of the wrong things. Within a few hundred miles they were beginning to strew the land with excess baggage. A large general store could have been started every twenty miles with what was discarded.

Most emigrants did not prepare well, and when it came to rearranging things a good many found they had been taken by the sharp merchants in the jump-off towns. The outfitters had no need to go to Oregon, or to California, to find wealth. They got theirs before the wagons started rolling beyond the Missouri.

Edwin Bryant, whose *What I Saw in California* was published in New York a year before the Gold Rush, wrote of the first night out on the trail: "Our provisions and cooking utensils, in the haste of departure, had been packed in the wagon without much regard for convenience, in case we should be obliged to make use of them; and we were consequently compelled to remove heavy boxes and trunks before arriving at our meal, flour and bacon, and pots and dishes for our kitchen table. Upon careful inspection we moreover found that sundry pots, skillets and frying pans we had specially ordered and paid for, were wanting."

For approximately the first forty miles, the Oregon Trail and the Santa Fe Trail were one. Somewhere near Gardner, Kansas the road split. Hiram Martin Chittenden wrote in his classic *American Fur Trade of the Far West,* "The Santa Fe Trail being the first established, a sign board was later set up to show where the Oregon Trail turned off. It bore the simple legend 'Road to Oregon.' . . . Surely so unostentatious a sign never before nor since announced so long a journey."

The first views of the broad, undulating prairie, whose rich black earth was garmented by lush grasses and swarms of wildflowers, thrilled the newcomers. David Jackson Staples, who went on to California in 1849, called the land east of the trail forks "the most beautiful country man ever beheld."

Later, of course, when the Trail became a highway, the immediate landscape lost much of its loveliness. The appetites of stock, the imprints of hooves, feet and wheels, the droppings of humans and stock, the scars of campfires, the discarded litter and the very impact of thousands of people and animals upon the country soon turned a virgin world into a dusty and unaesthetic stream of commerce.

Even a blind man, crossing the plains road, would have recognized it. If he did not stumble across the deep ruts—in many places there were at least several parallel tracks—his ears and nostrils would have told him where he was. For in the months of travel the Trail was seldom lonely for very long.

Jim Bridger, the famous Mountain Man, was not one to be shaken easily, but in 1859, while Jim was guiding a US

Army captain just arrived from the east, Old Gabe was so startled he couldn't believe his ears. The captain actually asked if there was any possibility of crossing the Oregon Trail without seeing it!

Indians who saw the Trail for the first time were amazed. The Jesuit mission builder, Father Pierre-Jean De Smet, probably the most famous of the "black robes" in Pacific Northwest history, and one of the ablest and most comprehensive chroniclers of the early Trail period, described the reactions of Indians he accompanied from their quiet settlements to bustling Fort Laramie in 1851.

"Our Indian companions," he wrote, "who had never seen but the narrow hunting-paths by which they transport themselves and their lodges, were filled with admiration on seeing this noble highway, which is as smooth as a barn floor swept by the winds, and not a blade of grass can shoot up on it on account of the continual passing. They conceived a high idea of the countless *White Nation* as they express it. They fancied that all had gone over that road, and that an immense void must exist in the land of the rising sun. Their countenances testified evident incredulity when I told them that their exit was in nowise perceived in the *land of the whites*. They styled the route the *Great Medicine Road of the Whites*."

Yet, for all its commerce, the Trail could fill the early emigrants, who came from settlements and from farms where neighbors were close and towns not too far off, with a terrible sense of isolation. "Even in Siberia," observed Chittenden, "there are occasional settlements along the route, but on the Oregon Trail in 1843, the traveler saw no evidence of civilized habitation except four trading posts, between Independence and Fort Vancouver." Within a decade, however, the "noble highway" was so choked with traffic that some travelers complained of claustrophobia.

Chittenden had a good eye for roads; he was a captain of

the Corps of Engineers. He also had a fine sense of history. He put them together to write: "Considering the fact that it originated with the spontaneous use of travelers; that no transit ever located a foot of it; that no level established its grades; that no engineer sought out the fords or built any bridges or surveyed the mountain passes; that there was no grading to speak of nor any attempt at metalling the road-bed; and the general quality of this two thousand miles of highway will seem most extraordinary . . . Before the prairies became too dry, the natural turf formed the best roadway for horses to travel on that has probably ever been known. It was amply hard to sustain traffic, yet soft enough to be easier to the feet than even the most perfect asphalt pavement. Over such roads, winding ribbon-like through the verdant prairies, amid the profusion of spring flowers, with grass so plentiful that the animals reveled in its abundance, and game everywhere greeted the hunter's rifle, and finally, with pure water in the streams, the traveler sped his way with a feeling of joy and exhilaration. But not so when the prairies became dry and parched, the road filled with stifling dust, the stream-beds mere dry ravines; or carrying only alkaline water which could not be used, the game all gone to more hospitable sections, and the summer sun pouring down with torrid intensity. It was then that the Trail became a highway of desolation, strewn with abandoned property, the skeletons of horses, mules, and oxen, and, alas! too often, with freshly-made mounds and head-boards that told the pitiful tale of sufferings too great to be endured. If the Trail was the scene of romance, adventure, pleasure, and excitement, so it was marked in every mile of its course by human misery, tragedy, and death."

The average American's mind-picture of the Oregon Trail is of a Conestoga wagon being pulled by oxen with a dog trailing behind or trotting alongside across the plains and mountains.

Actually, most wagons were not Conestogas, relatively few emigrants being able to afford the large, heavy, broad-wheeled vehicles built in southeastern Pennsylvania's Lancaster County, about sixty miles from Philadelphia.

Nor were oxen the dominant draw animals or dogs that sturdy. Horses and mules were as numerous as oxen and those dogs that survived generally wound up as wagon passengers.

An overview of the performance of Trail animals made in 1852 by John Hawkins Clark reflected the feelings of most emigrants:

"Good horses, good mules and good oxen are everything on a journey like this. Job in his day, immortalized the horse and clothed his neck with thunder; but he was silent on the mule, and for what reason I am unable to say. If he had made this journey and had used the mule as a motive power, he would no doubt have done him justice and left to succeeding generations his testimony of the mule's virtues. For our part we love the patient and hardy animal; their ears do not seem half so long as they did at the commencement of the journey. In every way they appear more endurable . . . Oxen are very reliable, patient and enduring . . . but they are more liable to get lame than either the horse or the mule. They will drink the poisonous water at every opportunity, and many of them are lost in that way, but with good watching they will make the trip. One would think a dog would make the journey very easily, but of the thousands who made the attempt very few succeeded in getting through. Those who had valuable ones let them ride. I know of no dog that made the entire trip on foot."

Those who took to the Trail in 1849, the year of the California Gold Rush, were only six years behind the first wagon caravan to reach the Far West. Until 1843 only a few wagons, three or four, perhaps, had reached Fort Hall, where they were left behind.

Eighteen forty-three was the year of the "Great Migration." Approximately one thousand people crossed the continent. They brought with them more than 100 wagons, almost 800 head of loose cattle, and just about 700 oxen. That year decisively proved the feasability of overland wagon transportation to the Oregon Country. Into the dawn of the twentieth century would the Oregon Trail—at least parts of it—still be in use.

Eighty miles from Independence the wagon trains crossed the Kansas River. By 1849 a ferry was here, which must have been a bonanza for its operators. In low water and light traffic the charge was a dollar per wagon; at high water and heavy traffic the fare was five times as much. If the water were high and the traffic light, a balance was struck. Animals were taken across at ten cents a head but generally the stock swam over.

The next fording was at Vieux Crossing, on the Big Vermillion. Here a Pottawatomie chief, Louis Vieux, sold supplies to the caravans. His men also helped the emigrants repair their wagons, which took a battering in the rough fording. Other Pottawatomies built bridges across the badly gouged prairie creeks and charged toll. The emigrants, enraged by what they considered an exorbitant levy, called the Indians crooks and swindlers. None of the whites seemed to see the irony in the situation.

Vieux Crossing was also a monument of sadness and a grim warning to those who followed the Oregon Trail after 1849, for in the green spring of that year a caravan buried almost fifty of its members, victims of Asiatic cholera, near the banks of the Vermillion. Those who came later must have shuddered when they saw the many gravestones, each marked with name and date.

Yet, as severe as the hardship of travel was on many, it proved to be the elixir for some. An example is the story told by eighty-five-year-old Sol Durbin in 1914, whose family had been with the Meek Cutoff Party of 1845.

Historic marker near the Vermillion River crossing, in early part of the Oregon Trail.

Courtesy State of Kansas

"In 1843 we went to Clinton City, Missouri," Durbin recalled. "My mother's health was very poor and father thought that a change of climate would help her. Mother's health did not improve, so we decided to go out to Oregon, where we heard the climate was very healthful. When we started from Missouri for Oregon mother was so poorly she had to be helped into the wagon. We did not expect her to live. She got strong and hearty coming across the plains and she spent nearly half a century here in Oregon. She lived to be ninety-three years old."

The Big Blue River was forded at Independence Crossing. Sometimes rafts had to be built, which meant a delay of several days. But the emigrants had no complaint here, near lovely Alcove Springs. While the men worked, the children played, the women washed and mended, the stock grazed leisurely. Fishing was sometimes quite good, couples walked soft-eyed or hot-eyed among the trees, meals were more carefully prepared, the air was sweet, and in the evenings joyful singing, usually religious, flooded the prairie. If a fiddler was along, there might be dancing.

Not everyone left the Big Blue in high spirits. Some did not leave at all. One was seventy-year-old Sarah Keyes, the mother-in-law of James F. Reed. Warned by her doctor in Illinois that she had not long to live, she insisted upon

James F Reed of the Donner Party carved his name and the date on a rock below the Alcove at Alcove Springs.

Courtesy State of Kansas

traveling West, to meet her only son, whom she thought was bound east from Oregon, at Fort Hall. She never made it, passing away May 30, 1846.

Her son-in-law's name is itself attached to harrowed legend, the Donner-Reed Party, better known as the Donner Party, which was snowbound on the eastern slope of the Sierra and suffered extreme deprivation and heavy casualties before being rescued.

Not all who began the Great Adventure saw it through. Some—a good many in the bad years—died. Others turned back, most of them before the Rockies were reached, a depressing number before a good start had been made. John Hawkins Clark, one of the more astute overland chroniclers, recorded the sad returning of those he met.

On May 10, 1852, he noted in his journal: "Met a young man with two small children returning to the states; said he had buried his wife and one child just beyond. We felt for the poor fellow as he every now and then turned his look toward the wilderness where lay his beloved ones, over whose graves the wild wolves would make night hideous with their dreadful howls as they struggled with one another for choice seats at the feast of human flesh."

Two days later Clark wrote: "Met some wagons returning to the states. The people with them looked tired and jaded, and had lost some of their number by smallpox. They said this was a hard road to travel and tried to induce us to return with them."

The following day, May 13, Clark penned an even bleaker picture: "Passed the grave of an immigrant, just buried, the wife and children still lingering over the new made grave, the company with which they were traveling having moved on. A more desolate looking group than that mother and her five children presented would be hard to find. An open, bleak prairie, the cold wind howling overhead, bearing with it the mournful tones of that deserted woman; a new made grave, a woman and three children sitting near by; a girl of fourteen summers walking round and round in a circle, wringing her hands and calling upon her dead parent; a boy of twelve sitting upon the wagon tongue, sobbing aloud; a strange man placing a rude headboard at the head of the grave; the oxen feeding near by, and the picture as I saw it was complete. We stopped to look upon the scene and asked the woman if we could be of any service. 'I need nothing,' she replied, 'but advice—where I shall pursue my journey or go back to my old home in Illinois.' We could advise nothing; the journey onward was a long one and it was something of a journey back, with no home when she got back. We passed on, but not without looking back many times upon a scene hard to forget."

A day later, on the bank of the Nemaha River, Clark observed: "There are many camps on the banks of this river; many are sick, some dead and great numbers discouraged. I think a great many returned from this point . . ."

Little more than a week later the humanistic Clark, who had embarked upon the long journey with the thought that cooperation, kindness, and love would mark the Trail, was shocked to find violence among the emigrants: "Passed the grave of a man found murdered. How strange that man will commit murder at all, and still stranger when he does it in a desolate country where there is so much need of aid and comfort from one to another."

The daily lack of cooperation Clark experienced prompted him to bitterly pen: "A word to all who expect to cross these plains: never get into trouble with the expectation of getting help; carry nothing but what is absolutely necessary, and mind your own business. There is but little sympathy for anyone on this road, no matter what may be his condition. Everyone thinks he has trouble enough and conducts himself accordingly. However, if one is stuck in the mud and there is no way of getting around, over or under, he may get a lift at the wheel, but then be cursed for having a weak team or for overloading or maybe bad driving."

As the Oregon Trail years passed the emigrants encountered travelers who had actually made it to Oregon, actually lived there, and were returning to "the states," some to bring back their families, others having given up on their dream. For the disillusioned, Oregon was too wet, too sickly, too hungry, too wild, too inhospitable, too damn hard to make a living, they explained, and exhorted the comers to return east with them. Now and then a wagon train halted to debate the matter, so moved were they by the tales of the experienced, and a few of the timid were turned around. But the westward army, cleansed of its deserters, moved inexorably on.

The trek through the Little Blue Valley was ordinarily delightful and the trail up the Little Blue River, though it ran through Pawnee country—which made some of the men itch for a fight but gave most of them the shudders—was normally not marked by hardship or grief, except when there was heavy rain or cholera.

Near the head of the Little Blue the emigrants turned northwest for the Platte River, rolling over low hills built of drifting sands by sweeping winds. Within a few years these hills had a name in emigrant lexicon: Coasts of the Platte.

Now, for most people, the land lost its charm. JT Kerns observed in his diary in 1852, that the sandhill country wasn't worth "three cents to the 100 square miles."

The Trail passed Fort Kearny, ground up the Platte, traversed the lean tongue of land lying between the South and North Forks of the Platte, followed the north bank of the South Fork, and then veered northwest to reach the North Fork of the Platte.

Already the buffalo, the deer and the antelope had almost disappeared from this region. Timber thinned out beyond the wooded dell of Ash Hollow, where the Trail first

Looking north on the Oregon Trail toward Ash Hollow. Just to the left of the highway at the bottom of the picture is the ridge with Oregon Trail ruts running north to the crest of Windlass Hill. Ash Hollow extends on north out of the top of the picture, lying mostly to the right of the highway, which splits this photograph.

Courtesy State of Nebraska

touched the North Fork. But to reach Ash Hollow the wagons had to descend Windlass Hill, the steepest mound the comers had yet encountered. It was a good training ground for future descents.

Now the journey settled down to drudgery, but no one could ever be sure what might happen. The oddest spectacles presented themselves. Enoch Conyers, who settled down to a good, long life in Oregon after his arrival in 1852, remarked in his diary: "We observe a spendid coach in which is seated four richly dressed young women, and a young man handling the lines. One of the young ladies was making music on an accordian, and another was playing a guitar; all were singing as they trotted by, gay as larks." Yes, trail life on the Platte had its light moments but was constantly sobered by death. In their journals, emigrant after emigrant noted the graves observed along the river.

The first of the great landmarks on the Platte was Court House Rock, so named because, to the early explorers and later to the emigrants, the wind-worn monolith, sprawled on an elevation, did look like a courthouse, especially from a distance. A smaller rock, at one side, came to be called Jail

Jail House and Court House Rock, near Bridgeport, Nebraska, were the first imposing landmarks seen by the caravaners in their trek along the Oregon and Mormon trails.

Courtesy State of Nebraska

House because, so went the reasoning, a jail house is always next to a courthouse.

From Independence the wagons had traveled 555 miles, more than one-fourth the distance to Oregon. Sixteen miles farther the emigrants were facing Chimney Rock, which Chittenden described as "a cylindrical tower of rock rising from the top of a conical hill" and which a perhaps more imaginative observer, in 1850, saw as a "big sweet potatoe hill with a pile of rocks on top."

Two or three days later, depending upon the speed of the particular train, the early emigrants surmounted Robidoux Pass, from whose summit they could see Laramie Peak, which some mistook for the Rocky Mountains, and reached

Oregon Trail ruts near Scotts Bluff in western Nebraska.
Courtesy State of Nebraska

Scotts Bluff, another prominent landmark and prominently mentioned in all Trail guides.

The pass was away from the river. In 1851 a shorter route, adhering to the Platte, was blazed through Mitchell's Pass.

Scotts Bluff earned its name and its legend from a fur trader who fell seriously ill while returning East in 1828 in a party commanded by WL Sublette. Two men were directed to stay with Scott, but the men, fearing for their own safety, abandoned him and reported to Sublette that Scott had died and that they had buried him. The following spring Sublette, making another expedition up the Platte, discovered the remains of Scott at the bluff. In his agonizing and desperate bid for life, Scott had crawled forty or sixty miles— depending upon the historian you believe—before he perished. Whatever the distance, it was a remarkable feat, though its ending was grim.

There was greenness, clear water, timber, and wild berries at Scotts Bluff. The emigrants would fondly remember this place as they trudged the next sixty-one miles, in gristly sand and suffocating dust, to Fort Laramie.

The fort, started as a trading post in the 1830s, was taken over by the US Government in 1849 for the protection of the caravans. For most wagon trains it was a key stop on the Trail. By the middle of 1850 the fort register showed that about 40,000 persons had or had been signed in. Men outnumbered women about forty to one and children outnumbered women about five to four. The numbers figured out roughly to about four people for every wagon, four people to every three oxen, twice as many people as horses, five times as many people as cows. Thousands who paused at Fort Laramie did not register and were not registered and many parties, rather than lose time at the crowded fort, swung around it and continued west. But the ratios along the trail then were probably the same as the fort registration.

Fort Laramie, prominent on the Oregon Trail. The fort was first built in 1834 and known first as Fort William, then as Fort John. It was used as a rendezvous for traders, trappers, and early-day explorers. It was purchased by the US Government in 1849 to protect the wagon trains. Emigrants paused here for supplies and rest. In 1890 the fort, having outlived its usefulness, was abandoned. In 1937 the State of Wyoming purchased the fort site from its private owners and donated it to the Federal Government, which in 1938 declared it a National Monument. It was redesignated a National Historic Site in 1960 and thereafter its buildings were restored by the National Park Service.

Courtesy State of Wyoming

For those who made camp at the stockade, and most did, the post provided an opportunity for repairs to be made, cargo to be rearranged and letters to be posted, though the mail service was miserable until the government took over the postal service. It was not rare, until late 1849, for the emigrants to have reached Oregon, or California, before their letters telling of their arrival at Fort Laramie were delivered in the East.

Here at the fort supplies were purchased and professional advice received. The strongest advice, to keep wagons light for the stiff pull over the Laramie Mountains, which were the Black Hills of emigrant lore, sometimes resulted in transferring supplies from wagons to mules and horses and leaving the wagons behind. Many emigrants sold or simply abandoned foodstuffs which later would have saved them from desperate hunger.

Leaving Fort Laramie, the emigrants continued their journey up the North Platte, whose terrain was sometimes to become so rugged as to push the Trail away from the river. But the first day out, though uphill, was a breeze, with the wagons pausing at Register Cliff, where every man, woman and child who could write scrawled his or her name on the rough rock.

Perhaps it was to relieve the monotony, perhaps it was their exhuberance of adventure, or a sense of history, or simply crude ego fulfillment, that the emigrants wrote or carved their names or initials on whatever they could: rocks, trees, skulls of buffalo and cattle, anything that would hold the letters of the alphabet. Sometimes they added the date.

If the first day beyond Fort Laramie was a treat, the first night was a luxury. The wagons were halted at Warm Springs campground, where clothes were laundered and leisurely councils held. Fort Laramie had been too hectic for much calm discussion.

Most large wagon trains elected a leader but his decision was rarely final. He could be outvoted by a committee, also elected by the men of the party, often referred to as the Council. One finds instances where the leader was replaced. The Council was the law-making body, generally called

Register Cliff, two-and-a-half miles southeast of Guernsey, Wyoming. Pioneers traveling the Oregon Trail registered their names on the soft limestone cliff as early as 1849.

Courtesy State of Wyoming

together by the leader, under whatever title he functioned—from captain to general. The Council was more interested in pragmatic results than in laying down general laws. As the trek continued, the codes of the Council were constantly revised. Jesse Applegate wrote: "It first took the state of the little commonwealth into consideration; revised or repealed rules defective or obsolete, and exacted such others as the exigencies seemed to require. The common weal being cared for, it next resolved itself into a court to hear and settle private disputes and grievances." By the time a wagon train reached its destination it might have run through enough rules to fill a book. The Trail was a great school for future legislators, attorneys and judges.

Justice on the Trail could be fair or heavy-handed, depending upon the kind of men in the Council, who served as the Court from which there was no appeal, and the nature of the situations. There was little ceremony in the trial, no need for men to play at being barristers, and scarcely any consideration for extenuating circumstances. The Court sought to go straight to the heart of the matter, define right from wrong, and mete out honest judgment. Offenses could range from shirking to forbidden sex, and punishments were usually based upon how seriously the crime jeopardized the harmony and effectiveness of the group or exposed the party to external danger. The guilty could be severely admonished, fined, lashed, or even expelled from the caravan. On one recorded occasion, a man who shot an Indian woman without cause was turned over to her people, who skinned him alive in full view of the emigrants.

Few wagon trains had professional scouts. All anyone had to do, after 1844, was to follow the beaten path. Alternate routes, such as cutoffs, were generally well-known and discussed long before they were reached. Impetuous decisions were not commonplace.

Nor was advice from a professional scout necessarily sound. Some of the Mountain Men who turned to scouting pretended to know much more about the West than they did, and some had lucrative reasons of their own for turning the wagon trains along devious paths. Had the Donner Party not been misled by a professional scout, they would in all probability have reached California without disaster.

Although trampling buffalo herds and Indian attacks have been most dramatized in fiction, there was far more danger from cholera and other diseases. Dysentary could become a problem; the scorching sun took its toll; brutal terrain exhausted draw animals and men; lack of good water was a constant curse for long stretches; shortage of edible flora reduced the numbers of stock; and when the emigrants miscalculated their food supplies, they suffered hunger.

Where Casper, Wyoming now stands, the wagon trains crossed the Platte and soon left it behind. In 1865, Fort Casper was built for protection against the increasingly embittered Indians. Until then the only sign of permanent humanity at the fording was Mormon Ferry. But even the enterprising Mormons, who did financially well with their rafts, were not there when the Trail was new. The emigrants then had to cross the river by their own devices, not all of which proved satisfactory.

Now, 794 miles from Independence, the Trail began to grind through broken, hilly, difficult country, putting the emigrants through their first real test. Few emerged heroic. J. Goldsborough Bruff, a highly respected chronicler of the California Gold Rush, wrote in near despair: "Great dissension in the company . . . All bad traits of the men now well developed, their true character is shown, untrammeled, unvarnished. Selfishness, hypocrisy, &c. Some whom at home were thought gentlemen are now totally unprincipled . . . Disaffected men of the company now talking about a property division."

Dead cattle and oxen were flopped everywhere. The alkaline water tasted horrible. Rattlesnakes cropped up in abundance. Worst of all, wagons were damaged descending sharp hills and the wagons were too heavy to pull up steep grades. Once again there was a discarding of equipment. Everything regarded as useless for the journey or too weighty was thrown to the side of the road. Kegs of gun powder were blown up, lest the Indians put them to their own use. As late as 1957, a man I visited at South Pass

Crossing the North Platte River in 1837 by the Sir William Drummond
Stewart hunting party. Painting by AJ Miller.
Courtesy National Park Service

City, Wyoming was still finding items which the emigrants
had thrown away.

There were forty-four miles of this jagged, pitted, lunar
terrain before the clear and lovely Sweetwater River was
reached at Independence Rock, which Father De Smet in
1840 had titled "The Great Register of the Desert."
Thousands who halted here did not continue until they had
inscribed on it.

Each time I pass Independence Rock (there is now a
Wyoming highway rest stop at its base), I climb high as I
can for a better appreciation of what life on the Oregon
Trail must have been like. The sweeping panoramas still
seem devoid of civilization and appear, when no cars are in
sight below, as though a wagon train might be coming

Independence Rock, the "Register of the Desert." Inscriptions on the rock date back to the 1830s. The number of pioneer inscriptions has been estimated to be between forty and fifty thousand.

Courtesy State of Wyoming

along. The emigrants who climbed the rock must surely have been awed by the vast sea of space engulfing them.

In a few miles the wagons passed through the narrow defile of Devil's Gate, a 400-foot high rift in a perpendicular granite barricade. Emerging, they saw Split Rock. It looked only a mile or two away. A day's march later it still seemed but a mile off, which it probably really was by then. Distance on the Great Plains was very deceptive for men and women raised in the shorter spaces and shallower horizons of their home country.

One more day and the wagons were confronted by a

gorge which forced the fording of the Sweetwater three times in less than a mile. Appropriately, the spot was called Three Crossings.

Now the emigrants raised their eyes toward the Rocky Mountains, but all they could see was a wide, gently rising, sandy plain. Still, the Rockies lay ahead. Some wagons halted to take account of their portent and to plan their pace for the many miles ahead.

Normally, the wagons were in movement about ten hours a day. Some caravans paused to rest on the Sabbath, though as autumn crept in there were fewer Sunday stoppings. Those who had been over the plains before urged all haste. Marcus Whitman, the famed missionary, urged the comers to move as fast and as hard as they could.

At the close of the day's march the wagons were drawn into a circle and campfires built. The first shift of night guard went on duty at 8 pm and within an hour or two most people, except the sentinels, were in their beds.

One of the finest and most detailed descriptions of life on the trail was penned by one of Oregon's most illustrious sons, Jesse Applegate, who arrived in 1843. The romanticism and literary embellishments of his essay, in contrast to the less pretty and more prosaic entries in almost all diaries, may perhaps be attributed to the time span: Applegate wrote *A Day with the Cow Column* no less than thirty-three years after his emigration. He prepared it in 1876 for the fourth annual reunion of the Oregon Pioneer Association.

Applegate's 1843 party contained many excellent people and a general state of amity, factors not always present in later caravans. The trail was virgin, generally ample of grass, and free of disease. There was also much more game and the Indians, still curious about the palefaces, were friendlier.

Here is a fragment of Applegate's graphic account:

It is four o'clock, A.M.; the sentinels on duty have discharged their rifles—the signal that the hours of sleep are over—and every wagon and tent is pouring forth its night tenants, and slowly kindling smokes begin largely to rise and float away on the morning air . . .

. . . Breakfast is to be eaten, the tents struck, the wagons loaded and the teams yoked and brought up in readiness to be attached to their respective wagons. All know when, at seven o'clock, the signal to march sounds, that those not ready to take their proper place in the line of march must fall into the dusty rear for the day . . .

It is on the stroke of seven; the rush to and fro, the cracking of whips, the loud command to oxen, and what seemed to be an inextricable confusion of the last ten minutes has ceased. Fortunately everyone has been found and every teamster is at his post. The clear notes of a trumpet sound in the front; the pilot and his guard mount their horses; the leading divisions of the wagons move out of the encampment, and take up the line of march; the rest fall into their places with the precision of clockwork, until the spot so lately full of life sinks back into that solitude that seems to reign over the broad plain and rising river as the caravan draws its lazy length toward the distant El Dorado.

Applegate's train was so large that it had to be split into two sections, the wagons in one and the loose stock in another. As the years passed the caravans became smaller, because of the need for speed and manageability. A twenty-wagon train midway on the Trail came to be regarded as somewhat formidable; seven-wagon trains were more numerous. Along the Trail large starting caravans divided into smaller groups and sometimes small groups banded together for protection and mutual aid. It was not uncommon for a family to pull out of one caravan and hitch up with another; some families were attached to three or four groups before they reached Oregon. And wagons traveling alone, at least for certain stretches, were not that all a rarity.

One thinks of a mountain pass as a gap in the mountains reached only after a steep climb. South Pass, the gateway through the Rockies which opened wagon travel across the continent, in no wise fits this description. You climb very gradually up a broad plain and then, before you really know it, you are at the crossing of the Continental Divide. The first time I saw it I was as dumbfounded as many of the emigrants had been.

Most popular history attributes the discovery of South Pass to Robert Stuart, a twenty-seven-year-old trader carrying vital papers from Fort Astoria to New York. Chittenden gives the credit to Mountain Man Etienne Provost. In all likelihood, the feasibility of South Pass had

South Pass, the Gateway of the Rockies. Over this easy upland way during open months of the year passed the high tide of covered-wagon migration.

Courtesy Wyoming State Museum

been investigated by many trappers and traders. It was certainly known to the Indians of the region.

A day beyond South Pass the emigrants were faced with the first of their critical decisions. Should they follow the Old Oregon Trail or take Sublette's Cutoff? In most cases the choice had been made beforehand, but some emigrants were uncertain what to do until they reached the forks. Sublette's Cutoff was shorter by about fifty-five miles, but it ground through arid, discomfiting sageland. The Old Oregon Trail was a much easier route. It followed the meandering Big Sandy River to the Green, that stream so intimately linked to the lore of the Mountain Men. In dry season the Green could be forded without difficulty or payment; when the water was high, rafts had to be built. That changed in 1847, when a group of Mormons, who were the champion commercial forders of the Trail, built a ferry, which did a thriving trade. A traveler in 1850 reported seeing "at least 200 teams waiting their turn to be ferried across." But there was consolation: the Green was clear and cool, the banks grassy and wooded.

Some of the wagons veered off the Old Oregon Trail north of the Mormon Ferry and followed a path that lay halfway between Fort Bridger and Sublette's Cutoff. There were many branch routes in these parts, a condition which existed in several areas of the west.

Across the Green the wagons on the Old Oregon Trail rolled southwest to Fort Bridger, built in 1843 by the legendary Jim Bridger. Many an emigrant swallowed his taciturn tall stories hook, line, and sinker, so enormous was his reputation, but the skeptics thought Bridger's prices stiff and concluded that he was more interested in making money than in helping them.

In a letter of December 10, 1843, Bridger explained his purpose here to a trader friend named Choteau: "I have established a small fort, with a blacksmith shop and a supply

Jim Bridger's original trading post
Courtesy Wyoming State Museum

of iron, on the road of the emigrants on Black's Fork of
Green River, which promises fairly. They, in coming out,
are generally well supplied with money, but by the time they
get there are in want of all kinds of supplies. Horses,
provisions, smith-work, etc. bring ready cash from them, and
should I receive the goods hereby ordered will do a
considerable business in that way with them. The same
establishment trades with the Indians in the neighborhood
who have mostly a good number of beaver in them."

For the emigrants, the fort—a minor one in the
perspective of western history—was not so small. Anything
bigger than two buildings must have looked as large as a
city to them. Added to their delight at reaching
"civilization" was the location: green, tree-lined, and veined
by snowwater streams aswarm with trout. Chittenden rightly
called it "an oasis in the desert."

After the Saints had developed their seed city, they blazed a road from Fort Bridger to Salt Lake City, and a substantial number of caravans bound for California took this route, especially after the discovery of gold. A few wagons bound for Oregon also plod this cutoff, but more than ninety per cent of the latter, after leaving Fort Bridger, followed a course north by northwest, and in seventy-six miles reached the Sublette's Cutoff Junction, in the verdant Bear Valley, where the grass was tall, the game plentiful and the fish in the mountain streams born to bite. At least so it was for the first decade.

Those who carried with them *Ware's Emigrant Guide to California,* published in 1848, could verify that the book was correct when it stated: "From the Big Sandy to the Green River, a distance of thirty-five miles, there is not a drop of water." (Actually, some emigrants figured the thirsty distances to be closer to forty or even fifty miles than thirty-five.) Little wonder the Cutoff was as well known by its second name, "Dry Drive." Many wagons crossed the long barren stretch without making camp, grinding forward day and night except for a pause during the hottest hours.

Now the Oregon Trail, practically reunited, followed up the Bear Valley to Soda Springs, one of the great oddities of the trek. The numerous hot springs, boiling fountains which gave off a strong vapor but whose waters when cooled tasted like soda water, aroused much excitement. The favorite of the comers was a miniature geyser which bore the name of Steamboat Springs. At regular intervals it erupted to a height of about three feet, much to the merriment of the children.

In a few miles the Trail parted company with the Bear and found the Portneuf River, the first link to the Columbia. Henceforth, every river crossed would be consumed by the Columbia which, in the end, surrendered itself to the Pacific. Though Fort Vancouver was still 800 miles distant, some emigrants felt that at last they were entering the Promised Land.

The Portneuf was swallowed by the Snake, on whose left bank sat Fort Hall, the third and least important of the four forts on the Trail. Hudson's Bay Company, which operated the post, offered efficient services and supplies at tolerable prices. By the time Fort Hall was abandoned in 1855, emigrants could avail themselves of other sources of supplies along this stretch of the route.

Two or three days after leaving Fort Hall, and after passing American Falls, which the travelers regarded with modest curiosity—by now they were becoming sophisticated voyagers—the Raft River was reached. Here was perhaps the most important fork in the road along the entire Trail, for at this point the California-bound wagons turned south.

Some Oregon-bound wagons, starting in 1846, did turn south, following the California road for 300 miles before turning west on the newly blazed "Applegate Trail." Initially it proved to be more of a disappointment than a triumph. It was later shortened and improved and became a "direct link" between the Old Oregon Trail and the southern valleys of western Oregon but it never could compete with the parent road in popularity.

No river the emigrants encountered was to be as despised as the Snake. It flowed through wasteland, gritty miles of sagebrush and choking alkali, where at times the oxen were hock-deep in dust. From the trace along the south bank the weary travelers would see the broad river but more often than not they were barred from the stream by the precipitous bank. To see water so closely and yet not be able to reach it was agony in its crowning hour of hell. Here and there springs appeared, but by the time the emigrants could discern the good from the poisonous water, many cattle lay dead. The emigrants would go miles out of their way to find a decent watering hole; there was no assurance that another would be located before thirst wrecked their dreams.

Trees were so scarce that wild sage was used for fuel; they were now beyond the range of buffalo chips, the fuel of the Great Plains. Sometimes, when wild sage did not suffice, the emigrants broke up their wagons for burning, which in part accounted for so many iron parts of the prairie schooners being found on the trail.

And then there were the Indians, each week more resentful at the massive intrusion. They stole horses and later, in desperation, turned to violence the emigrants called massacres. Some years later this part of the trail was stained with blood, white folks' and red folks', though no one could tell, looking at the blood, which had belonged to whom.

The land was a disaster: parched, thorny, furnace hot. Water was scarce, but at Thousand Springs sprays and

On the Oregon Trail in 1837 with the Sir William Drummond Stewart hunting party. Painting by AJ Miller, a member of the party.
Courtesy National Park Service

gushes, cascading down the porous rock banks, provided some wet touches. Still, the springs, believed to be the outlet of buried rivers, were more of a scenic diversion than practical help.

Reports spread that there was good grass on the north side of the Snake. The first crossing was at Salmon Falls. It was no easy operation, and there were casualties.

By far the greater number of wagons, however, continued churning down the south bank. JT Kerns thought the country "too poor to buy a shirt." The statement, taken from his 1852 diary, was read to the forty-second annual reunion of the Oregon Pioneer Association, in 1914. The old timers, who remembered the days on the Trail more clearly than what had happened to them a year ago, chuckled appreciatively.

"The plodding oxen, the complaining wheels and the dust-burdened" emigrants continued along the weary lengths of the cursed Snake to Three Island Ford, where the wagons and stock and people were brought across, by one means or another, to the north bank.

Some emigrants, fearful of a Snake crossing, maintained a route along the south bank. "It was a barren, burnt-to-death waste," Kerns scribbled in his diary. A day later he added: "Bad luck to the man who is such a sinner as to have to seek refuge in such a country as this." The entire passage through Idaho was marked by nameless graves. Kerns reported to his diary: "Saw six graves." Three days later he wrote: "A Mr. Stone's wife died of cholera this evening after camping." She was buried early the next day, "in as decent a manner as circumstances would allow, and after paying our respects to her, we took up the line of march. Had an unusual allowance of dust to the mile today." The land was "almost destitute of Indians and all other kinds of vegetation."

Kerns' party, weary to the core, reached the Owyhee

Site of Three Island Crossing on the Snake River
Courtesy Idaho Historical Society

River almost three weeks after they had passed Three Island Ford. Beyond the Owyhee they rejoined the main trail.

Once the main trail emigrants set foot on the north bank of the Snake they turned away from the river. They had had enough of its cruelty, but the path they chose was also Dantean in its grotesque hellishness. The many graves by the sides of the road attested to the gruesome character of the alkali flats. Some placed blame for the deaths upon the spring water, heavy with alkali. More and more of the despondent travelers observed that, from one end of the Trail to the other, there was a high correlation between the frequency of alkali springs and pools and the large numbers of fresh graves and dead stock.

Three days after Three Island Ford, the mainstream

Fort Boise on the Snake River
Courtesy Idaho Historical Society

wagons rolled into the sweet valley of the Boise River. The stream ran fresh, trout was plentiful, the grass excellent. Fat jackrabbits were all over the place and they made for juicy eating. Humans and stock took on fresh life in the idyllic setting.

It took the emigrants about two days of easy travel down the Boise River to reach Fort Boise, on the Snake. The fort, a Hudson's Bay Company trading post, was a keen disappointment to those who had counted on obtaining much-needed foodstuffs. The trains stayed there only long enough to be ferried across the Snake, into which the Boise runs.

As the Oregon Trail matured, more ferry enterprises across the Snake were started. They operated from up the river clear down to Farewell Bend. But the ferry most closely associated with the Old Oregon Trail was about four miles south of present Nyssa, Oregon. The emigrants were now 1,585 miles from Independence by the most traveled road.

Those who had expected to wander through a garden of greenery beyond the Snake soon had second thoughts. The first sixteen miles, northwest through Cow Valley, were dry as bones. For those who had neglected to take water, parched lips came quickly. The distance to the Malheur River seemed long as doomsday to the thirsty. But at last the Malheur was reached, where Vale now sits, the center of a vast irrigated area, and at legendary Warm Springs the emigrants found water hot enough to have been boiled by the devil. This did not deter the women from a welcome opportunity at laundering.

Across the Malheur the Trail bent north, sometimes west and sometimes even east, rolling over low hills and up draws for about twenty-three miles to meet the Snake again. Here the river swerved north and the pioneers aptly named their point of departure with the stream "Farewell Bend."

Not all the caravans adhered to the beaten path. Everywhere there loomed the possibility, cutoffs were blazed. At Vale, in 1845, Mountain Man Stephen H. Meek, brother of the redoubtable Joe Meek, piloted a wagon train straight west, instead of turning north, as the other emigrants did. Aflounder in the sagebrush wastes and jumbled hills, the pioneers suffered from hunger and exposure, and buried many of their dead before breaking through to the Deschutes, which they descended to The Dalles. No other wagon train in Oregon history had as many casualties.

The disaster of Meek's Cutoff Party did not discourage later wagon trains, seeking a shorter way to the Willamette Valley, from following the path of the anguished party. The route was improved yearly, through better knowledge of where grass and water could be found, and became one of the three main trails into Western Oregon. The other two were the Old Oregon Trail, by far the most popular route, and the very arduous Applegate Trail, pioneered by Jesse Applegate in 1846.

Farewell Bend, where the Oregon Trail left the Snake River and wound into the Burnt River and Powder River valleys. Just around the bend to the north was the pioneer Olds Ferry.

Courtesy State of Oregon

The last-named route, the Applegate, plowed through the Black Rock desert of Nevada and Surprise Valley in California, crossed Modoc County, and followed the Lost River into Oregon, near present Merrill. Then it crossed the Coast Range, approximating state highway 66, and reached present Ashland, which was not settled until 1852. From there the Applegate trace wound into the Rogue River Valley and continued north through the Umpqua Valley and into the Willamette Valley, where the earlier emigrants settled.

Those who formed the vanguard had it most difficult. In its first year the Applegate Trail was almost as much an ordeal as the odyssey of Meek's "Lost Wagon" party. Tabitha Moffet Brown, who later had as much as anyone to do with the germ of Pacific University, was a widow in her sixties when she drove her own ox-team across the plains, accompanied by an even older relative. Her description of the 1846 caravan on the route blazed by Jesse Applegate is as graphic as any recorded on that merciless trek:

> We had sixty miles of desert without grass or water, mountains to climb, cattle giving out, wagons, breaking, emigrants sick and dying, hostile Indians to guard against day and night, if we would save ourselves and our horses and cattle from being arrowed and stole.
>
> We were carried hundreds of miles south of Oregon into Utah Territory and California; fell in with the Clamotte and Rogue River Indians, lost nearly all our cattle, passed the Umpqua Mountains, twelve miles through. I rode through in three days at the risk of my life, on horseback, having lost my wagon and all that I had but the horse I was on. Our families were the first that started through the canyon, so that we got through the mud and rocks much better than those that followed. Out of hundreds of wagons, only one came through without breaking. The canyon was strewn with dead cattle, broken wagons, beds, clothing, and everything but provisions, of which latter we were nearly all destitute. Some people were in the canyon two or three weeks before they could get through. Some died without any warning, from fatigue and starvation. Others ate the flesh of cattle that were lying dead by the wayside.

The new-broken Meek and Applegate cutoffs were so disaster-ridden that Governor George Abernathy was moved to issue a manifesto warning of the dangers involved. Written April 22, 1847, the circular was distributed to the emigrants before they reached the cutoff points.

"A number of the emigrants of 1845 took a cut off, as it is called," the circular began, "to shorten the route, leaving the old road; the consequence was, they were later getting in, lost their property, and many lost their lives. Some of those who reached the settlements, were so broken by sickness, that it was some months before they recovered sufficient strength to labor.

"A portion of the emigrants of 1846 took a new route, called the southern route," the circular continued. "This proved very disastrous to all those who took it. Some of the emigrants who kept on the old road, reached this place [Oregon City] as early as the 13th of September, with their wagons, and all got in, in good season, with their wagons and property, I believe; except a few of the last party. While those that took the southern route, were very late in reaching the settlements—they all lost more or less of their property—many of them losing all they had and barely getting in with their lives; a few families were obliged to winter in the Umpqua mountains, not being able to reach the settlements.

"I would therefore recommend you to keep the old road," Abernathy concluded. "A better way may be found, but it is not best for men with wagons and families to try the experiment."

The Indians Mrs. Brown feared in 1846 were to become more aggressive in the next quarter century, until the destruction of Captain Jack's band of Modocs in 1873. With their ancient lands taken from them before their eyes the Indians grew desperate. Since they had no recourse to politics, and could negotiate only from a position of weakness, they took direct action, often characterized by violence. Probably the most blood-letting occurred ten miles southeast of the present town of Tulelake, California. Here, in 1852, the Modocs wiped out ninety Oregon-bound travelers. Since then the site has been known as Bloody Point.

Two members of the ill-fated Stephen Meek "Cutoff" Party of 1845 lie buried here, on the old Conroy homestead, northeast of Tygh Valley. A more fitting grave marker has replaced this primitive pioneer memorial.
Phoebe L Friedman

One thing was certain. The ruts of the wagon trains were the first models of roads in Oregon. From the Rogue River Valley into the valleys of the Umpqua and the Willamette, stage coaches followed the Applegate Trail and the original US 99 from Grants Pass to Eugene was rarely out of sight of the trace scratched out in 1846.

The sagebrush route of Meek's Party was to become, in large measure, the Willamette Valley and Cascade Mountain Military Road, which stretched from Ontario to Albany and took four years to build, 1864 to 1868. Later, this pike was the most important link between western and central Oregon. Wagon trains up to half-a-mile in length carried sheep and wool from the range country and returned with fruits, vegetables, other food supplies, and manufactured goods. Settlements sprang up to service these mercantile caravans and the stage coaches which rattled from the banks of the Snake to the curve of the Willamette. Some of the youth who followed Meek's "short cut" returned east of the Cascades on the Military Road as middle-aged men and women in search of new homestead land.

On June 15, 1905, six decades after Stephen Meek led his weary flock into the desert, an Oldsmobile dubbed "Old Scout" reached Vale, the first automobile on a trans-continental run to enter Oregon. "Old Scout" continued west, roughly following the steps of Meek into central Oregon, but continuing west where Meek turned north. On June 21 the Oldsmobile, after passing through Sweet Home and Albany, arrived at Portland. A few of those who had been with Meek were there to see it. What thoughts they must have had! Actually, emigrants who crossed the plains in 1845 as children of ten could have seen airplanes fly if they had reached the age of eighty. And some did.

The Old Oregon Trail, after reaching Farewell Bend, was more or less paralleled in large sections by the first laying out of US 30. There are still places where the modern highway literally covers or runs shoulder to shoulder with the emigrant road.

Many years ago I met an elderly man whose parents, at age twenty, had come by wagon to Oregon in 1850. He was born the following year. He recalled that his mother had told him that when the emigrants reached Farewell Bend a preacher in the party exclaimed: "Praise God! The worst is over! Now we enter Beulah Land!"

The preacher did not have his facts straight, any more

OREGON HISTORY

FAREWELL BEND, THE LAST CAMP ON THE WEARY JOURNEY ACROSS THE SNAKE RIVER PLAINS. HERE THE OREGON TRAIL LEFT THE SNAKE RIVER AND WOUND OVERLAND TO THE COLUMBIA. HERE CAMPED WILSON PRICE HUNT, DEC. 23, 1811; CAPT. BONNEVILLE, JAN. 10, 1834; NATHANIEL J. WYETH, AUG. 25, 1834; LT. JOHN C. FREMONT, OCT. 13, 1843.

OREGON STATE HIGHWAY DEPARTMENT

Historical marker at Farewell Bend, near Huntington.
Courtesy State of Oregon

than we writers, following the lead of the emigrants, refer to the green pastures of early Oregon as Beulah Land. *Harper's Bible Dictionary* defines Beulah as "the name given to Palestine after the Exile when it was repeopled and restored to God's favor." The emigrants had not been in exile and there is no evidence that the Oregon Country had ever fallen out of God's favor, but the preacher's enthusiasm was sincere and it was shared by many even less familiar with biblical lore. (The town of Beulah, in Malheur County, was named for the daughter of the first postmaster and gives no clues as to how the first white settlers felt about the land around them.)

Those who came to Farewell Bend later, when the issue of statehood for Oregon was settled, found Olds Ferry, which did not go out of business until the third decade of the twentieth century, when a paved road and all its appendages rendered the historic ferry completely obsolete. It had been used by emigrants on still another cutoff—fording the Snake at present Weiser and following the north side of the river to Farewell Bend, where the crossing was made.

On a hillside to the left of the old highway near Huntington the last imprints of the old wagon wheels have not yet been completely erased. Five miles further, at Lime, whatever wagon scars still exist are to the right. If you want to place the Old Oregon Trail in a modern setting, then the Trail crosses the road at Lime.

You have only to take one look to see how forsaken and wretched the country is. It was no better—indeed, much worse—for the emigrants. This was no hymnal Beulah Land; it was the Devil's garden of Hell, and some emigrants actually considered it the roughest stretch of the entire journey from the Missouri to the Willamette.

John C. Fremont, who was not easily disturbed and was an old hand at packing through unpleasant terrain, said of the Burnt River Canyon: "The common trail, which leads along the mountainside at a place where the river strikes the base, is sometimes bad even for a horseman." For the wagons, bumping through the stony canyon, it was all bad.

John C Fremont
Courtesy Oregon Historical Society

Ten miles a day "up and down the sideling mountains" was considered good distance for those parts, "enough to hide all despairing sinners," as JT Kerns woefully observed. The trail crisscrossed the Burnt River, crossing it at least once a mile and in some stretches every quarter mile.

On the third day out of Farewell Bend the wagons sloped into the welcome vistas of the Powder River Valley. The exhausted comers gave thanks and continued on a course more north than west. Until Baker was founded, born of the Eastern Oregon gold rush in the early 1860s, the Old Oregon Trail passed about six miles from the site. After 1863 many caravans angled for Baker, to take on supplies or to have some repairs done at the blacksmith shops.

Some of the emigrants, of course, caught the gold fever and sprinted off to the streams and mines, on occasion selling or abandoning their wagons in Baker. There are supposed instances of men "jumping" caravans to head for the gold while their women folk continued westward. At least I was so told by a couple of old timers in Baker some decades ago, and if I cannot, for lack of other documentation, attest to their veracity, their account sounds plausible. One needs only to imagine what behavior will emerge in any given situation, and we know the effects of the California Gold Rush on families, plans, and careers.

To the right and left of the emigrants flowed the Powder River, a clear stream with the leap of a squirrel and the brain of a lynx. Looking farther left, the horizon was a shadow-tinted range topped by five peaks, the smallest more than 8,000 feet elevation. The emigrants knew the range's name: Blue Mountains, "from the dark-blue appearance given to them by the pines," observed Fremont.

Not far from what is now Haines the caravans passed Lone Pine Stump, the amputated, mortally-wounded remainder of a once graceful pine that had reigned in solitude on an extensive plain. French trappers had called it *L'Arbre Seul* and for them and for others who came early to Oregon it had been an important landmark. In 1843, for some obscure reason, the tree was cut down. Chittenden ascribed the act to a "needy emigrant," but Fremont, who arrived later, found the tree "stretched on the ground," so it had not been chopped up by its feller, who had swung an "inconsiderate emigrant axe."

Fording the Powder, the pilgrims in search of a land of

promise crossed the ground on which North Powder town was to rise in the 1870s and passed within a short distance of where a child was born on December 30, 1811 to the Iowa Indian woman, Marie Dorion, whose French-Sioux husband, Pierre, was a scout for the overland Astorian party led by Wilson Price Hunt.

Although this expedition suffered so many hardships that historians have found it facile to call the party "ill-fated," it did establish a route which was to be followed, in parts, by the Old Oregn Trail.

There was one big hill to climb—Kerns wrote that it was "the most difficult and highest hill we have yet seen"—and then the descent into the breathlessly handsome Grande Ronde Valley, "the best and most beautiful place we have seen on the whole road, or in fact in our lives," added Kerns.

Fremont was equally impressed. "It is a place . . . where a farmer would delight to establish himself, if he were content to live in the seclusion it imposes."

Captain Bonneville, who had come earlier in 1835, was excited by the color of the camas root, which blanketed the valley. "When the plant is in blossom, the whole valley is tinted by its blue flowers, and looks like the ocean when overcast by a cloud."

The circular, table-flat, rich-earthed Grande Ronde Valley, encased by the forested slopes of cool mountains, appeared as an ethereal garden to many of the emigrants. They could not say enough nice things about it.

It is still magnificent scenery. I penned these notes, which appear in my *Oregon For the Curious*: "Cove, a town of 376 nestled in a far corner of the Grande Ronde Valley, overhung by the Wallowa Mountains. The houses, cherry orchards and green plots on the glistening rises of the dew-washed vale northeast of Cove comprise one of the prettiest pictures of rustic Oregon. From Cove you can see clear across the valley to the West—a beautiful saucer upon which sunlight spills wonders."

And three sentences later: "In summer the Grande Ronde Valley between Cove and Union is dotted with stacks of hay on open fields, and between the haystacks cattle graze. Framing these scenes are cherry orchards, velvety and luxurious in the pools of their shade. And beyond them all—the purple loom of the Wallowas."

It occurred to more than several of the pilgrims that the Grande Ronde Valley might be a fine place to settle down, but their compass was set for the Willamette Valley and they would not fall short of their goal. They had come too far to give up before they reached the land they had vowed to themselves and they would not be tempted by a splendid garden, however much it appealed to them. Later, some of the emigrants wondered aloud about the blindness of their follow-the-flock mentality when everything they had come west for was before their eyes in the Grande Ronde Valley.

Almost two decades after the first wagon trains rimmed through, a few of the emigrants retraced their route to stake the first claims in the prairie that had remained constant in their dreams. In the winter of 1861 they holed upon the flat and when spring came a man named Ben Brown moved his family five miles south, to the south bank of the Grande Ronde River, where he put up a log house right at the edge of the great schooner road. Wagons were still a-coming—and plenty—and freight haulers and stages, too, now. He had to make a living, of course, and preferring to do something other than farm he converted his house into a tavern. Soon a few other rough-hewn structures arose, and so another settlement dotted the map. The town, if it could be called that, was more-or-less named after Brown.

Every settlement warranted a post office. When one was established in May 1863, Brown demanded immortality but the meeting held to choose a name selected La Grande, in tribute to the beauty of the site. Rarely were the settlers so imaginative. That, or Brown was mighty unpopular. Perhaps his whiskey was too weak and too expensive.

From sunflower mornings to paintedcup skies the wagon trains rolled on, the clink of rim against rock and the moan of wheel in dust giving way to the chant of iron crossing the fertile vale. For fifteen lovely miles the refreshed caravans moved through the Grande Ronde Valley until they reached the hem of the Blue Mountains. They had gleaned by the Old Oregon Trail 1,751 miles. The long and worst was behind them, they told themselves, though no one discounted the hardships ahead. Those who came in the first years of the Trail knew that they would be going to places without roads or schools or doctors around or maybe even neighbors close by and that whatever was going to be built would have to be done from scratch: houses, barns, schools, fences, stores, bridges, settlements. One wonders if the early comers realized that the land and the taming of the wilderness would wear out the first generation. Much of the second generation stayed on the farms of their parents, the earthbreakers, but by then the land had begun to change hands and sons were beginning to leave for the towns and trades. Little of the pioneer land remained in the ownership of the third generation.

Although they had some doubts about the Blue Mountains crossing, the emigrants undertook the ascension with gusto. The trail was steep and rough and the oxen strained as the wheels bit furrows into the soil. But the exhilaration of the gentle breezes, the plentitude of wood for fire, the ready sources of clear water and, above all, the gossamer, dreamy, pastel magic of the uplifted hills and their soft hazy recesses more than compensated for the difficulties of vehicular movement.

The wagons beat a true path up the southeast slope. When the railroad was laid out it followed the caravan ruts.

The highway took the same course. Some faint creases of the old trail can still be found on the left side before the summit is reached and on the right side after the summit is passed.

The Blue Mountains crossing was considered a likely source of trouble and in 1844 Major HAG Lee, one of those names which flits across a page of history like a fly darting between sugar cubes, established Lee's Encampment. In 1863 a small stage station was opened by the brothers Meacham, Harvey and Alfred, Alfred coming up from California, where he had been a Gold Rusher. Two years later they built a larger facility, known as Meacham Station and Mountain House. Harvey was killed seven years later, when a tree fell on him. By this time Alfred was Superintendent of Indian Affairs, an appointment of General Grant. A year after his brother's accidental death, Alfred almost joined him, courtesy of Captain Jack's band of Modocs. On April 11, 1873, on a flat of the Lava Beds, in northern California, the desperate Indians resorted to a favorite white stratagem, bushwhacking the enemy at a peace parley. General ERS Canby, after whom the Willamette Valley town was named, and the Reverend Eleazar Thomas were killed and Meacham severely wounded and left for dead. After he had been rescued and nursed back to health by Winema, a Modoc woman, Mecham continued to deal with Indians around the country until he died, in 1882, in the safety of Washington, DC.

A few miles beyond Meacham the caravans pulled up at Emigrant Springs. It had good grass and water and was to be a favorite with comers as long as the great wagon trace was in existence. Eight decades after the first prairie schooners left a thin and faint shadow upon the Blue Mountains, a large stone marker was erected in honor of the pioneers. It was dedicated by President Warren G. Harding who, before that summer of 1923 was six weeks old, had passed into his own last sunset.

On a warm day in 1936, a middle-aged man gave me a ride from Pendleton to La Grande and at Emigrant Springs he paused to walk about a bit. I followed his footsteps and his remarks with equal faith. Suddenly he turned to me and said: "My grandfather talked of chawing with Ezra Meeker here in 1852."

For a man who didn't chase politics and wasn't obsessed with setting up banks or buying up land, Ezra Meeker was about the best-known person who came across the Trail. Certainly the most peripatetic of all the emigrants, he seems to have gone everywhere in Oregon and points north. A perceptive, sophisticated journalist whose view was longer than his contemporaries, Meeker was almost as widely read in Oregon as he was in San Francisco and back east. In his later years he retraced the Oregon Trail by ox team, automobile, and airplane.

There lay but a few hours between the leaving of Emigrant Springs and the arrival at the summit of Emigrant Hill. With cries of "Hallelujah!" and "Glory be!" the tanned and hardy folks looked down into a sea of tall, softly rippling grass, a shimmering vale of emerald sheen. On a clear day, when the skies were free of buttermilk churn or fluffy clouds spun out like cotton candy or wind-slatted rain that pelleted down like buggy whip handles, the great snowheads of Mount Hood and Mount Adams, more than 100 miles away, popped up like hazy dandelions on the blue-burnished slope of the western horizon. On a very clear day, when the sun scoured the skies, the peaks looked twice as big as they were.

It took the covered wagons four days to cross the fifty-mile-wide range, but no one wrote of suffering. John Zeiber penned in his journal: "A fine stream of water divides us from the next hill; grass has been good and plenty for days. The pine timber grows from 100 to 180 feet high and our camp fires of dry pine make the cool nights comfortable . . . We passed through the pines and over some of the best farming lands we have seen on the route . . . The pines grew thicker and taller and the openings presented the most charming views . . . This day we left the Blue Mountains and really they proved the pleasantest part of our journey."

In the first years of the Trail, a significant number of wagons angled north from the eastern fringe of the Umatilla Valley to the mission station Marcus and Narcissa Whitman had built at Waiilatpu, "the place of the rye grass." Dr. Whitman had helped guide the wagons of the "Great Migration" of 1843 over the way he had first traveled to the far end of the continent in 1836, the year he and his wife had establishd the mission. A true believer in Manifest Destiny, Whitman had turned Waiilatpu into a provision base, a rest camp, and a hospital.

From the mission the trek took a turn due west, to Old Fort Walla Walla, and then down to the great gap of the Columbia, where the river was followed on its left bank to The Dalles.

Traffic to the Whitman Mission had already considerably thinned by the time the Whitmans were slain by the Cayuse, in the late autumn of 1847, and after that the Waiilatpu road was practically abandoned.

The first important point west of the Blue Mountains on the main emigrant turnpike—and it truly became a turnpike toward the close of the fifth decade—was the Umatilla River, near the site of present Pendleton.

For almost two decades the comers made camp on the land that became Pendleton before the Umatilla Valley was recognized "as fitting for wheat," as a pioneer native son once chronicled.

In 1851, when during the late summer and autumn scarcely a day passed without a caravan rattling through, a trading post was established. So little value was placed on the grassy earth that even when there were several stations in the area, a ferry operator could talk a squatter into swapping 160 choice acres for a team of horses.

Ruts and wagon tracks of the Oregon Trail in Umatilla County, Oregon.

Courtesy State of Oregon

The ferryman's name was Moses E. Goodwin and he had one tenant on his tract, GW Bailey. Both men teamed up in a shrewd power play to have the county seat moved from Umatilla City to Goodwin's farm. In 1868 Bailey was elected county judge and a year later the records were moved to his house. The farm became Pendleton but was not incorporated until 1880. By that time Pendleton had become a cattle center, with cowboys taking on one last snort before they started the long drives across the mountains into Idaho, Wyoming, and Montana. The scene seemed wild and melodramatic to the thinning lines of emigrants who were still dribbling west.

At the Umatilla River a branch of the Oregon Trail followed the stream forty-four miles to the Columbia River. Umatilla Landing, at the confluence of the Umatilla and the Columbia, was founded in 1863, not to serve the wagon trains bound for settlement but to supply the frenetic gold mining in Idaho. It was known as Umatilla City when it was the county seat, from early 1863 to late 1868. Covered wagons then heading west were a novelty in this river town, primarily because the branch route which meandered down the south bank of the Columbia was too cramped for widespread use.

The main road continued north by northwest, to where the village of Echo is now to be found. South and west of the hamlet the creased traces of the Trail are still plainly visible.

As early as 1851 the Umatilla Indian Agency was located here. Evidently it wasn't enough to provide a feeling of security for in 1855 a fort, under the leadership of an old Indian campaigner, Major Granville O. Haller, was erected. The major named the stockade after his wife, Henrietta. The town itself was named after another woman, Echo Koontz, daughter of one of the first settlers in these parts.

Fort Henrietta merits little attention in the diaries of the emigrants. To be fair, few of the comers of 1855 and later were keeping diaries and those that were compiled were generally considered too "recent" by the pioneer association for reading or printing. The real "romance" of the Old Oregon Trail resided in the first decade of wagon migration—1843 to 1853.

An eight-mile county road, linking Echo to Oregon 207, roughly parallels the wagon pike. Then for thirty miles there is no smooth road of any kind to follow where the emigrants trudged. Only one paved road breaks this gap,

Oregon Trail ruts west of Echo.

Phoebe L Friedman

which crosses Juniper and Sixmile Canyons. This is Oregon 74, and the Old Oregon Trail wound through where the village of Cecil now clings to the earth.

In this gap area the scene today is not a world apart from

thirteen or fourteen decades ago. True, wheat grows where wild grass did, and there are other signs of man's hand, but the topography is still wild and sweeping: a rippling, uneven sea of troughs and slants of slopes and swells of hills; rough draws and washes; hillocks in the distance that seem to swirl out of nowhere; and puffs of dust that look like Indian smoke signals. There still remain visible portions of the Trail, the sharpest being in the vicinity of the old post office of Ella, seven miles east of Willow Creek, which skims past Cecil, and Wells (or Well) Spring, another five miles east. The spring, upon which the emigrants seem to have drawn heavily, was heartily noted in journals of the early years.

A seven-mile road west of Cecil, which runs into a county road continuing on to Oregon 19, provides the closest approach to today's motorist for following the Oregon Trail. Rough terrain forced the crude pike to assume the form of a broad "V", which the seven-mile road cuts across at the lower end.

There is another gap of seven miles, across Eightmile Canyon, before the wagon trace is met by another paved road, Oregon 19. Here, seven miles south of Arlington, stands a historical marker honoring WW Weatherford, who came by here in 1861, a barefoot boy of seventeen driving oxen, as he had across the plains and hills. Later he settled five miles south of here, became the first wheat farmer in Gilliam County, and lived to be eighty-two. By then, in 1926, he had seen trains bound for Chicago, gasoline-powered tractors replace horses, combines, the magic of electricity, radio, and that contraption that must have made the prairie schooner seem like a stone age relic, the airplane.

East and west of the Weatherford Marker, a few miles each way, the tatoos of the wagons wheels are still imprinted on the plain.

A paved road the shape of a scythe adheres to the next seven miles of the Trail as it ground through Alkali Canyon. Here, too, are faint blurs of the mighty migration.

Old Oregon Trail marker seven miles of Arlington, on Oregon Highway 19.

Courtesy State of Oregon

Two miles north of the old Rock Creek post office station, at a point where the paved road meets a partial-gravel lane angling southeast from Blalock, the wagons pushed on due westward, clinking and clanging and bouncing and rubbing while the emigrants lifted their eyes to the green Cascades and felt their pulses quicken.

In four miles they came to the John Day River, with Deep Canyon on one side and Diamond Butte on the other. The land seemed harsh to most of the comers, but its scenic impact could not be denied. It would be a good place to come back and see some time, they said, but very few returned for another look. Those who did, with scarce exceptions, settled on the plains of what are now Gilliam and Sherman counties.

They crossed the John Day, cold in the crisp of autumn, by fording or floating best as they could. Those who arrived after the Trail was pounded into a high road found a ferry at the river.

There is no feasible way to follow by car the next stretch of the bending trail. Seen as dots on a map, the route sketches this pattern: a long climb to the top of a hill, then a short dip into a trough, and finally a rise to a hill which breaks into a plateau. Altogether, it took the early emigrants about two days to travel from the west bank of the John Day to where Wasco is now sited.

After the Barlow Road, the last of the great cutoffs, was hacked out across the Cascades; some wagons which took it branched off the main trail within three hours after crossing the John Day and followed a course which brought them past the later towns of Grass Valley and Tygh Valley.

Wasco was a child of the Old Oregon Trail, born in 1869 as Spanish Hollow to sell supplies and services to the comers. Whatever touches of the traces remain are found southwest of Wasco, between Mad Spring Canyon and Spanish Hollow.

It is now nine miles from Wasco to Biggs, by way of US 97. The wagon route, to the left of the highway, was longer. At the point where Biggs leans against the Columbia, many emigrants had their first glimpse of the Great River of the

Barlow Trail marker

Courtesy State of Oregon

West. They were impressed, but those who knew they would have to use it as a road were not without apprehension. The Columbia swept past them as though it had devoured a thousand caravans and had stomach to gorge a thousand more.

A half-day of travel brought the now itchy pilgrims to the next formidable obstacle, the Deschutes River. It was running mean and rocky in a tricky channel and the first comers had to do some hard-headed calculating before they began the crossing. The prairie schooners were floated across and the livestock hollered and whipped into the river to swim. When the Deschutes looked too difficult to take in one crack the emigrants used an island at the mouth of the stream to divide the crossing into two parts.

After a while the Indians of the local Columbia River area, old hands at swapping services and goods, offered to transport women and children to the far shore in exchange for bright colored shirts and other items that took their fancy. When the river was rough they did not lack for customers.

A low, horseshoe-shaped falls at a rock reef marking the upper end of a long rapids drew the attention of the emigrants, who by now were experienced sightseers. Coming in the fall, they did not witness a far more spectacular scene: Indians netting and spearing salmon trapped in the boiling pools of a cavernous trough.

For perhaps hundreds of years fishing stands on the rocks had been passed from father to son. Robert Stuart, the Astorian, observed in his journal: "Here is one of the first rate Salmon fisheries on the river . . . the fish come this far by the middle of May, but the two following months are the prime of the season—during this time the operator hardly ever dips his nets without taking one and sometimes two Salmon, so that I call it speaking within bounds when I say, that an experienced hand would by assuidity catch at least 500 daily."

Early travelers knew the falls simply as The Chutes, a name given to all such falls and rapids on the Columbia. Later, the place was called Celilo Falls until it was drowned by a dam in the 1950s. A hundred years before the Indians had signed a treaty with the US Government permitting them to carry on their ancient livelihood until the sun no longer arose. But a world which can produce a bomb brighter than a thousand suns can also extinguish a few in the name of progress.

The emigrants did see the old village of Wishram, which Lewis and Clark described in their *Journals*, which Washington Irving spoke of in his *Astoria*, and which contributed prominently to Edward Curtis' artistic presentation of North American Indians.

Near the falls the early comers saw some Indian lodges, which eventually gave way to wooden shacks and salmon-drying sheds.

In 1863 a fourteen-mile long portage railroad was opened, to avoid some of the river's turbulent waters, but the railroad was for commerce, not for caravans seeking new land.

From the falls the caravans left the river to travel inland to The Dalles. Since the river curves, the inland route was more or less direct.

The Dalles derived its name from the French word for flagstone and was used by the French-Canadian fur traders to describe the now submerged river rapids flowing swiftly through a narrow channel over flat basaltic rocks.

Many years before the first wagon train arrived, the area, called by the Indians Winquatt and Wascopam, was already an exciting place. As a navigation breakpoint it became a crossroads of Indians for hundreds of miles around. Lewis and Clark spoke of it as "the great mart of all this country." It had permanent villages and during the salmon run thousands of men, women and children flocked here to fish and barter. Like every cosmopolitan setting, it had its swindlers and sharpies, its thugs and robbers, and there, too, was the clearing house of Chinook, the *lingua franca* of the Pacific Northwest. When the voyageurs came, French words were bastardized into the Chinook lexicon; when the British and American arrived, the same with English.

The first white settlement was a Methodist mission established in 1838. It was abandoned nine years later. A temporary stockade erected during the Cayuse War of 1847 gave way to a permanent military post, Fort Dalles, which ceased operations in 1867. All that is left of the fort today is a single building, the surgeon's quarters, now a museum.

By Chittenden's computations the emigrants had traveled on the Old Oregon Trail 1,934 miles since leaving Independence, but the end was not yet in sight, and the frustration of being so close and yet so far could be unnerving.

The Columbia lay pressed against basaltic cliffs and hills and it was impossible for the wagons to continue due westward. Stock might be driven by torturous paths along the bank or across the Cascades inland or swum across the Columbia and led down an Indian trail through a thick forest to Fort Vancouver and then swum back across the Columbia. The loss of stock in the first years was tragically high.

In the dawn of wagon train migration, The Dalles was as far as the Trail wound. Ezra Meeker penned a poignant portrait of the final encampment on the Old Oregon Trail. "Those who took passage felt that the journey was ended. The cattle had been unyoked for the last time; the wagons had been rolled to the last bivouac; the embers of the last camp fire had died out . . ."

Many wagons were left behind at The Dalles by emigrants who took to the Columbia there. These included not only the comers who arrived before the Barlow Road was opened but people who came years after the wagon route was blazed through the Cascades. These latter persons were mainly those who were too tired and sick when reaching The Dalles to even contemplate the arduous mountain journey or those who arrived too late and dreaded Cascade snows and bitter cold.

Almost every kind of river craft imaginable was used to carry the emigrants and their luggage—and sometimes their wagons—down the Columbia to Fort Vancouver or, later, sometimes just to the mouth of the Sandy River. The wagons were generally broken down before being loaded on the craft, but sometimes wagons were floated wheel-less down the river. The mortality rate of the floated wagons was no cause for celebration.

A barge voyage of up to ten days was not uncommon and before it was over many of the passengers were bone-weary and seasick. The comers were subjected to heavy rains, rough waters, sometimes painful portages, hunger and little sleep, but the vilest elements must have been the powerful headwinds, which not only halted the craft in their tracks but actually, at very blowy times, pushed the rafts,

Exhibit in Fort Vancouver National Historic Site halls, Vancouver, Washington.

Phoebe L Friedman

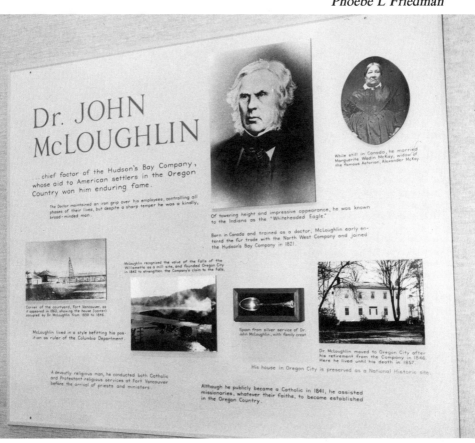

longboats, barges, and sailboats back. That must have been the acme of frustration: to be put ashore until the winds abated.

The costs were high, too, especially after the rivermen saw what profits could be had. Finally the Hudson's Bay Company's western headquarters at Fort Vancouver was reached, and for the early emigrants there was a warm reception, led by the hospitable Dr. John McLoughlin, the six-foot-four, massive-framed, legendary "White-Headed Eagle." He provided food, clothing, and supplies to the needy and had the emigrants ferried across the Columbia to the northern lip of the Willamette Valley, now Portland. Here the emigrants preceded south to begin a new life.

One of the turning points along the entire Trail came in 1845, when a party of pilgrims, many of them weak and sick and low on provisions, found a shortage of river craft. Samuel K. Barlow, turning despair to determination, led his party over the mountains, around the south slope of Mount Hood. In reality, he did not break entirely new ground but followed an Indian trail which had been used by emigrant herders to drive cattle across the Cascades.

"God never made a mountain that he had not made a place for some man to go over it or under," said Barlow, who carried the title of Captain because of his leadership of a caravan.

On October 1, 1845, a start was made to scratch a wagon trail across the cordillera. The entire party numbered nineteen men and women, besides children. "Their able assistants," as William Barlow, Samuel's son, recalled long years later, "were seven horses, thirteen wagons, sixteen yoke of cattle and one dog."

The expedition had sufficient provisions for two months, enough money to purchase more, and their cattle and horses were in hardy shape. "The greatest deficiency we felt," remembered William Barlow, "was the lack of good tools.

Old rusty axes and saws, young and tender muscles, and big trees were quite incompatible. But pluck and necessity compelled action, so we hacked away and went on."

There was little difficulty on the east side of the Cascades, where the pine and hemlock were thinly spaced. "But on the west side the trees were thick and the underbrush made every yard or foot even an impassable barrier to our wagons, till ax, saw, or fire demolished or burned the barriers away."

Near Mount Hood two of the party decided to turn back. William H. Rector, who had helped Captain Barlow stake out the trace, announced: "We have found a good route for a road, but it will be a very hazardous journey this time of the year. I dread the possibility of the danger for my wife, so we have concluded to return to The Dalles."

A critical decision had to be made: the emigrants were cold and their food was running out and their stock were taking a battering. Two of Barlow's sons were detailed to drive the cattle down the Indian trail and into the Willamette Valley. Goods were cached, the wagons left behind, and a cabin built for the men who would guard them. Captain Barlow's third son, William, and John M. Bacon, a tailor by trade, were dispatched to the house of Philip Foster, below the mountains, for supplies. Women, children, and what provisions remained were packed on horses and the party took off for the valley beyond.

The going was fearsome: through dense forests, across huckleberry swamps and torrents and over the broken hills of the range's western face. A foot of snow left the horses nothing to eat but laurel, which the party thought to be poisonous, especially after a horse died. Finally, on December 23, the half-famished pioneers reached Foster's farm, the first on the Oregon Trail in the Willamette Valley. Forty-eight hours later, on Christmas Day, they arrived in Oregon City. It had taken them eight months and twenty-

Fort Dalles, the last military outpost on the Oregon Trail.
Phoebe L Friedman

four days to come the 2100 miles from Fulton County, Illinois.

The following year, 1846, Samuel Barlow applied for a charter to construct a wagon road over the path the party had taken. Authorization in hand, about forty men were hired and work was begun, Barlow supervising the operation. The road was about eighty miles long, William Barlow said, sixty-five miles of it "cut through the primeval forests, canyons, creeks, and rivers of the Cascade mountains and slopes."

By the time the Barlow Road was completed there were still emigrants arriving at The Dalles. Some turned northward, to follow the new route. Before 1846 was out, 145 wagons and 1,559 head of livestock passed over the new pike.

The judgments of those who took the Barlow Road differed. Reactions depended on the weather, the fortitude of the travelers, the condition of the road at the particular time of travel, the physical stamina of the individuals, the strength of the draw animals, and the amount of provisions carried. For most, the Cascade crossing was far from being a picnic. Those who were exhilarated by the sweep of the forests and the snow cone of Mount Hood were vastly outnumbered by the men and women who cringed before the barrier that lay between them and the fertile prairies they had journeyed so far to reach.

Some men had all the spirit taken out of them when they contemplated the worst of the nerve-wracking task. Some women folded to the earth, sobbing. Everyone had to dismount and mothers with new babes in their arms were forced to push themselves up the slopes. Youngsters who could not climb the muddy hills were carried by their parents, already weak and tired from the many miles of toil behind them. Cattle and oxen were worn to a nub and faltered repeatedly, though often they were pulling empty wagons, the contents having been unloaded and hauled piecemeal upon the backs of the weary plodders. At some points, particularly one, the descent was so steep the wagons had to be let down with ropes. In that section of the Barlow Road which still bears some vestige of the original pike, rope scars can still be found on some trees.

Theodore Wygant, who crossed in 1850, still had sour memories of the Barlow Road when he dictated his reminiscences forty-six years later from the diary he carried on his way to Oregon.

"For over eight days," he recalled, "we struggled through snow, rain, mud, and cold and witnessed suffering and despair among the poor emigrants, beyond anything we had before encountered—deserted wagons, hundreds of dead cattle mired in the mud, with only their backs sticking out,—cattle lying dead around wagons, with the emigrant families and their camp fires near, the people waiting for help to come to them from the Willamette Valley; such were the scenes that we passed through the Cascade Mountains, ourselves nearly all the time on foot, picking our way as best as we could and driving our poor animals."

Two years later Enoch Conyers noted in his journal: "We are now camped at the foot of the Cascade Mountains and three miles from the 'Barlow Gate' where toll is supposed to be taken for the great benefit to be derived by the poor emigrant, worn out by his long trip of two thousand miles across the country with an ox team, who now has the privilege of paying a few paltry dollars for crossing the last range of mountains between him and civilization." At Barlow Gate, where they camped in a "beautiful place," Conyers party found no one to take toll, which did not disturb him. "The poor worn out emigrant is not one bit sorry."

The roughest part of the Barlow Road was behind the corners when they arrived at the western toll gate. Passage was five dollars per wagon and ten cents per head of stock. The toll could be paid in cash, note, or kind. The long trek had cost the calico pilgrims much more than they had anticipated, and many arrived almost destitute. In the first years, half of the persons using the Barlow Road could not pay. Some of them never honored their debt. The Barlow Road continued as a toll pike until 1912. By then it was quite passable.

It took the caravans about two weeks to travel from The Dalles to Oregon City via the Barlow Road. Today, of

Barlow Road at Smock Prairie

Phoebe L Friedman

course, the drive by automobile is an easy one and can be
easily accomplished in two hours.

Today's motorist can follow the Barlow Road from The
Dalles by taking US 197 to Tygh Valley, a favorite covered
wagon campground. From here a paved road leads west six
miles to the hamlet of Wamic, a sometime "east gate" toll
station. Here the real Barlow Road begins. A narrow dirt
road westward, not recommended for most passenger
vehicles, is the one remaining portion of the pure pike that
cannot be reached by highway. It snakes thirty-two miles

through the dusklight of tangled woods, often edging precipitous slopes, to Barlow Pass, on Oregon 35. Above Smock Prairie, near Wamic, the hillsides still bear the ruts of the battered wagons.

Before long other wagons reaching Wamic angled south and furrowed a road along the White River. It entered present Oregon 216 and became an alternate part of the Barlow Road, a cutoff of a cutoff, traditional along the Oregon Trail. The state highway continues to US 26, which lopes north to Government Camp.

In 1849 a detachment of the First US Mounted Rifles, which had crossed the plains and come up from The Dalles on the Barlow Road, lost more than half its horses and mules in trying to get around Mount Hood. So arduous and perilous was the trail that forty-five wagons were abandoned. The warning sign they posted: "Government Property—Do Not Touch," gave rise to the name of Government Camp.

US 26 follows with a high degree of faithfulness the Barlow Trail. West of Government Camp, descending the seaward slope of the Cascades, the emigrants looked down the dizzying plunge of Laurel Hill—so named because the rhododendron bushes reminded the comers of the laurel they knew back east—and prepared for the worse. Two miles of swift drop awaited them.

"The road on this hill is something terrible," a distraught Enoch Conyers lamented in his journal. "It is worn down into the soil from five to seven feet, leaving steep banks on both sides, and so narrow that it is almost impossible to walk alongside of the cattle for any distance without leaning against the oxen. The emigrants cut down a small tree about ten inches in diameter and about forty feet long, and the more limbs it has on the better. This tree they fastened to the rear axle with chains or ropes, top and foremost, making an excellent brake."

Laurel Hill, with Mount Hood in the background. For many takers of the Barlow Road, this was the most difficult section of the Oregon Trail.

Courtesy State of Oregon

Off Laurel Hill the going was easy and there was little grumbling when the wagons had to ford Zigzag River, a tributary of the Sandy. A mile farther the emigrants reached Lower Tollgate, the end of the Barlow Road, and stepped upon the hem of the Willamette Valley. Now thoughts were concerned with where to settle.

From Lower Tollgate to Oregon City there was no single path. Generally, the early wagons followed the Sandy River to present Sandy (by way of present Marmot Road, where many parties bivouaced at Rock Corral), and turned toward Eagle Creek, where Philip Foster operated a farm, grist mill, store, and restaurant. Foster's farm was the site of the last great encampment and the opportunity for the weary travelers to have their first home-cooked meal in months. The next morning the Clackamas River was forded and in less than another day the emigrants arrived at Oregon City.

There was no definable end of the Oregon Trail—as, in truth, there was no one jump-off on the Missouri River (half-a-dozen places have claimed that distinction). The strongest bid for such honors has been made by Oregon City, where caravans generally dissolved themselves in the first years of wagon travel.

Celebrations upon reaching Oregon City, or any other breaking-up point, were brief, if at all. The emigrants were too busy wondering and inquiring about where and with whom to go. Speculation was rampant and ill-advice sent many a family on a wild goose chase. Eventually there was a sorting out and settling down, though there was constant change and upheaval and a bag of loose ends.

A rule of thumb for some comers was to locate near the farmsteads of relatives, friends, and neighbors who had arrived before them. In time, some Willamette Valley communities were comprised almost entirely of people from the same midwestern county. A case in point is the area of Benton County known as Irish Bend, where the children of Erin followed one another to the flat prairie of the Willamette River.

Those who made it to the end of the Trail had little time in the beginning to look back. The concern for almost all was first in surviving and then establishing commerce and communities which would enlarge their lives.

Later, when there was time for leisure—for picnics, reunions, and historical societies—a looking back began to take shape. It grew as men and women aged and thus clung the more fiercely to the bedrock of their pioneer importance. Year by year their trail experiences became more meaningful. In a state that changed so vastly during their own lifetime, they reaffirmed their pioneer spirit in a surge of memories.

Whatever else the pioneers had done with their lives, they had one distinction no one could take from them: they had come the long, hard way to seed Oregon. They were, in their glory, the sons and daughters of the Fabulous Trail.

Some Who Didn't Stay

For the emigrants crossing the plains, Oregon should have been their final destination. That was the way they had planned. But some could not put a halt to their moving. A few went north but most turned south, for California. Others kept going—elsewhere, anywhere.

The situation was prophetically seen by Captain Avery Sylvester, a Massachusetts skipper who witnessed the arrival of the Great Migration of 1843, the first wagon train to reach Oregon and made up significantly of Missourians.

"They are well adapted for pioneering," wrote Sylvester, "and to this end to civilize and endure, and devote their attention. As soon as schools and churches make their appearance, and the chase becomes scarce, they sell their lands for the most that they can get, and retire to the West, where they take up new lands, shove back the Indians, and prepare the way for more advanced civilization. . . . What turn they will make is more than I can tell, but one thing is sure, this place will hold but a few of them, and that few the most civilized. The others will sift out to California and for a new Texas, most likely. In this way the US will be enabled to take honorable possession of a great part of Mexico."

Prominent among the 1843 arrivals was Peter Hardeman Burnett, who solemnly vowed to hitch his wagon to the future of the new land. Soon he became the area's foremost propagandist. "I consider Oregon as superior to California," he crowed. "The climate of that country is too warm for men to have any commercial enterprise."

Peter Burnett
Courtesy Oregon Historical Society

Burnett's broadsides, featured in many an Eastern newspaper, were not entirely selfless. He and a fellow traveler of the plains, Morton Matthew McCarver, had founded a town called Linnton (now part of Portland) and were working overtime to sell lots. Some innocents, pondering the long trek to Oregon, might have been a little

Morton Matthew McCarver
Courtesy Oregon Historical Society

more skeptical had they known that Burnett and McCarver were in the real estate business.

You can safely guess what happened to Peter Burnett, who had so strongly warned the folks back home about going to California. He went there himself. When Linnton couldn't make it as the great port of the Willamette, Burnett turned to farming, politics, and law, and did well at all three. Upon the creation of Oregon Territory, Burnett's cousin, President James K. Polk, appointed him judge of the Territorial Supreme Court, but by the time the news reached Oregon, Burnett was headed for the gold mines. Two years later he was elected California's first governor.

McCarver also made tracks for California and was a delegate to that state's constitutional convention. Unable to get his own way—excluding Negroes from the state—he returned to Oregon. After a spell he was off again, this time to Tacoma, Washington, where he died.

Another of the 1843 comers to leave Oregon was Henry H. Hunt, who hauled a set of mill irons across the plains. The next year, at what is now Clifton, he built a sawmill and in 1845 was shipping rough-cut lumber to the Sandwich (Hawaiian) Islands. Six years later, having made his fortune, he sailed off for California, setting an example for multitudes of the affluent in the century to follow.

There were, of course, others before Burnett, McCarver, and Hunt.

The Revolutionary War hero, Robert Gray, who brought the first ship into the Columbia, shrugged away all possibility of a profitable trading post being built at present Astoria and returned to sea, never to come back to the Great River of the West.

Lewis and Clark had no intention of staying permanently in Oregon. They left two weeks ahead of their scheduled departure, wondering if they would ever get the dampness out of their bones.

Philip L. Edwards, who came with Jason Lee in 1834 and was second to Ewing Young in command of the great cattle drive of 1837, was probably the most versatile and gifted of the early Oregonians. He returned east with Lee in 1838 to drum up reinforcements for the Methodist missions and saw Oregon no more.

Thomas Jefferson Farnham, organizer of the near-disastrous Peoria Party, reached his private mecca, Oregon, in the autumn of 1839. Before he could find heaven, the rains came. Mired in mud, Farnham booked passage on the first ship bound for New York. Until he returned west—to California—he spent a lot of time denouncing the "Oregon Bubble Burst."

Lansford Hastings, like Farnham an attorney and author, also had a vision of paradise, but in 1843, after a year in Oregon, he led a caravan of fellow-disillusioned to California. Determined that no one else be misled, he worked indefatigably to convince Oregon-bound emigrants that they would do better in the southland.

In 1845 William B. Ide was one of those who turned off the trail for California. The next year he entered the pages of history as "General" Ide, commander-in-chief of the thirty-three-man, ragtag army that hoisted the Bear flag above Sonoma and established a very short-lived independent republic with Ide as president.

Samuel Hancock, a leader of the caravan from which Ide split off, didn't think Oregon such a bad place. Nonetheless, for reasons of his own, he moved on eventually to Whidbey Island, Washington.

The propaganda war on Oregon began long before the first wagon train set out from Independence, Missouri. Probably the most ardent publicist was Hall Jackson Kelley, a Massachusetts schoolteacher whose obsession became the promotion of the Oregon Country. He turned out books, pamphlets, and letters in such quantity as to provide continuous reading for his fans. When he was twenty-seven or twenty-eight, he wrote, "Word came expressly to me to go and labor in the fields of philanthropic enterprise and promote the propagation of Christianity in the dark and cruel places about the shores of the Pacific." A few years later, after he had started to paint the Oregon Country in the lavish colors of the Garden of Eden, he "announced to the world" his intention to settle Oregon. That was in 1824. Ten years later he finally made it to his dreamland, arriving penniless at Fort Vancouver.

He didn't stay long. Dr. John McLoughlin, the chief factor of the post, had little tolerance for fanatics, and he shipped Kelley out the following spring. That didn't stop Kelley, back in Boston, from resuming his agitation for American settlement of Oregon, but by then stronger voices were speaking out.

One of the more articulate champions of Oregon was Senator Linn of Missouri. In 1838, summarizing all he had read, Linn declared that the Oregon Country "may almost be considered tropical," and an eastern writer, equally informed, stated that "oranges, lemons, citrons, pomegranates, and vegetables common to the warm climates can be cultivated here." To enhance his credibility, the latter added that cotton would do well along the shores of the Columbia River.

Just as early, there were those who argued the other side. John B. Wyeth in 1833 quoted a W.J.S., who supposedly had been to the Pacific Northwest and back and had described his experiences in two 1832 issues of *New-England Magazine.*

Wrote Wyeth: "He says: 'Do the Oregon emigrants seek a fine country on the Oregon River? [Undoubtedly the Columbia.] They will pass through lands to get to it of which they may buy two hundred acres for less than the farther expenses of their journey.'

"He tells those who may reach St. Louis, that they will find there many who have been to Oregon, and found no temptation to remain there."

Wyeth ends with a plea: "It is devoutly to be wished that truth may prevail respecting those distant regions. Indeed the sacred cause of humanity calls loudly on its votaries to disabuse the people dwelling on these Atlantic shores respecting the Oregon paradise, lest our farmers' sons and young mechanics would, in every sense of the phrase, stray from home, and go they know not whither—to seek they know not what."

Few of the great trailblazers who wandered through the Pacific Northwest remained in the Oregon Country. Only the name of Peter Skene Ogden comes readily to mind. Joe Meek and Ewing Young were about the only real Mountain Men who came to Oregon to live out their lives. Black Harris died in Missouri; Osborne Russell, who lost an eye while blasting rock at Oregon City, passed away at Placerville, California; Doc Newell's life came to an end at Lewiston, Idaho; James Clyman breathed his last in California's Napa Valley.

An unheralded Oregon arrival of 1845 was James W. Marshall, a New Jersey carriage maker. He took a swing around the Willamette Valley, found it too damp and too hungry, and hied himself off for California. There, at present Sacramento, he was engaged by John A. Sutter to build a sawmill on the South Fork of the American River, at a place afterward called Coloma. One January morning of 1848—Marshall thought it was the nineteenth but it seems more likely it was the twenty-fourth—he was checking the tailrace when something odd caught his eye. Stepping into the lower end of the race he found upon a rock, six inches below the surface of the water, one or two pieces of gold. The rest is history.

Along with others at the discovery site was Charles Bennett, an 1844 Oregon emigrant who left the Willamette Valley three years later and wound up at Sutter's Mill. Both Sutter and Marshall mention Bennett in their accounts of the gold findings, which appeared in the November 1857 issue of *Hutchings California Magazine*.

Sutter wrote: "In the fall of 1847, after the mill seat had

James W Marshall
Courtesy Oregon Historical Society

been located, I sent up to this place . . . a number of laborers . . . and a little later I engaged Mr. Bennet from Oregon to assist Mr. Marshall in the mechanical labors of the mill."

Marshall noted that when he discovered gold, Bennett was then at the house, "sick." The next day, the wife of one of the workers at the mill made some experiments upon the gold "by boiling it in strong lye, and saleratus; and Mr. Bennet by my directions beat it very thin."

That ought to have set the record straight, but for the rest of his life Bennett claimed that it was he who had first seen the gold, and so it is recorded on the marble shaft above his grave in the Odd Fellows Cemetery at Salem.

When news of the gold discovery reached Oregon early in August 1848, practically the entire adult male population decamped. Women were left behind to work the farms, tend the stores, conduct prayer meetings, teach, doctor, and carry on the affairs of society. Early in September the Reverend George Henry Atkinson, a newcomer to Oregon City, reported in dismay:

"During the last two weeks our town has been in a state of high excitement. Our lawyers are going or gone. Our mechanics have left their shops in many cases. Our three physicians decided to leave. Some of our merchants decided to dispose of their merchandise, or to close business and leave. Several preachers left camp meetings and religious duties to follow their fleeting people. We are left with women and children."

A more pungent commentary on the decampment was a poem composed by John Carey and printed in the November 10, 1848, issue of the *Oregon Spectator.* It reveals more graphically than scholarly prose the temperature of the gold rush fever in Oregon.

> At sound of gold rush both young and old
> Forsook their occupation.
> And wild confusion seemed to rule
> In every situation.
>
> The doctor cocked his eye askance,
> The Promised wealth descrying,
> Then wheeled his horse and off he went
> And left his patients dying.

The preacher dropped the Holy book
And grasped the mad illusion.
The horseman left his flock and crook
Amid the wild confusion.

And then I saw far in the rear
A fat, purse-proud attorney
Collect his last retaining fee
And start upon his journey.

So many Oregonians stayed on in California that their vote provided the margin in electing ex-Oregonian Peter Burnett as governor of the new state.

As far back as the early 1840s there was constant changing of states by the unsatisfied. Californians departed their drought for the rain of Oregon, and Oregonians fled their wetness for the arid spaces of California. When migrating parties met along the trail they would strenuously argue, with each side putting down the land left behind and urging the others to change their minds. There seem to have been no winners.

However boring, one must return to the gloomy rain as a prime factor that caused people, who had come with hearts aglow, to hit the road again for drier and sunnier climes. An early example is Charles Howard Crawford, a young minister in the Cumberland Presbyterian Church, who arrived overland in Oregon in 1851. He really wanted to stay, but the damp winters drove him to take passage to San Francisco. By 1858, though, Babylon on the Bay didn't have enough sin for a vigorous conservative preacher to combat, so Crawford sought choicer pickings in the rough town of Stockton.

He gave Oregon one more try, returning in 1862 to spread the gospel among the Powder River miners. He was in his element here, among roughnecks, compulsive gamblers, good men gone to seed by drink, sinners in the clutch of the devil, vigilantes and their hangings. Two years was all he could take, and he never set eyes on Oregon again.

Another man who made it safe to Oregon and then took off for California was Buffalo Bill—but not the Cody of penny-thriller fame. This Buffalo Bill was in reality William Havens, who jaunted off on foot from his 1851 wagon train—when Cody was a five-year-old—to shoot a buffalo in a herd seen nearby. The caravan moved on, and it took Havens two days to catch up. He was empty-handed, but he had a whopping good story in explanation. As related by Charles Crawford, Havens said: "I got near enough to shoot a buffalo and it made him mad and he took off after me. When the others saw him running they ran too and I was chased by a large herd. They were all throwing their tails 'wiggletree, waggletree, wiggletree, waggletree.'"

It seemed highly implausible to Haven's listeners that he could fully observe the tails of the buffalo thundering after him while he fled for dear life. After the laughter subsided he was named Buffalo Bill, and to his dying day he was called that.

Some people couldn't make up their minds and kept crossing and recrossing the continent. John L. Burres, for whom a state wayside on the John Day River is named, described in his memoirs an experience near Green River, while Burres was Oregon bound in 1854:

> Here we met the first people going east, one Man Wife and three babies. The babies were the two oldest in baskets one on each side the horse while one was carefully packed in the middle on top the horses back. When first married this couple crossed the plains [to] the Willamette Valley [but] the winter was too wet for them. They had a child born there. When spring came with good weather they crossed back to Missouri. There the second child was born. They found Missouri too cold and moved back to Oregon where the third baby came to see them. But it was too wet for them and they

were on their fourth trip across the plains to
Missouri again. Uncle Charley asked them It isn't
very profitable is it [and] they said well it's a
healthy way of living. How long they kept this
game going or which state they finally settled in I
never knew.

Burres had his own trait of indecision. After trying
California and Washington Territory he staked out a claim
near Albany. Then in 1880 he and his family moved to the
Pendleton area. Next he halted for a while in Sherman
County. His final stop was Goldendale, Washington.

People pondering on moving west to Oregon were often
torn betweeen the rhapsodic letters of the settlers, who may
have been trying to justify their coming out, and the
embittered backtrackers, who depicted Oregon in the most
vile and nauseating terms. If everybody who arrived in
Oregon before territorial status had stayed here, the country
might have doubled its population.

Within Oregon, people kept changing their minds on the
character of the land and the worthiness of its settling. Time
and changing conditions had more than a little to do with
shifts in opinion.

Peter Burnett, who came in 1843, was ecstatic about the
white folks he found. "I never knew so fine a population, as
a whole community, as I saw in Oregon most of the time I
was there," he reminisced. "They were all honest, because
there was nothing to steal; they were all sober, because there
was no liquor to drink; there were no misers, because there
was nothing to hoard; they were industrious, because it was
work or starve."

This rather sanguine state of affairs was of relatively short
duration as the east caught up with the west. Reports of
Paradise foundering became as numerous as the rhetoric of
Paradise found. In 1851, two months after he had completed
the long haul from Springfield, Illinois, where he had been a
neighbor of Abraham Lincoln, the ever-opinioned David

Newsom set forth his impression of the territory in a letter to the *Illinois Journal*: "Oregon has been much overrated and men's expectations have been raised too high! You will find as many sharpers and swindlers at The Dalles, Portland, and Oregon City as you can guard against."

Less than two years later David Newsom was writing of hard times for the comers: "The old Oregonians, or 'wheat boilers,' as they are commonly called here, have reaped a golden harvest off the emigrants of 1852 . . . . The emigrant's money went first; then their remnant of stock, and then their credit and labor; and now that Spring has arrived, poor fellows, they have nothing left upon which to begin the world.

"Many thousands are now in Oregon, who are entirely destitute of the means of subsistence. They are restless and discouraged, and look on the dark side of the picture."

Some of the destitute and discouraged dragged themselves off to California, where at least they could be warmer. Some others returned and threw themselves on the mercy of relatives and friends for a fresh start in the old land. Almost every county in Missouri, Iowa, Illinois, and Indiana had at least one family who had tried Oregon and given up.

Newsom also warned, a month after his previous letter, of expecting too much out here. Emigrants, he cautioned, "seem to think that nothing is really neccessary but to reach Oregon, and here fall into the arms of the kindliest people on earth, and *live*! But on arriving, they soon discover their mistake, and find that men have human nature here as well as elsewhere."

Somehow the sparsely settled country appeared to some idealists as virgin land in more ways than one. For them, Oregon was—or should be—untarnished by the sordid political and business ethics of the East. For them the most bountiful crop on the frontier was virtue. The Golden Rule guided every path, and from every hill there echoed the

Sermon on the Mount. Their experiences on the trail should have taught them better, but their illusions were really shattered when they learned that Oregon was a new beginning only in time and space and not in morality.

Some of the idealists left Oregon during the territorial years because they felt the country had become too corrupt. David Newsom complained in 1855: "We are cursed with bad legislation and bad laws. The laws here are made right under the fumes of the brandy bottle." Those who moved on to California in search of cleaner politics quickly found they had gone from the bottle to the still.

Few pioneer families held their lands after the second generation. "There is ironical significance," observed Charles Henry Carey in his *History of Oregon*, "in the fact that the lands for which these original settlers hungered, and for which they braved almost incredible hardships, and for which they endured almost innumerable deprivations to make them more fruitful, have largely passed from the possession of their descendants."

Twenty years earlier, at the turn of the century, TW Davenport surveyed an area "100 square miles on the east side of the Willamette Valley, in Marion County" and found that "sixty-six percent of the donation land claims have passed out of the possession of the donees and their descendents."

Weary, defeated, seeking a respite from their toils, at least some of these pioneers departed for other parts of the state, or for other Western states, or back to where they had started.

The first great rush to Central Oregon began shortly after the turn of the century, when the greedy railroads and unscrupulous land promoters lured thousands of eastern, southern, and midwestern families to the High Desert. Gaudy brochures, flamboyant posters and pie-in-the-sky newspaper ads promised rich land at low cost, bountiful crops, feasible transportation, modern schools, available market centers, good roads, ample water and whatever else could turn the minds of the innocents.

Lies, all lies. The land was harsh, the soil unyielding, rainfall was scant, transportation was far off and market centers as far or farther. From Arrow it was ninety-five miles to the nearest railroad point; from Fort Rock, fifty-three miles "by the new road"; from Stauffer, ninety-five miles; from Summer Lake, sixty-five miles; from Warner Lake, a mere forty miles; and some settlements were more than 100 miles from the closest railhead.

Roads were far between and bad, schools had to be built, doctors were often two days away.

The wind seemed to blow constantly. There were few trees for shelter. All attempts to plant orchards failed. Wood had to be hauled long distances to build homes, most of which never got beyond the stage of shanties.

"The country was very undeveloped," remembered John Jenkins whose family came out from Minnesota in 1912 to settle on land five miles from Sink, in northern Lake County. "There was only a post office at Sink and no place else to obtain needs for a distance of at least seventy to ninety miles. There was no water so it had to be hauled from Sink."

The homesteaders worked themselves to the bone to dig wells but few succeeded in reaching water. (Apart from the land promoters and town merchants, the only people on the High Desert to make money were the professional well diggers, and most homesteaders could not afford them.)

Digging a well was "found to be very difficult because of the rock formation which required extensive blasting with dynamite," recalled John Jenkins. "There were no outer buildings for storage and so the dynamite was stored under the beds in the shack we called home. As the hole for the well deepened a windlass was constructed atop the hole.

An abandoned ranchstead on the High Desert
Phoebe L Friedman

This enabled my mother to raise the nail keg that was used to remove the debris from the bottom of the well after having been filled by my father. After that was done father had to be raised by my mother . . . Then the dynamite had to be set and father would yodel for help and had to be raised to the top again. Before the fuze could be lighted, juniper logs had to be laid across the well. This process continued until the well was fifty-three feet deep with no sign of water. At that depth the only rope we had broke and with no replacement and with very little prospect of water the project had to be discontinued.

"There was not only a shortage of water but also of food, particularly meat. To provide for our meat, mother would set a trap each night for rabbits, as there were many of them. There were so many in fact that rabbit drives were organized from time to time." (Naturally, the rabbits consumed whatever vegetables managed to grow.)

When the homesteaders cleared the sagebrush, the wind blew the soil away. The bunchgrass was too rich for horses and many died. By the time the nation became aroused to World War I the towns had begun to disappear, less than a decade after the first had been established. Some of the men went to the shipyards to seek work; others, with their families, returned home. By 1920 most of the settlements were gone. Without exception the others were vacated within a few years or enfeebled.

The family of John Jenkins was typical in its despair and lost dreams. The only water the family had was hauled, the stock were dead or dying, the land grew nothing but sagebrush and bunchgrass. Others in the same condition could only plod away, too poor to go home. The Jenkins family was luckier.

"With no future in sight," said John Jenkins in 1991, "mother saved us from complete ruin by making it known she had money that she had earned during her years as a seamstress before marriage that could finance our return to Minnesota. Father was more than happy to take advantage of this opportunity and we returned to Tracy, Minnesota on April 29, 1913."

The remains of two of my favorite Oregonians are outside the state, one to the south and one to the north. The first went of his own volition, the second was exiled as a prisoner of war.

I have often spoken of Charles Erskine Scott Wood as the Leonardo da Vinci of Oregon. He was, as lawyer, soldier, scholar, writer, humanist, and advocate, as completely talented, integrated, and far-seeing a figure as the state was ever privileged to know. A companion of artists and bohemians, mentor to Portlander John Reed (whose ashes lie under the Kremlin Wall), courtroom defender of socialists and anarchists, corporate attorney, as much at home with cowboys as with financiers, and as at ease with

Charles Erskine Scott Wood
Courtesy Erskine Wood

the penniless as with the overstuffed, CES Wood was for all
seasons. By the linear standards of Oregon he was an
anachronism, an oddity who could be forgiven because he
was colorful, a freethinker who could be tolerated because

Medallion of Chief Joseph, owned by Erskine Wood
Phoebe L Friedman

he was deeply imbedded in the power structure. He was
wealthy and he was famous and, because of that, society
could overlook his abiding sympathy for the Indians, his
irreverent ideology, and his sometimes shocking liberal
views. His last years were spent with his second wife, the
gentle and concerned poet, Sara Bard Field, in Los Gatos,
California. Cremated, his ashes were spread on a hillside
under a spreading oak.

Chief Joseph the Younger—the Indian half of the mutual
admiration society of Joseph and Wood—was in his own
way as gifted and heroic as his white friend. Joseph was a

Erskine Wood

Phoebe L Friedman

compelling orator, a philosopher who would have been at home among the weighty sages of his time, and a patriot of his people.

After losing their land to white expropriators, Joseph and his Nez Perces sought to reach Canada and freedom. Less than two days short of their goal the end came, in the Bear Paw hills of Montana. He was first exiled to what is now Oklahoma and later placed on the Colville Reservation in arid north-central Washington. There he died of a broken heart. And there he lies today. Despite all his pleas, Joseph was not permitted to return to his beloved Wallowa Valley, his valley-of-the-winding-waters, where his adored father was buried.

Wood in California, Joseph in Washington. Between the spreading oak on the hillside of Los Gatos and the grave at Nespelem on the Colville Reservation there lived in Vancouver, Washington a man who knew both. Erskine Wood had written lovingly of his father and of his father's trusted friend, Chief Joseph, with whom Erskine as a lad had spent two summers on the isolated reservation. Upon his death in 1983 Erskine Wood was buried in Portland's Riverview Cemetery. He was, thus, one of those who did stay.

The Good Life In Oregon

The good life in Oregon is at Lonerock, Leslie Gulch, Whiskey Run, Shaniko, on the Silvies River, at Strawberry Lake, and at a passel of other places you won't find listed in the glossy travel folders.

The good life in Oregon is plowing up a scruffy slope in search of Oregon Trail wagon ruts; tramping the beach below Cape Ferrelo at dawn for Japanese glass floats or sea-sculptured driftwood; breathing the musk of juniper ridges through the open window of the only motel room in a dot on the desert a hundred miles from the nearest city; rummaging through the moss-covered garbage heaps of an abandoned mining camp; packhorsing into the glacier-coated Eagle Cap Wilderness of the Wallowa Mountains, the "Switzerland of Oregon"; lurching along the sand dunes south of Florence; pitching camp on Hart Mountain, where prong-horned antelope roam at day and coyotes call at night; stumbling across a vine-covered cemetery that hasn't had a fresh grave for seventy-five years; talking to old buckaroos who started wrangling before the first automobile honked its way into the Blitzen Valley; snapping pictures of a pioneer church that had been turned into a sheep barn; cooling your feet in a lake reflecting the face of South Sister; pausing at the side of a dirt road in sparsely-settled Wheeler County and exclaiming, "Look, no smog!" and, well—a thousand other inexpensive and unstructured pursuits, all of which Oregonians relate to the outdoors.

Oregon isn't a great resort state. Apart from Salishan, the

Taj Mahal of Coastal inns; Sun River, at the eastern hem of the Central Cascades; and Kah-nee-ta, the Indian spa on the Warm Springs Reservation, there aren't many swanky resorts. Dude ranches are about as few.

Oregon does have some major tourist attractions. The best-known, of course, is Crater Lake National Park. After you have seen Crater Lake, everything else in the state is anti-climactic—except the southern coast, of course. But Crater Lake buttons down for the summer after Labor Day and early in autumn the snow arrives. Also, Crater Lake to many Oregonians is tourism-bounded: a calendar picture thing people here are trying to get away from.

The Oregon Coast, the unspoiled parts of which are equal in rugged beauty to any coast on this planet, is less formal, and there are still beaches where you can stroll a mile or two without meeting another soul or where you can build a fire at night without having to inhale anyone else's smoke. That, too, is part of the good life, away from the Coney Island highway strips and pompous motels. From Brookings, near the California border, to Port Orford, where the West bends against the West in a surge of awesome magnificence, the Oregon Coast achieves its grandest dimensions and contouring and is farthest from the madding crowd.

Oregon Caves National Monument, "The Marble Hall of Oregon," is also highly-publicized, and rightly so, being the most exciting and exquisitely-carved complex of caverns on the Pacific slope. And there are such privately-owned ventures as Sea Lion Caves, where herds of the ocean mammals colonize in a deep recess of an ocean shelf, and compounds where tame deer eat out of your hand. All of these pull in large numbers of tourists. And like every other state, Oregon has its share of festivals, salmon bakes, chicken and turkey roasts, regattas, county fairs, historic celebrations, river floats, timber carnivals, and agricultural fiestas.

Herding sheep on the high plains of central Oregon.

Jim Hughes

Then there are the growing number of folk pageants, headed by two of at least regional stature: Scandinavian Festival at Junction City, and Mt. Angel's Bavarian-like Oktoberfest.

Finally, with apologies to all other activities which have been omitted, there are the rodeos—so many that nobody seems to know them all, because some are not professional or accredited or anything else that smacks of official respectability. But there is as much spirit and drama at the All-Indian Rodeo, below tiny Tygh Valley, or at the

The welcome mat is out at Alkali Lake Station.

Phoebe L Friedman

Imnaha River Canyon, in Wallowa County.
Courtesy State of Oregon

ramshackle, dungy grounds of the Paulina Rodeos, which mainly draw ranchhands from the Ochoco hills, as there is at the internationally-renowned Pendleton Round-Up, the most extravagant bite-the-dust show this side of Cheyenne or Calgary.

The Pendleton Round-Up, which rings down the curtain on Oregon rodeos, coming in mid-September, is easy to reach. Pendleton is astride Oregon's cardinal east-west highway, I-84, and is serviced by multi-daily air flights and bus runs. The city, largest in eastern Oregon, has numerous lodgings, but tourist accommodations are sold out months before the Indians set up their tepees back of the arena and downtown is transformed into a false-front cow-trail railhead.

Paulina, on the other hand, doesn't have such restrictions on housing, simply because there isn't any in the frontier hamlet of thirty, where the general store is also the post office, tavern, and gas station. (No lube jobs, or anything like that; just a couple of pumps leaning against the store.)

You have to look close at an Oregon map to find Paulina. First you locate Prineville, on US 26. It's a big town in these parts, better than 5,000 people, and the seat of Crook County. It has another distinction: "Rockhound Capital of the USA." Thousands come here yearly to dig into the free chamber of commerce claims for plume, moss agate, obsidian, and thunder eggs.

From Prineville a blacktop county road takes off eastward for Post and Paulina. It galumphs through deep rock canyons, mounts a vast plateau, and passes a silent world of sage hummocks, choppy hills, tumble-down shacks, sagging fences, and far off the pavement, a few stock ranches. It also runs alongside of, for thirty miles, the Crooked River, deeply etched in Oregon history and folklore.

Down this twisty stream, in 1845, came the battered, grimy wagons of the lost, dispirited Meek Cutoff Party. Somewhere along their confused route, at the Crooked or another river or creek, several nuggets were said to have been picked up and placed in a wooden water container, giving rise to the state's most embedded legend, the Blue Bucket Mine.

None of the emigrants, as the tale goes, knew that the butter-colored bits of metal were gold. The awareness came only after gold was discovered in California. It was followed by frenetic searches, with expeditions scouring central and eastern Oregon. The Blue Bucket Mine was never found but the Argonauts did unearth gold near present Baker City, setting off a boom that saw the overnight skyrocketing of a hundred gold camps, few of which survive even as ghost towns.

Twenty-five miles out of Prineville the first settlement is reached—Post, in the geographical center of Oregon. Blink twice and you'll miss it. The entire town is only a store and a sleepy Grange hall, and its total human population consists of husband and wife, who sell groceries, stamps, and gasoline.

Paulina, thirty miles beyond Post, was quite a burg in the homesteader days. As late as the 1920s it had three general stores, a barber shop, a blacksmith shop, and a two-story hotel. A restaurant operated until 1945. But the exodus of homesteaders and the combining of small farms into a few large ranches, plus the building of a decent road to Prineville, drained the life blood from the town. Paulina today is down to the store, an elementary school (high school students are bused to Prineville), a simple community church—formerly the schoolhouse at Beaver Creek, the pioneer Congelton ranchstead, and the Pau-Mau Club.

The club, a sun-blistered frame hall, is the parlor, oasis, stock mart, and civic forum for residents of a 2,500-square-mile area. They bounce in from the sage washes, the pine coves, and the wild horse hills for companionship, refreshment, trading, and gossip. Gone are the days of the monthly dances, country stomps which, except for the ear-splitting amplified guitar shock waves, were throwbacks to homesteader hoedowns. No longer do signs request patrons to check their guns, knives, and clubs at the door. Paulina is mighty civilized now, but at rodeo time, on Labor Day, the whooping-it-up echoes the blustery past.

Paulina tells something about what Oregonians regard as the good life. The hamlet is far off a state or national highway, it has a pioneer flavor, the land offers numerous photo possibilities, the tumble-down cabins invite scrounging for old bottles and other collector artifacts, and the Crooked River adds historical lore.

There are so many places to visit in Oregon without putting out a cent for admission. Jacksonville, in the southern part of the state, is a living museum of the mid-nineteenth century, when the town thrived from gold mining. You can spend hours in the sprawling cemetery on the hill, the museums, and the old (and sometimes quaint) buildings that comprise downtown and the nearby residential sections. Stores which in the 1850s and 1860s were occupied by butchers and bakers and harness makers are now the shops of artisans. Jacksonville has become Oregon's Carmel.

Lonerock firehouse and "post office"
Phoebe L Friedman

Shaniko, on US 97, is more recent, dating back only to the turn-of-the-century, when it was the wool shipping center of America. But its raw atmosphere and feral environment (the snow peaks of Mt. Jefferson and Mt. Hood frozen like coned clouds in the blue-burnished sky above the ochre-purple plateau) give Shaniko a "Western" mood which in contrast makes Jacksonville appear genteel and bourgeois.

Then there's Lonerock, southeast of Condon, with its tight fistful of humans and its tradition that the eldest citizen is mayor. Each house has a woodshed and separate underground cellar, as the homesteaders did a century ago. Near the great rock that gives the town its name the old church stands, seldom used now, but pretty as ever. And down the dirt street are the once viable enterprises which have been bolted for decades and decades.

Old homestead at Boyd

Ralph Friedman

Nehalem River near the end of its run.

Ralph Friedman

Towns like these are all over Oregon. Towns such as Westfall, which two decades ago had a post office but not a single resident within its platted boundaries; Drewsey, which gained the name of "Gouge Eye" in its hectic frontier days, and which had the most picturesque general store in the state; Golden, a charming weatherbeaten tintype hidden in the bend of a lonely country road; the ghostly gold camps of Bourne, Granite, Greenhorn, and Cornucopia; Hardman, which in approach looks alive, because of the buildings that line the highway, but is nigh deserted, another homesteader settlement molding toward dust; and dozens and dozens more.

There is supreme pleasure in browsing Oregon roads,

Wahkeena Falls, on Columbia River Scenic Highway.
Courtesy State of Oregon

whether they be the ocean loops of US 101; the highways which adhere to clear and spirited waters, such as the Umpqua, the Santiam, the McKenzie and the John Day; pikes across the mountains, with viewpoints reaching out to a jumble of color and form; or High Desert traces that slowly slither off into purple rangelands and lavendar hills.

Scenic roads are many. Those which come quickest to mind are the Columbia Gorge Scenic Highway, with its profusion of waterfalls; Century Drive, with its incredible variety of mountains, lakes, forests and volcanic flows (as well as the only Osprey Preserve in the nation); Deschutes River Canyon Access Road, leading into the primitive chasm and passing Sherar's Falls, where Indians fish from

Fossil Beds of Grant County
Courtesy State of Oregon

Anthony Lake at the foot of Gunsight Mountain.
Courtesy State of Oregon

wooden platforms above the boiling Deschutes as their ancestors did centuries ago; Hells Canyon, leading to the lip of the deepest gorge on the continent; Steens Mountain Scenic Drive, rising to 9,000-foot-high Fish Lake and then looking 5,000 feet to the historic Whitehorse Ranch, remote on the edge of a borax desert; Hat Point, gaping a mile down at the Snake River; and Upper Imnaha Canyon, where the Wallowa and Seven Devils mountains thunder above the isolated, strung-out picturebook ranches.

There is as much adventure in following roads scarcely

Goose Creek, below Broken Top Mountain.

Courtesy State of Oregon

known to outsiders: from Wagontire to Fort Rock, across a graveyard of homesteader towns; from Gold Beach to Wolf Creek, up alongside the tumultuous Rogue and through mountains which only a few decades ago were trackless save for the mute and overgrown paths of early prospectors; from Frenchglen to Fields, an outland desert hamlet which has changed little since it was a twenty-mule-train stop; and from Elgin to Troy, sixty-three miles through a forest primeval that is sheer magic every mile. And more, dozens more. Come explore for yourself; the whole state off the main highways is a treasure map.

For many Oregonians the good life is searching for agatized myrtle at Whiskey Run, or Greenhorn fern at

Scotts Mills County Park, in the heart of the Willamette Valley.
Phoebe L Friedman

Oneonta Gorge

Courtesy State of Oregon

Greenhorn, or jasper at Sunflower Flats, or the striking agate in Deadman Canyon, or obsidian at Glass Buttes or . . . I could go on for pages. Rockhounding is a prime avocation in Oregon.

For other Oregonians the good life is trolling for salmon at Winchester Bay or throwing out their lines for steelhead on the Chetco or trying for Rainbows and Eastern and bass and carp at one of several hundred rivers, lakes, creeks, and reservoirs.

Few states in the nation have as excellent a system of state, national, county, and corporation parks as does Oregon. Some state parks are so popular that reservations are mandatory, but I have camped at state, Forest Service, Bureau of Land Management, and county parks where only a small fraction of the campsites were taken, and on occasion I have found myself the only dweller for the night.

The good life in Oregon is bird-watching at the Malheur National Wildlife Refuge and spending the night at the Frenchglen Hotel, a frontier hostelry sixty miles from the nearest motel. A mile from the inn stood the headquarters of P-Ranch, made famous by the legendary Pete French, whose soul still rides the wind racing over the rimrock buttes. Although he has been dead for almost a century, gunned down by a homesteader while be basked in glory as the cattle king of Oregon, Pete French is talked about in Harney County as though he had been shot only yesterday.

The good life in Oregon is hiking along one of the hundreds of mountain trails, or trudging to high waterfalls not seen from a road, or riding the Canby Ferry back and forth across a dreamy bend of the Willamette River, or photographing covered bridges, or seeing green-soaked meadows roll through the Waldo Hills with the current of a snow-fed river, or just sitting on an autumn hillside and watching the leaves turn color.

What I am trying to say—and I know I will never

Covered bridge over Elk Creek, west of Drain.

Phoebe L Friedman

Rhododendrons along a rushing stream below Mt. Hood.
Courtesy State of Oregon

succeed, any more than anyone else really can—is that the good life of Oregon is Oregon itself: its unblemished Coast, its waters, its mountains, its valleys, its leathery cow towns and dusty desert hamlets, its compelling scenery (ranging from an early rural church at Sodaville to the Grand Canyonesque formation of Owyhee Lake and the stunning cliffs of Leslie Gulch), its fishing and rockhounding and indigenous museums and legends and history and its old people who want to tell their stories now, while they still have breath.

Oregonians have turned to an exploration of their state, doing it informally and as they please, without time schedule, fanfare or restrictions. And in their discoveries they have found the good life, as can you.

A Quiet At Gouge Eye

There is general agreement among chroniclers of Oregon folklore that Drewsey, near the northeastern corner of Harney County, began life as Gouge Eye. But Castolia Drinkwater, who was born in these parts in 1887 only four years after the area was peopled by palefaces, was sure Gouge Eye was never more than a nickname.

"They had so many fights and wild times and gouged each other's eyes out in those early days that folks got to calling it Gouge Eye," she told me some years ago. "But the proper name is Drewsey."

One of my favorite tales about Gouge Eye—or Drewsey—concerned the town drunk. The story was spun out for me in the 1930s by a Harney County cowpoke who handled a bottle as happily as he did a lariat. One day, the yarn goes, the town drunk sloshed down more than usual and, full of fire and bravado, staggered from saloon to saloon, taunting, "I can whip any SOB in this town." Finally he came to a saloon where the town marshal was snoozing in a chair at the card table. Hoisting himself to confront the lawman, the seedy soak repeated his boast. Without opening his eyes, the lawman hauled off and knocked the challenger stiff. When he awakened about twenty minutes later, the drunk crawled out of the saloon, lifted himself groggily, and lurched down the street hoarsely shouting, "The town marshal can lick any SOB in this town."

Castolia Drinkwater listened with stoic patience while I

Drewsey post office circa 1905.

Courtesy Alan Williams

told her this tale and replied neutrally, "There are a lot of stories."

Some writers hold that Drinkwater Pass, on US 20 three miles west of the turnoff to Drewsey, was given the name by emigrants who found potable water, just as Stinkingwater Pass, ten miles west of the turnoff, derived its designation from the disagreeable fumes of mineral springs along a nearby creek, which was tagged with the same odorous label.

"I don't know about Stinkingwater Pass," said Mrs. Drinkwater, a tall, big-boned woman with an air of serenity in her deep-pooled eyes, "but Drinkwater Pass was named after my family." Her parents were pioneers here and so were the parents of her late husband.

Castolia Drinkwater

Phoebe L Friedman

"The town was much bigger when I was young," Mrs. Drinkwater recalled. "We had one hundred, maybe one hundred-fifty people then. Only got forty now. Always been cattle country. And sheep—but more now."

Former IOOF Hall in Drewsey

Phoebe L Friedman

Drewsey slouched two and a half miles off US 20, but in atmosphere it seemed far removed from the national highway, where cars whizzed by at seventy miles per hour. Scarcely an outsider drove into the town which, but for the out-country gas station, looked as if it were built for a John Ford Western. Sequestered among splayed sagebrush, which in true frontier mystique spread to the gossamer swales of plastic hills, Drewsey was genuine leather, sweat-stained, and wind-scarred.

Some of the sagging wooden structures had to be at least ten years older than the IOOF building, put up in 1910. The

Catholic Church, no longer used as such, in Drewsey.

Phoebe L Friedman

old Catholic Church, no longer used and sleeping in a bed of arid stubble, couldn't be much younger. By any standard, the Community Church, erected in 1930, was a Johnny-come-lately.

Apart from the gas station there was only one important business in town, the Porter Sitz Co. general store. It was started before 1885, said Mrs. Drinkwater.

Her husband purchased the store in 1909. Upon his death in 1936 she took over the operation. She still owned the store when we were there, running the financial end from a paper-and-ledger-piled desk long-set on a platform in the rear. The merchandising management was left to Sam Burt, a breezy, wizecracking quick-mover who had been with the store since 1934.

Drewsey in the early 1900s

Courtesy Alan Williams

In all probability the Porter Sitz Co. general store was the most general general store in Oregon. In essence, it was the old-fashioned mercantile establishment which retained its horse-and-buggy character while adding modern wares. It carried groceries, frozen foods, hardware, dry goods (from suits and dresses to bolts of cloth and bedding), shoes and boots, grain, stock salt, toys, auto supplies, and a host of etceteras.

The goods overflowed the shelves and were hung from the rafters, jammed on counters, and heaped on the floor. Somehow, though, the customers knew exactly where to go and, if a newcomer didn't, Sam Burt precisely led the way. If the store could be seen as a haystack, he could find a needle in it.

Contemporary Drewsey
Courtesy Alan Williams

One thing the store was not: cash-and-carry. Most folks paid only once a month, the way it had been for nine decades.

Violence had become rare in Drewsey. An eye hadn't been gouged for more years than anyone could remember. "If you want to see that kind of rough stuff," said Mrs. Drinkwater laconically, "you have to watch television."

Postmoretem: Castolia Drinkwater died in a nursing home in Burns November 14, 1985, at age ninety-eight.

Sam Burt passed away in Drewsey July 27, 1984, fifty years after he had gone to work at the Porter Sitz Co. store.

The Porter Sitz store burned down in July 1979. It was rebuilt of steel in the fall and winter of 1979–80 as a storage facility.

By 1990 the IOOF building was gone. The old Catholic Church was privately owned. A new Catholic Church was holding mass Saturday evenings. The Community Church was still functioning.

In 1993 Drewsey had a population of twenty-six, a convenience store and post office, a cafe, and a gas station. The John Ford Western look of the countryside still remained.

Another Look At John Wayne

Could the United States Army fighting the Indians in the last century be as cruel and crude and stupid as depicted in the movie *Dances With Wolves?*

Yes, if we are to believe a letter written to the *Owyhee Avalanche* of long-gone Ruby City, Idaho Territory in 1865 by a prominent resident of southeastern Oregon.

The correspondent was Edward Watts Inskip, the proprietor of a fortified stage coach station and store known as Inskip Rock House, or Inskip's Station, fifteen miles west of Jordan Valley.

Inskip had trouble with the Indians. So did all the other whites in the area. The Indians had been pushed out of their homelands, and they struck back any way they could. The army was called in to deal with the "hostiles", and from the soldiers Inskip really learned the meaning of trouble. After a rather traumatic experience, he fired off this letter to the newspaper:

> Ruby Ranch, Lower Cow Creek
> November 28, 1865
> Eds. Avalanche: On the evening of 18th inst., we were visited by a bunch of cutthroats (commonly called New York wharf rats) in the shape of the "U.S.A." Regulars. They stole everything they could get their hands on about the ranch—flour, rice, sugar, coffee, potatoes, liquors, hay to sleep on, and robbed the corral of the fence posts and wood pile for fuel—and when I called on the officer to put out a guard to stop such depradations, he said it was a wet, bad evening,

but he would make all right in the morning. But when morning came, I was told by the same officer that they were going out to fight the Indians, and I should not begrudge the soldiers a little "straw." The same officer also came to me and said I might trade with the soldiers for anything but their arms and it would be all right, and even wanted to sell his own overcoat; but on the following morning said all clothing traded for should be returned, and positively refused to pay for anything his men stole—which amounted to at least a hundred dollars. One of his men, too, loaded his gun in the house and then deliberately discharged it through the roof, the ball striking a collar beam and rafter and throwing splinters all over the table where eight men were at dinner. I applied to the officer to take the men away, but he only told the man not to shoot in the house and let him go at large. These men also cut open each other's haversacks, and stole their contents. But I will give two soldiers credit; they remained sober and tried to keep the rest in their places, and told me that several of their comrades had rings with them for cutting pockets so as to steal their contents. Now Messrs. Editors, I think these men are more to be dreaded than the native Indians of the country, and I also believe New York sent them out here to get rid of them, and place them in a weak territory where we need help instead of a den of thieves.

Yours truly,
E.W. Inskip

Was Inskip an exception? Were the soldiers he accused of hooliganism of a vastly different breed than their comrades scattered elsewhere throughout the West? What happens to the image of John Wayne if there is some truth in Inskip's charges?

Unfortunately, soldiering in the West was sometimes not done by the best of mortals. Many of the men who joined the army were unschooled, often from the unemployed, or the poorly paid, or the drifters, who took out on the Indians their own frustrations.

Sheep Ranch House, in vicinity of Inskip's Station, was built about 1865 as a way station and fortification in case of Indian attacks. Note port holes.

Mike Hanley

In their biography of Colonel Benjamin Grierson (*Unlikely Warriors*) William H. and Sherley A. Leckie say of Grierson's recruiting problems in 1866, "Of fifteen men who arrived in November, one deserted after a few days, another was arrested by civil authorities in Leavenworth City and thrown in the 'calaboose' and a number of others turned out to be sickly and unfit for any kind of duty." This incidence could be multiplied to the point of sadness.

Desertions were not infrequent at the Western posts, with

the Volunteers being the worst offenders. During the Persian Gulf War, it was estimated that fully one-third of the Reserves called to duty did not show up. The Volunteers did better, or worse, taking holidays when they chose or simply going home to stay, despite their terms of enlistment.

Lieutenant Theodore Talbot, who served at the Columbia Barracks (Vancouver) and Astoria from the spring of 1849 to the close of 1852, was not optimistic about the men under him. "Talbot related their efforts to beat the black market, their attempts at suicide, their drunkenness, eccentricities, and all the emotional eruptions caused by close confinement during long winter months," wrote Robert V. Hine and Savoie Lottinville in their *Soldier of the West.* "In general, Talbot saw the army as filled with partiality and wastefulness, as ridiculously underpaid, and as hopelessly undermanned."

On June 11, 1849, Talbot wrote to his mother: "Some of our men have attempted to desert. Their plan was discovered and frustrated. Out of some 30 or 40 concerned in the plot, only seven got off. They were pursued the same night and retaken without loss. The only true way [to keep them contented] is to increase their proper military pay." But this was not done.

It was not rare for posts to be vacated without formality. In 1862, when the paymaster arrived at Fort Umpqua, near Reedsport, he found all the troopers absent, having gone hunting. Evidently the officers had also departed.

Officers as well as enlisted men went AWOL. Brevet Major General George A. Custer, after experiencing mass desertions in his Seventh Cavalry, left his command in frustration to join his wife in Fort Riley, Kansas, and for this indiscretion was court martialed and found guilty.

On some posts there was as much friction between the men as there was hostility between the soldiers and the Indians. Bitterness among officers was as rampant. Talbot, speaking of the "Regt. Mounted Rifles" which arrived in Oregon City in the early fall of 1849, declared, "there appears to be but little harmony among the officers of that Regiment." At that point, three officers of the regiment were facing court martials.

(In a "procedure almost without precedent in the records of Military Courts," Talbot relates his experience as a member of a General Court Martial. The president of the court, Brevet Lieutenant Colonel Backenstos, "was deemed by the Court to have been guilty of gross disrespect in the face of the Court, and was arraigned and tried by the Court." Later, Backenstos was arrested for his part in a "violent personal affray" with the assistant surgeon of the post.)

Grierson's perceptive and candid sister, Louisa Semple, wrote that officers at Fort Sill, Oklahoma—her brother excepted—were a "bunch of drinking, swearing, gambling, domineering men," many of whom were also "shiftless."

The abuse of Indians by soldiers was on occasion equalled by the abuse of the soldiers by their officers. In Grierson's command, wrote the Leckies, "A few officers were inclined to mistreat their men and quickly established reputations as being graduates from the 'knock down and drag out' school."

Soldiers, particularly officers, who demonstrated sympathy for the Indians suffered from the bigotry of their comrades in blue and often remained in lower rank because of this discrimination. A prime reason Grierson, a true Civil War hero, did not advance up the line, state the Leckies, "was the racial prejudice aroused against him because of his enlightened treatment of blacks and Indians. Grierson was years ahead of his time in defending the rights of both."

Grierson commanded Black enlisted men, first called Buffalo Soldiers by the Cheyenne because the hair of the Blacks suggested to the Indians the wooly hides of the bison.

No one on the plains seemed to see the irony of one oppressed people oppressing another oppressed people; all most white officers and enlisted men could see, through the blood in their eyes and the poison in their hearts, were the "niggers" and the "Injuns," and many an officer refused to command or cooperate with the Buffalo Soldiers.

In its anxiety to create in the public image a record of massive victory, the army often used "body counts," much as it did a century later in Viet Nam. These "body counts" were often as distorted as those across the Pacific. In the killing of Indians, the army included the elderly, women and children, the infirm and the sick, without identifying them as such. Subtract these from the casualty lists and many encounters ended with more dead soldiers than Indian warriors.

Still, the defeat of the Indians was manifest from the beginning of conflict; they were outnumbered, outgunned, outmounted, and outsupplied; they lacked consistency and endurance (some of them were marvelous light cavalry and superb guerillas but their tradition of waging quick skirmishes failed them in longer battles and in designing campaigns); and they were too fragmented, with members of some tribes actually helping the soldiers at war with other Indians.

Suicide was not an everyday occurrence in the West of the army but neither was it regarded as unthinkable. The primitive, frustrating life on the frontier could drive even the best of men to madness. Writing to his mother on September 25, 1850, Talbot discussed the attempted suicide of Major John Hathaway, a West Pointer who had served with distinction in the Mexican War.

The literature on army life in the West is replete with references to the frequently mangy, boring, demoralized conditions in the frontier posts, especially the smaller ones. There is more disgruntlement than cheer in these accounts;

the food sometimes scarce, more often unappetizing; the mounts needed replacements; clothing requisition was far behind schedule; housing was too often crude; and the Indians did not improve matters, breaking treaties they had been forced into; killing, kidnapping settlers on the fringe of emigration; raiding farms and setting fire to houses and barns; appropriating the stock of settlers; and acting as though they believed the land really belonged to them.

The one commodity both soldiers and Indians verily had in common was whiskey. Bootleggers flitting through the area sold their illicit product with even-handed impartiality, much as arms merchants did in Europe and later in the United States and China. When strict officers, such as Grierson, spotted the booze, they ordered it spilled on the ground, but as often the whiskey was undetected until drunken war whoops rent the prairie.

Small posts dotted the West and their size and isolation added to the demoralization and frustration of the soldiers. (Ironically, at least sixteen posts bore the name of Indian tribes or bands, and in a gross show of insensitivity, at least one post was built on the site of an Indian burial ground.) As early as 1853 the large, far-flung number of army stations was challenged by Jefferson Davis, then Secretary of War, who called the policy "injurious to the discipline, instruction, and efficiency of the troops, and it is believed that it often invites aggression by that exhibition of weakness which must inevitably attend the great dispersion of any force."

In the final analysis, soldiers in the West could scarcely be expected to be angels. They too often came, as a journalist wrote in the 1870s, "from the dregs of society" (though there were many good and decent men everywhere), were brought up believing every horror story imaginable about Indians, were quick to seize upon anything that would satisfy and dissipate their frustrations, and were carrying out

Suttler's store at Camp Warner, 1869.
Courtesy Oregon Historical Society

an immoral national policy: "The only good Indian is a dead Indian," said a famous general.

Unhappy, bigoted men, who felt the country owed them everything for fighting its war, these were the kind of soldiers Edward Watts Inskip found on the lava plain of southeastern Oregon.

Charbonneau: The Going Home

The first time Jean Baptiste Charbonneau saw Oregon he was nestled in a cradleboard. The next time, more than sixty years later, Oregon was to be more than a transient layover.

You may remember Jean Baptiste as "Pomp," the infant whom Sacagawea carried on her back to the Pacific with the Lewis and Clark Party. He was the only member of that expedition ever to set foot in the Pacific Northwest again. Only Patrick Gass, who died in 1870 at the age of ninety-nine, survived him.

A Lemhi Shoshone, Sacagawea was captured by the Minnetarees when she was scarcely a teenager and swapped down the line until she landed in the hands of Toussaint Charbonneau, a "squawman" from Montreal who had taken up with the Mandan Sioux.

Charbonneau then was about forty-five and still a pluralistic girl chaser but he married Sacagawea, the latest of his Indian wives, perhaps to keep her from other men.

Lewis and Clark first saw Sacagawea on November 11, 1804 when, looking like a child though about sixteen and pregnant, she walked into their camp near the Mandan Villages of present Bismarck, North Dakota. Three months to the day later, Baptiste was born.

Sacagawea underwent difficult and prolonged labor. To alleviate her suffering and hasten delivery, Lewis followed the advice of a French trader who had lived among the Missouri River tribes for fifteen years, administering a medication consisting of two rattlesnake rings crushed in a

Statue of Sacagawea, Pomp on her back, in Washington Park, Portland.

Courtesy State of Oregon

little water. Ten minutes later the baby emerged. Always the scientist, Lewis observed in his field book, "What effect it may really have had it might be difficult to determine."

The captains saw a useful role for Sacagawea. She would be their guide to the far Upper Missouri and their liaison with the Shoshones. Charbonneau was at first a problem. He did not endear himself to Lewis and Clark but if he did not go, he asserted firmly, neither would his wife. Reluctantly the captains assented, reasoning that the French-Canadian would earn his salt as an interpreter. But Charbonneau was more; he was the only member of the party who could easily communicate with Sacagawea. In her home country she spoke to Charbonneau in a common tongue. He translated to the French-speaking members of the expedition, who in turn transformed the message into English to the captains. In reverse the process was from the captains to the interpreter to Charbonneau to Sacagawea to the Shoshones. (Twenty-five years later Baptiste would need no lingual links in or out of the wilderness.) So, in the late afternoon of April 7, 1805, among those in the small flotilla that started up the Missouri, were Sacagawea, Charbonneau, and Jean Baptiste.

William Clark, who took a fancy to Baptiste, called the baby "Pomp," using it in the affectionately humorous Shoshone idiom to mean "Little Chief." Later he hitched the name onto one of his own boys.

There came the day when Pomp outgrew his cradleboard. Soon he was a toddler and could shuffle his feet around the campfire as one-eyed Peter Cruzat sawed away on his fiddle. Watching the child move his tiny moccasined feet, Clark was impelled to call him "my little dancing boy."

Coming down the Yellowstone River northeast of present Billings, Montana homeward-bound, Clark's detachment passed a mighty, flat-topped butte. Clark climbed it, two-thirds of the way up carved his name and the date (July 25,

Missouri River. The Lewis and Clark party boated up and down this stretch of the stream.

Courtesy Missouri Resources Division

1806), and called the butte "Pompy's Tower." Today, as it has been for a long time, the "remarkable rock" is known as Pompey's Pillar.

Upon the return of the party to the Mandan Villages, Clark energetically sought to persuade Sacagawea and Charbonneau to let him have Pomp to raise as his own son. The parents declined. Clark then proposed that he set the French-Canadian up in business in St. Louis if Charbonneau would take Sacagawea and Baptiste with him. Again he was turned down.

National Park Service ranger kneels by a dugout canoe similar to those used by the Lewis and Clark party, on grounds of Fort Clatsop National Memorial.

Courtesy State of Oregon

Historical marker near site of Fort Clatsop.

Courtesy State of Oregon

Replica of Fort Clatsop
Courtesy State of Oregon

A few years later however, the family did move to St. Louis and Charbonneau, who had been with the Indians for ten years before he saw Sacagawea, may have made an effort to adapt, but soon wearied of civilized trappings. Sacagawea, always eager to please, tried to imitate white manners and dress but the closer she came to white ways, the greater grew her yearning to return to the home of her people.

In April 1811, with Baptiste along, Charbonneau and Sacagawea went up the Missouri River on a keelboat with the Manuel Lisa Party and helped build Fort Manuel, a fur-trading stockade. Charbonneau was put on Lisa's payroll and for a time things went well for the family, but Sacagawea did not have long to live. Her obituary was penned on December 20, 1812, by John Luttig, a responsible reporter: "This evening the Wife of Charbonneau a Snake Squaw died of a putrid fever she was a good and the best Women in the fort, aged abt 25 years she left a fine infant girl."

Charbonneau was not at Sacagawea's side when she passed away. He had gone off on a fur-buying trip, was long overdue and feared dead. Luttig took the eight-year-old Baptiste and the lad's sister, Lizette, to St. Louis. There, on August 11, 1813, he applied to the Orphan's Court for appointment as their guardian. It is probable he was doing this to keep the children intact and safe until Clark, now governor of Missouri Territory and superintendent of Indian affairs, returned to the city. With Clark back in St. Louis, his name replaced Luttig's on the application for guardian-ship. Nothing further is known of Lizette except that, according to Lean Wolf, an ancient Hidasta, she died during a smallpox epidemic at the age of twenty-five.

By 1819 Charbonneau was back in St. Louis and employed by Clark as interpreter for five months. Baptiste was there, too, and at Clark's urging was entered in an Indian school where, according to Bernard De Voto, he stayed "some years" and "learned French and English, ciphering and Roman history." Then, at eighteen, he met Paul Wilhelm, Duke of Württemberg, Germany, whose entire life was devoted to the study of natural science. (Jean Baptiste must have looked younger than he was, for the duke took him to be sixteen.)

Paul was probably the first of European nobility to travel to the American West. Having everything of sophistication, intrigue, and comfort at home, he hungered, he wrote, "for the vast silent place and the simple life among free unaffected children of nature." He was twenty-six when he made the first of his seven visits to America. During a trading post run upstream from the mouth of the Kansas River he was introduced to Toussaint and Jean Baptiste Charbonneau. Toussaint, he noted, "later served me in the capacity of interpreter," but it was Jean Baptiste to whom Paul turned for companionship.

In Jean the duke found a young man not encumbered by family tree, in tune with nature, a spirit free in the wilderness, a child of the earth. Joining his fortunes with Baptiste, Paul vicariously bound himself to the great open sky. Since he had to return to Europe, and wanting a living force of the West by his side in the old land, he proposed that Jean come with him. Clark approved and the two took off. All this we surmise, for in Paul Wilhelm's *Travels in North America 1822–1824*, he says only that Baptiste "joined me on my return, followed me to Europe, and has since then been with me."

Paul's castle was Baptiste's home and he accompanied the duke on royal European visits. No doubt, Baptiste learned the amenities of country living, studied the classics and acquired a proficiency in languages—reading and speaking German, French, and Spanish and becoming more fluent in English. With the Indian tongues he already knew, he became a broader linguist than his blue-blooded mentor.

After six years, when Paul decided to take another look at the aborigines, Baptiste went with him, arriving in St. Louis late in 1829. Clark granted permission for the duke to boat up the Missouri to observe the Indian villages, and Baptiste may have gone along. Somewhere along the river they parted company, perhaps at the earth-mound lodges of the Mandans. In all probability they did not meet again or correspond.

Sacagawea's expedition babe, now twenty-four, turned

Jean Baptiste Charbonneau was born in a Mandan dwelling such as one of these. These earthlodges are at Fort Lincoln State Park in North Dakota.

Courtesy State of North Dakota

Mountain Man. In the fall of 1830 he was with a party of trappers, led by Antoine Robidoux, which got lost trying to cross the Snake River plains from American Falls directly to Wood River in Idaho. The ordeal, described by JH Stevens, a member of the party, suggests that the trappers may have erred their way into the Craters of the Moon.

Dry in the "burning atmosphere" of the lava beds for two days, the men had the "most maddening desire for water." Luckily, they found a stream near the camp of John Work's Hudson's Bay Company Snake Brigade, but Charbonneau was not as fortunate. Separated from the others while scouring the lunar landscape for water, he came across Work's party at night. Unaware that there was another group of white trappers in the area, he suspected a bivouac of hostile Indians and retreated to the lava beds. It took him eleven days of agonizing and treacherous travel to reach the Snake River, where he fell in with still another contingent of white trappers. He stayed with them until meeting the Robidoux party, which had found its way back to the Snake by going up the Wood and down the Big Lost Rivers. The harrowing experience was fixed long in Baptiste's mind, for he spoke of it many years later.

There is no detailed record of Baptiste's life as a Mountain Man. If he kept a journal, none has been found. If he wrote letters, only one has been discovered—an official statement penned in California. No writer ever interviewed him. There is no physical sketch of him; he is as vague a portrait as is Sacagawea. Practically all we know of him comes from the words of others. It seems strange that so educated a man should have such disregard for written expression.

His companions were of a ruder school than the kind he had known in Württemberg. For a spell he rode alongside Joe Meek and for a while he hooked up with Jim Bridger, "Old Gabe" himself. Meek and Bridger were barely acquainted with proper English, but they were honor students of Rocky Mountain College, the open-sky institution of the Mountain Men. So were the rough, boisterous, flinty, go-for-broke trappers Baptiste met at the Green River Rendezvous of 1833 in Wyoming, and later at Bent's Fort and Fort Vasquez, both in Colorado.

Like all true Mountain Men who had outlived the beaver trade, Baptiste took whatever work came his way, as long as it fitted his outdoor disposition: interpreter, hunter, and boatman among other chores. It was on one of his trips boating furs to St. Louis that he came face to face with John

COUREUR DU BOIS

A mountain man as sketched by Frederic Remington.
Courtesy Oregon Historical Society

C. Fremont, headed West to begin a career as the overdescribed "Great Pathfinder."

"Mr. Charbonard," as Fremont remembered him, was

Jim Bridger
Courtesy Oregon Historical Society

camped along the Platte River in northeastern Colorado. Baptiste welcomed him with a hearty greeting and served an excellent meal of boiled beef tongue and mint julep, washed down with strong coffee that had sugar in it, a rare treat so far from a city.

Another vignette of Baptiste at the same spot was drawn by Rufus Sage, who noted that the camp of the boatmen "was under the direction of a half-breed named Chabonard, who proved to be a gentleman of superior information . . . There was a quaint humor and shrewdness in his conversation, so garbed with intelligence and perspicuity that he at once insinuated himself into the good graces of listeners, and commanded their admiration and respect."

It is too bad that Sir William Drummond Stewart, for whom Baptiste drove a cart in 1843, kept no journals. Otherwise we might know what, if anything, he observed of the equally sophisticated son of Sacagawea. Stewart was then forty-four, six years older than Baptiste. He had been a captain of the King's Hussars, was a veteran of Waterloo, owned a castle or two in Scotland, authored third-class romantic novels, was the patron of Western artist Jacob Miller, lived high on the hog in the wilderness, and knew the Rocky Mountain country a lot better than most Americans. He was on his second and last visit to the West, headed for his Camelot of Green River, which the Mountain Men called the "Seedskeedee."

Another of Stewart's party of ninety-three persons and forty-three carts and light wagons was William Clark Kennerly, a nephew of William Clark. Kennerly, wrote John Bakeless, "used to tell in after life how he had personally known the boy Baptiste while he was in school in St. Louis" and that Clark's son, Jefferson, was among the many white travelers in the West whom Baptiste served as interpreter.

Kennerly reported that two hotheaded men in the caravan pushed a shouting match into a fight—common in the mountains, where things went wrong so easily and tempers flared so readily. "The whole cavalcade stopped to witness it," Kennerly said, "while Charbonneau ran excitedly about, keeping a ring around the combatants with his heavy whip and shouting for no one to interfere." He, too, could be high-strung and quickly roused to fire, as others who met him observed.

In that same year Baptiste sold land inherited from his father for $320. There is no record of when the senior Charbonneau passed away. Late in his seventies he married a fourteen-year-old Assiniboine prisoner, and the wedding was marked by "a special charivari." How long that bond lasted or how many brides he took after that is a blank in history. The last heard of the old man is that, according to a letter by Joshua Pilcher, who succeeded Clark as super-intendent of Indian affairs, Charbonneau reached St. Louis in the summer of 1839 "tottering under the infirmities of eighty winters, without a dollar to support him. This man," wrote Pilcher, "has been a faithful servant of the Government—though in a humble capacity."

In all likelihood, Baptiste readily spent the inheritance money. He never accumulated enough wherewithal to lift him above the gentle side of poverty. (When he died he left no will and had nothing to leave.) Zenas Leonard, writing of Rocky Mountain life in 1834, knew many like Baptiste: "Scarcely one man in ten, of those employed in this country ever think of saving a single dollar of their earning, but spend it fast as they can see an object to spend it for. They care not what may come pass to-morrow—but think only of enjoying the present moment."

Like the Mountain Man he was, Jean Baptiste was ever on the move. Eighteen forty-four found him at Bent's Fort, where an observer noted Jean's hair hanging down to his shoulders, and added: "it was said that Charbonneau was the best man on foot on the plains or in the Rocky Mountains." Considering the elegant company Baptiste kept, the compliment was superb.

Undoubtedly the meatiest description of the fur trappers, "the real pioneers of the Far West," was penned by a young Englishman, George Frederick Ruxton, who traveled through the country from late 1846 until his death in St. Louis at the age of twenty-seven in August 1848. No one else captured so keenly the idiom of the Mountain Men, and in his series of articles for *Blackwood's Edinburgh Magazine*, Ruxton thrice places Baptiste among them.

In the first instance, the oldest of a group of Rocky Mountain College students is doing some reminiscing as his camerados puff silently on their pipes "whilst the buffalo 'hump-ribs' and 'tender loin' are singing away in the pot."

The narrator recalls:

"Bill Bent—his boys camped on the other side of the trail, and they was all mountain men, wagh!—and Bill Williams, and Bill Tharpe (the Pawnees took his hair on Pawnee Fork last spring); three Bills and them three's all 'gone under.' Surely Hatcher went out that time, and wasn't Bill Garey along, too? Didn't him and Chabonard sit in camp for twenty hours at a deck of Euker? Them was Bent's Indian trappers upon Arkansa. Poor Bill Bent! them Spaniards made meat of him. He lost his topknot to Taos. A 'clever' man was Bill Bent as I ever know'd trade a robe or 'throw' a buffler in his tracks. Old St. Vrain could knock the hind-sight off him though, when it comes to shootin'. And old silver heels spoke true, she did: 'plum-center' she was, eh?"

Among the trappers gathered to spend the winter at a mountain valley called Brown's Hole, which spills over northwest Colorado into Utah, were "Chabonard and his half-breeds."

In Ruxton's last reference to Baptiste he portrays a band of trappers, their mules loaded with beaver pelts, camped on a creek near Taos, New Mexico. Their number includes such legendary figures of the Southwest as Dick Wooton and Kit Carson, and with them "Chabonard a half-breed, was not lost in the crowd."

In the rough company of the Mountain Men, Jean Baptiste was bound to both fit in and stand out. He could decipher as well as any of them the dim clues of the beaver, the faint marks of the travois, and the imprint of moccasin, but where few trappers could read English beyond an elementary level, Baptiste could handle German, French, and Spanish with ease. He could speak the Rocky Mountain language (alien to outsiders) as fluently and as cussedly as any of the trappers, and he could converse on their own terms with college dudes who came west for scenery and shooting. Refusing to live either as an Indian or white, but only as himself, he linked himself to the most democratic family in the nation, the people of the open sky.

With the close of the fur trade, brought about by the indiscriminate slaughter of beaver and fashion changes in London, the Mountain Men dispersed. Some went to farming, a few took jobs in towns and cities. The restless and promotional types became guides for Oregon and California-bound emigrants. Baptiste and several others turned to scouting for the military; it was as steady a paycheck as a freelancer might expect.

Baptiste's last job for the military was in 1846 as a guide for the Mormon Battalion, which was organized by the US government to, in simple words, wrench California away from Mexico. The battalion started from Fort Leavenworth, Kansas, and by the time it reached Santa Fe it was so disorganized and malcontent that General Stephen Watts Kearny, who had overall responsibility for the outfit, appointed a new commander, Philip St. George Cooke, jumped from captain to lieutenant colonel. At Santa Fe, forty-one-year-old Jean Baptiste Charbonneau signed on.

The red-shirted Baptiste, nudging along a stubborn army mule, is cited often in Cooke's journal. For instance, the day Jean Baptiste's mule kicked him and ran away, Jean angrily tracked it for miles before he could get within shooting range. He then brought it down with unerring aim. By God, no damn critter was going to get away with that!

A few days later, in late November, Cooke wrote of "Charboneaux" on a hill chasing grizzly bears. "I saw three of them far up among the rocks, standing conspiculously and looking quite white in the sun, whilst the bold warrior was gradually approaching them. Soon after, he fired, and in ten seconds again; then there was a confused action and we could see one fall, and the others rushing about with loud and fierce cries that made the mountain ring. The firing having ceased whilst the young bears were close by, I was much alarmed for the guide's safety; and then we heard him crying out in Spanish, but it was for more balls, and so the cubs escaped. The bear was rolled down and butchered before the wagons had passed."

With the arrival of the Mormon Battalion in San Diego on January 30, 1847, the eighteen consecutive years of Jean Baptiste Charbonneau as a Mountain Man came to a close. His next and last nineteen years were, except for the final few days, to be lived out more prosaically in California.

San Luis Rey is a modest settlement north of San Diego. It is the site of the San Luis Rey de Francia Mission established in 1798 by the Franciscan Fathers along *El Camino Real* (The Royal Highway) and second only to Santa Barbara Mission in its design, beauty, and extent of remains.

Both in the village today and in the "Old Mission" there is no record of Charbonneau ever having been there. In reply to my query, a historian of the area wrote that none of the families of the early settlers—"The first recorded came in 1864"—had ever heard of Charbonneau.

Yet there was a settlement at the mission site, largely composed of Indians. With the American military in control, Baptiste was appointed *alcalde* of San Luis Rey in November 1847.

His responsibilities, as mayor and judge, were the "care and protection of Indian servants and ex-neophytes, as well as the keeping in check of gentile bands." No doubt he took his duties seriously, but his stay in office was neither happy nor long. Reports reached the military that their *alcalde* was a ringleader in an Indian-uprising plot, and a serious investigation was undertaken. Baptiste, signing his name as "John B. Charbonneau of St. Louis, State of Missouri," vigorously defended himself, charging that his chief accuser, an Indian named Paulino, had lied.

Baptiste was not cut of bureaucratic cloth; no Mountain Man was. He would rather stand up to a wildcat than be stung by flitting rumors and biting politics. In July 1848, he submitted his resignation. He had given the office his best, he said, but there was bitterness toward him because, being a half-breed, the whites thought he favored the Indians too much. His quit letter was accepted and he departed the south of California for good.

Gold had been discovered at Sutter's Mill on the American River six months earlier and the word had spread as fast as the wind could carry it. Sailors left their ships, farmers their plows, ministers their pulpits, and doctors their practices to rush to the hills. Jean Baptiste Charbonneau was in the first tidal swell of argonauts, but luck was not with him. Like most hopefuls, he did not strike it rich; unlike most of the disappointed, he stayed on in the gold country.

He seems to have gone first to Murderer's Bar on the Middle Fork of the American River, where El Dorado and Placer counties meet. Jim Beckwourth, in his biography, tells of finding "my old friend Chapineau housekeeping and stayed with him until the rainy season set in." The son of a white Southern planter and a quadroon mother sharing a cabin with the son of an Indian mother and a French-Canadian father—this was ethnic democracy under the pines. What a writer would have given to sit in on the

Jim Beckwourth
Courtesy Nevada Historical Society

palavering of the two old Mountain Men—one with the reputation of being the biggest liar west of the Mississippi and the other who could recount tales of royalty! There was enough here to burn the lamps long after midnight.

The *Historical Souvenir of El Dorado County*, published in 1883, relates that "Of first settlers at Murderer's Bar may be mentioned . . . Jim Beckwourth and Shabanau," and Thompson and West's *History of Placer County* declares that in June of 1849, "Tom Buckner's heart gladdened by the appearance of other men at his camp, in the person of J.B. Charbonneau, Jim Beckwourth, and Sam Myers." (Buckner's Bar was opposite Murderer's Bar.)

Baptiste must have moved about the area some. The 1860 federal census of Placer County shows his address to be Secret Ravine Post Office, a mining camp out of Auburn. A year later, according to the Placer County directory of 1861, "John B. Charbonneau" was a clerk at the Orleans Hotel in Auburn.

Nothing more is heard for five years. Then a small obituary in the *Owyhee Avalanche* of Ruby City, Idaho Territory, dated June 2, 1866, brought this sad news:

"DIED—we have received a note (don't know who from) dated May 16, '66, requesting the publication of the following:

"'at Inskip's Ranche, Cow Creek, in Jordan Valley [Oregon] J.B. CHARBONNEAU . . . of pneumonia; one of the oldest trappers and pioneers, he piloted the Mormon Brigade through from Lower Mexico in '46; . . . was en route to Montana.'"

A fuller obituary was printed in the *Placer Herald* on July 7, 1866. After detailing (not always correctly) Baptiste's life, it concludes with a warm portrait of him in Auburn:

"The old man, on departing for Montana, gave us a call, and he said that he was going to leave California, probably for good, as he was about returning to familiar scenes. We felt then as if we met him for the last time.

"Mr. Charbonneau was of pleasant manners, intelligent, well read in the topics of the day, and was generally esteemed in the community in which he lived, as a good meaning and inoffensive man."

THE PLACER HERALD.

AUBURN, JULY 7, 1866.

THOMAS BOYCE, North East corner of Montgomery and Washington streets, San Francisco, is authorized to solicit advertisements and subscriptions in that city for the Herald, and receipt for the same.

J. J. KNOWLTON & CO., Advertising Agents, corner of Kearney and Sacramento streets, are authorized to solicit advertisements and subscriptions for the Placer Herald, and receipt for the same.

STAGE LINE TO GEORGETOWN.—Mr. Orr has put on a line of four horse stages between Auburn and Georgetown, El Dorado county. The stages leave Auburn every morning at 9 o'clock, after the arrival of the cars from Sacramento; and the morning stages from Georgetown connect with the down train that connects with the San Francisco boats. At present the mail service on this stage route is tri-weekly, but the contractor expects that the postal department will soon authorize it to be carried daily.— The Express matter from San Francisco and Sacramento goes by this line. The stages cross the American river at Rattlesnake, but upon the completion of the new road at the junction of the North and Middle Forks they will adopt that route, which will be much shorter.

I. O. O. F. ELECTION.—At a regular meeting of Auburn Lodge No. 7, I. O. O. F., the following officers were elected for the ensuing term: John Harwood, N. G.; D. W. Spear, V. G.; Thomas Jamison, R. Secretary; A. N. Gambell, P. Secretary; E. T. Holley, Treasurer; S. B. Woodin, A. N. Gambell, Miles Furniss, Trustees. The installation will take place on Saturday evening, the 7th inst.

GOOD QUARTZ.—A piece of quartz may be seen at the American Hotel, taken out this week, from the fifty foot level of the Charles Mallett claim, which would be called good rock any where. It contains a streak of auriferous sulphurets through the center, several inches in width (which we are informed is a characteristic of the vein at present) while the rock, in color and texture, is just what experts desire to see. We are informed that the quartz prospects handsomely in gold.

CLIMATE OF MONTANA.—A friend writing from Montana, illustrates the severity of the seasons there, when he says it has become a trite saying that they "have nine months winter and three months cold weather."

HOT WEATHER.—The thermometer stood at 103 and 106 degrees in Auburn, on last Sunday. Since then it has moderated, so as to be endurable.

☞ The "Fourth" was generally celebrated in the large towns and cities of the State. At San Francisco the celebration was the finest ever held in that city.

☞ We suspect the printers in Nevada county are still celebrating, as we have not received an exchange from that quarter since the "Fourth."

☞ The new Radical organ, for some time announced, has commenced publication in San Francisco, under the name of the

DEATH OF A CALIFORNIA PIONEER. — We are informed by Mr. Dana Perkins, that he has received a letter announcing the death of J. B. Charbonneau, who left this county some weeks ago, with two companions, for Montana Territory. The letter is from one of the party, who says Mr. C., was taken sick with mountain fever, on the Owyhee, and died after a short illness.

Mr. Charbonneau was known to most of the pioneer citizens of this region of country, being himself one of the first adventurers (into the territory now known as Placer county) upon the discovery of gold; where he has remained with little intermission until his recent departure for the new gold field, Montana, which, strangely enough, was the land of his birth, whither he was returning in the evening of life, to spend the few remaining days that he felt was in store for him.

Mr. Charbonneau was born in the western wilds, and grew up a hunter, trapper, and pioneer, among that class of men of which Bridger, Beckwourth, and other noted trampers of the woods were the representatives. He was born in the country of the Crow Indians—his father being a Canadian Frenchman, and his mother a half breed of the Crow tribe. He had, however, better opportunities than most of the rough spirits, who followed the calling of trapper, as when a young man he went to Europe and spent several years, where he learned to speak, as well as write several languages. At the breaking out of the Mexican war he was on the frontiers, and upon the organization of the Mormon battalion he was engaged as a guide and came with them to California.

Subsequently upon the discovery of gold, he, in company with Jim Beckworth, came upon the North Fork of the American river, and for a time it is said were mining partners.

Our acquaintance with Charbonneau dates back to '52, when we found him a resident of this county, where he has continued to reside almost continuously since—having given up frontier life. The reported discoveries of gold in Montana, and the rapid peopleing of the Territory, excited the imagination of the old trapper, and he determined to return to the scenes of his youth.— Though strong of purpose, the weight of years was too much for the hardships of the trip undertaken, and he now sleeps alone by the bright waters of the Owyhee.

Our information is very meager of the history of the deceased—a fact we much regret, as he was of a class that for years lived among stirring and eventful scenes.

The old man, on departing for Montana gave us a call, and said he was going to leave California, probably for good, as he was about returning to familiar scenes. We felt then as if we met him for the last time.

Mr. Charbonneau was of pleasant manners, intelligent, well read in the topics of the day, and was generally esteemed in the community in which he lived, as a good meaning and inoffensive man.

The announcement of Charbonneau's death in the *Placer Herald*, July 7, 1866, page 2, column 2.

Courtesy California State Library

Barn at Ruby Ranch, site of Inskip's Station, was built in 1865. Stage coach was rebuilt by Jordan Valley rancher Mike Hanley.

Mike Hanley

In 1874 there were four graves at the fortified stage station on Inskip's Ranch, built of southeastern Oregon lava rock, by rancher, storekeeper, and amateur doctor, Edward Inskip. For many decades there was common folklore in Jordan Valley that one—and there was general agreement on which one—held an Indian or "half-breed." The issue was resolved through the investigation of Mike Hanley, a valley rancher, and later confirmed by professional researchers. In his 1973 book *Owyhee Trails*, Hanley wrote, "I clearly marked it a few years ago as a historical point of

The first marker put up over the grave of Charbonneau. It was designed, inscribed, and erected by Jordan Valley rancher Mike Hanley.

Mike Hanley

interest that should be preserved." Today the grave, more formally noted, is a National Historic Landmark.

You look past the grave and see Jean Baptiste Charbonneau plodding down the western slope of the Sierra.

It is spring, and with damp winter past, he ought to feel young again; but he is sixty-one, not as strong as he used to be, and people speak of him as elderly.

Behind him, on the banks of the American River, he has left his last camerados, the washed-out miners who never had the real feel of gold in their hands and who stayed on after the gold had gone. He is wifeless, childless, his parents long departed, and no trace of any family. With two companions he is bound for Montana Territory.

Why do some friends in Auburn believe he is headed for Alder Gulch to hunt for gold? The gulch has all been staked out; the rush started three years ago, and Jean knows that three years after gold was found at Sutter's Mill, all the placer streams in the Mother Lode were just about worked out.

And why do others in Placer County think he is going back to his people? He has no people in Montana, and none in the Mandan Villages where he was born, and none in the Rocky Mountain country, with all the Mountain Men having disappeared from there ages ago. The most permanent home he ever had was along the American River.

Down the western slope of the Sierra he trudges, and passes through Sacramento. Is he aware that in the little village of Franklin, twenty miles to the south, death had come the year before to Alexander Hamilton Willard, blacksmith, gunsmith, salt-maker, and hunter of the Lewis and Clark Party?

Willard was an indomitable soul. He was seventy-four, and the veteran of two Indian wars, when he drove an ox team across the plains. At Franklin he did a little blacksmithing, then spun out his years rocking on the porch of his frame house and regaling anyone who cared to listen about his days with the Corps of Discovery. There is no evidence that Willard and Baptiste, no more than fifty miles apart for thirteen years, knew of each other's presence.

Up in Butte County the three travelers veer off onto the Chico-Ruby City road. At the end of each day Baptiste is very tired, but he does not complain. He will reach his destination; he always has. He tells this to one of the two men, who asks quietly, "Is death a destination or a final interruption?" Jean smiles wearily. "That is a philosophical question," he replies, and puts the coffeepot back over the fire.

At Susanville he begins to cough and a day later is spitting out rust-colored phlegm. His companions want to stop for a while, but every Mountain Man has known aches and chills. Once they get out of the highlands here . . . And summer is coming.

But the coughing increases, and there is a tightness in his chest. Sometimes it seems to his friends that he is fighting for breath, and he is feverish.

At Inskip's Station he must halt. He tells his companions to go ahead; he will be all right. But they stay.

Where is Doc Inskip now? Is he away from the station? Or does he try to help? But what can he do? The infection is too deep.

Jean lies there, slipping in and out of mind. He wants so much to remember how it was being carried in the cradleboard on his mother's back; he has tried so hard over so many years to remember, but somehow he cannot reach through the fog of time. But he sees, through his mother's telling him as a small boy, Meriwether Lewis doctoring him and William Clark tossing him in the air and catching him with a hug, and Scannon, the big dog, licking his face, and the big black man, York, looking into his eyes and laughing with shining white teeth, and John Colter and George Drouillard steadying him as he shuffles in his moccasins by the campfire to the fiddle of Peter Cruzat and the sing-song calling of John Potts.

What happened to them all? Potts dead under a shower

of Blackfeet arrows, Drouillard killed two years later by the Blackfeet because the wind was blowing the wrong way and his friends could not hear his shots, Colter to be the first white man in the Yellowstone Canyon. Cruzat, Cruzat, where has he gone, where is the fiddle?

In and out of mind he slips. There was the duke and those places in Europe and Sir Stewart and the Mormon Battalion and the colonels and the generals and the strange time at San Luis Rey. They are hard to see, they flash by too quickly. But here is Jim Bridger riding down the trail. *Gabe! Gabe! Hold up a spell.* And the Sublette brothers at Rendezvous. Bill Williams hip-deep in snow. Caleb Greenwood lean and hungry as a winter wolf. Kit Carson

Present gravesite of Charbonneau
Courtesy State of Oregon

ten feet tall in the saddle. Jim Beckwourth spinning another yarn in the smoky cabin.

But whose faces are these, whose? And why can't he hear them speak? And the beaver streams getting mixed up, the mountains where they shouldn't be, the sky whirling and swirling over him as he falls off his horse.

Everything so dim now. The fog, that fog. And then, inside his cradleboard, he hears his mother cry: "The big water, the big water! Now we can go home."

Great Day At Harney

Harney's most unusual day may have been in the summer of 1912, when Governor Oswald West rode into town and made a speech at the local church. A governor had never come to Harney before, and didn't afterward, but there wasn't anyone like Os West for getting out into the sticks.

About fifteen miles northeast of Burns, Harney was a homesteader village settled on the high plateau of Rattle-

Historical marker near Burns
Courtesy State of Oregon

snake Creek in 1885, five years after the last troops marched
out of Fort Harney, two miles to the north.

By the late 1930s Harney was dead. Its obituary was
written in *Oregon: End of the Trail*, published in 1940: "It
is a ghost town with only one occupied house and two or
three inhabitants. Rabbit brush and sage flatten in the wind
about its tottering walls; jack rabbits leap along the one
street, and rattlesnakes sun on the deserted step of the store,
whose counters and showcases are still standing."

The last time we were there only a couple of fatigued
barns gave any clue to the location of Harney. But when Os
West came astride his patient mare into the rough-cut, dust-
clod town, Harney had two saw and shingle mills and was a
wool and livestock shipping point. It had a school, a
Presbyterian church, a post office, a livery, a general store, a

Harney County Sagebrush Orchestra playing near Harney while the
town was alive and active.

Courtesy Oregon Historical Society

Independence Day celebration, 1914, in Harney. The entire population
and all of its automobiles are present.

Source unknown

saloon and a population of more than a hundred women,
men and children, not counting the rancher folk who fled
out of loneliness and boredom to spend the night at friends'
homes in the bustling settlement.

West was on his way to a conference of Western
governors in Boise when he arrived at Harney. Two days
earlier he had been entertained at Wagontire by Bill Brown,
the famous stockman. (See *Tracking Down Oregon*) What
happened at Harney—and a following anecdote—was told
by West in the December 1949 issue of the *Oregon
Historical Quarterly*. It is a gem of wagon-day life on the
open spaces:

The ghost of Harney: "Rabbit brush and sage flatten in the wind about its tottering walls." This, too, has long been gone.

Courtesy Oregon Historical Society

Leaving Burns, I headed for Harney, where I hoped to deliver an afternoon's speech. Calling at Fred Haines' General Merchandise store, I declared my wishes (Fred was a hard-boiled Republican) and asked about a hall. He said they used the church for such purposes. I then inquired as to the custodian. And was advised that the town marshal was the man. I then asked where I could find him and was advised that he owned and operated the town's only saloon. Crossing the street to the saloon, I found sitting at card tables, or standing around the room, about forty sheepherders and packers. The marshal was officiating behind the bar. After making known my wishes he stated that he would be glad to open the church for me.

Abandoned homesteader's cabin near Harney
Phoebe L Friedman

Although a pronounced prohibitionist, I didn't have the crust to ask such a favor without setting up the drinks for the crowd. After the ceremonies at the bar, the marshal said: "All of you get the hell out of here. I'm going to lock up. We are all going down to hear West make a speech." After he opened the church, he rang the steeple bell, which brought the few women of the village on the run to see what was about to happen. After delivering a lousy speech, I headed for Vale.

Let me skip a year or two. I am dispensing justice from the Governor's chair. The Harney County Sheriff dropped in with news that the next time down he was bringing a friend of mine to the Pen. Asking for particulars, he informed me that my Harney marshal-saloon keeper had engaged in a shooting match with two would-be competitors and winged one of them.

"Well," I said, "When you bring him down drop in here on the way to the Pen"—and he did so. I had a pardon prepared for my Harney friend and as I handed it to him, I said, "Brother, go thy way and shoot no more."

That was Oswald West—wise, tough, honest, and compassionate. And always close to his people. Towns can empty and drift away, but legends and great individuals remain alive and deeply rooted in our heritage. No one combined legend and individualism more preciously than Os West when he was telling about Oregon of the homesteading frontier.

A Muted Whisper Of Marysville

*Then goodbye to heavy bread, and the rugged paths
I've tread.
I am going to a country where I shall be better fed.
Then goodbye to mouldy beans, and to dismal, dark
ravines.
I shall have a better prospect now, for I have ample
means.*

California Gold Rush Song

An ore cart slept near an old cabin on the shoulder of Little Canyon Mountain, about four miles above Canyon City. It was the only intact remnant of Marysville, a long-forgotten mining camp of the great Grant County gold fever.

A dim trail off a corner of the cabin tumbled down a steep slope into a wan clearing, where the main part of Marysville had stood. The tire tracks were barely perceptible; it didn't look as though there had been anyone here for months.

At one time there were more than fifty shacks on the small shelf of the mountain. As late as the 1950s two of the early cabins still clung to earth, but evidently someone had torn them down for whatever usable lumber remained. All that was left of Marysville when we saw it were a couple of heaps of splinters, a few dented cans, and the rusted body of a flivver piled against a brambled bank.

In this clearing of pine forest, who could tell where the store perched or who lived at what spot? If you hadn't known that on this ground there was once a community called Marysville, you could never have guessed there had even been a town here.

Ore cart at Marysville

Phoebe L Friedman

One day in 1862, some tired prospectors, in weary search of the mythical Blue Bucket Mine, stretched out on Whiskey Flat. Billy Aldred, spotting some interesting looking stuff across Canyon Creek, waded over. Having no sluice pan at hand, he stripped, knotted the sleeves of his underwear, filled the longjohns with the gravel soil, recrossed the creek, and fell to washing dirt. Another gold rush was on its way.

Even before the sluice panning had run to pure gravel, the miners attacked the hills. Camps sprang up overnight, peaked like Roman candles, and almost as soon were deserted and gone from memory. Nobody knows where most of them stood. Marysville lasted longer than most.

There are a score of vacant grounds or graveyards of rubble in Grant County that once teemed with life. Yet not a word of many of these camps was left behind.

Come to one—a slapped-together, here-today-and-gone-tomorrow hillside scatter skidding down to a ravine. Look deep, listen hard, and still the scene does not take on life. Where were the chroniclers who could draw a picture of bone-aching miners complaining of ague, or of grimy muckers warming up their pots of caked beans under smoky lamps? No one left a description of what must have happened: the ribald cries of success and the profane mutterings of defeat, the pious gathering in prayer under a tree on Sunday morning while the still rollicking heathens rolled dice across the clearing, the jugs of cider being guzzled down on a Saturday night, and the awkward, impromptu sashaying and do-si-doing of sweat-splotched men who had no women for company.

No historians here, no journalists to tell of hauling water from the cold creek, of lonely laments of family and the girls who stayed behind, of tall stories that broke the wind into laughter, of vows that made the moon blush. There was no time for reporting; the drive for gold consumed all energies. And why try to see history in this grubby, ramshackle mudpool when there were a hundred others like it? There was never a post office here; no one called it home—unless it was a floater who drawled poker-faced that his hat was his home, and he wouldn't leave home under any circumstance. You could make up a story (probably true) about the fellow who asked the name of the camp because, he explained, he had to go on to Canyon City the next day and, in case anybody asked, wanted to tell where he had been up against the elephant.

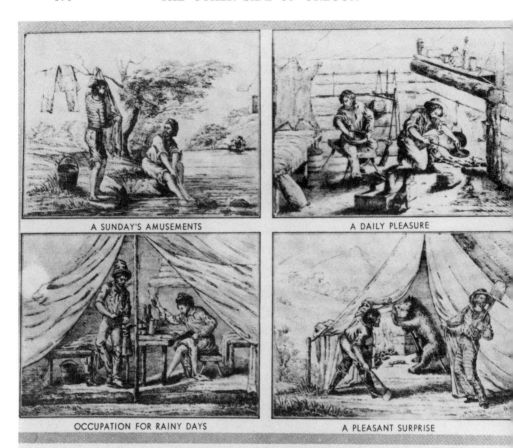

A SUNDAY'S AMUSEMENTS

A DAILY PLEASURE

OCCUPATION FOR RAINY DAYS

A PLEASANT SURPRISE

SUNDRY AMUSEMENTS IN THE MINES

Sketches of gold camp life that appeared in *Harper's*, October, 1856.

Courtesy Oregon Historical Society

Marysville boomed into a settlement before anyone knew it or cared. The miners were followed by gamblers, saloon men, dancehall women, storekeepers and their families. The place actually had a school, with all of twenty-one pupils. But it was all of short duration. When the mining started to run down, the dancehall ladies left first, and close behind them went the gamblers, the saloon men, and the families. The school emptied, then the store faded—and the bugler blew retreat for Marysville. At least, unlike the camps that were obliterated in every way, its name and location are still known, even if only to a few.

There was something else that distinguished Marysville from almost every other Oregon ghost camp I had seen: a small, tangled apple orchard. If it had been planted by the miners it seems odd, because it was so close to where the center of the village must have been. If it were planted later, by whom? My own guess is that the orchard was the work of a hermit—at least an outlander who liked living apart from others—who may have worked the mines for gleanings after the miners had departed.

All up and down Little Canyon Mountain, on its sides and deep into it, there was multitudinous evidence of mining: shafts, holes dug to chase after veins, tailings, and miners' cabins. It seemed almost eerie, in the twilight, to find shacks and houses back of the trail, where only four-wheel drives were at ease. On the upper slopes, the dwellings did not have electricity, and some were deserted.

I strongly urge you not to go up to the mountain without a guide. And don't test any of the mine shafts; a slip could be fatal. Go to Marysville, inhale a gob of history, and return to Canyon City before the sun sets. And when you think of Marysville, see it as people who acted upon their own drudgeries and desperations just as you might in a similar situation.

> The tall pines wave, and the winds loudly roar,
>   No matter, keep digging away;
> The wild flowers blossom round the log door
>   Where we sit after mining all day.
> A few more days and our mining all will end,
>   The cabin so rich will be dry;
> The tools on the bank shall be left for a friend,
>   Then, my Log Cabin Home, good by.
>   California Gold Rush Song

William Hanley: A Fine Feeling For Life

> Dreamers . . . there's two kinds. The kind that rides along and lets thoughts flicker across their minds and the kind that sees a vision and rides off to make it come true. Got to lift your mind to far off, sometimes, to see things, same as your eyes. With youth it all looks close and quick, but Time develops problems.
>
> Nothing so pure and restful as space . . . just keep moving through it.

In 1930 there was published a book which briefly basked in the glow of local sales and today is virtually forgotten, which is sad, because *Feelin' Fine!* is in its own way a literary classic of ranchers and homesteaders in eastern Oregon and, above all, of a most unusual man. It deserves a rebirth in popularity—if for no better reason than to better understand Oregon, for how can we know the ground upon which we dwell if we do not comprehend the trails to our places in the elements?

Feelin' Fine! was "Bill Hanley's Book" and was "put together" by Ann Shannon Monroe, a Portland author who took upon herself "the role of Boswell," and "began collecting his utterances."

"Also," she explained, "I have come into possession of jottings made by him through his later years at the close of day among his cattle and horses and birds on his great ranches, and in the thick of men in busy city streets concerning things a man may think but seldom speak: sometimes serious, sometimes humorous, always deeply penetrating, and at times so poetically beautiful that I have had to pause in awe before the scribbled sentence found on the back of an envelope, on a telegram blank, on a hotel bill—and scrap of paper across which the stub of a pencil chanced to travel."

The book's title was wisely derived from the closing phrase of some of Hanley's short jottings. For instance: "Went over the railroad they're finishing through Poison Creek Canyon. The old canyon was one of my first adopted homes in my boy days. Lived at its mouth two winters . . . big winterings for deer. The sides would be covered with little bunches of them feeding . . . Feelin' fine!"

William Hanley was already a legend when the book was published. He owned and operated five ranches, totaling almost 25,000 acres, most of which had been barren before Hanley put in irrigation. His 6700-acre Bell A Ranch, three miles out of Burns, was widely regarded as one of the finest in the West. His OO (Double O) Ranch, now a wildlife refuge, was eight miles from gate to front door.

Bell A Ranch, near Burns, founded by and long the property of William Hanley.

Phoebe L Friedman

Hanley's fame as scientific rancher, environmentalist, good roads enthusiast, and grassroots philosopher spread far beyond eastern Oregon, where he was known as "the Sage of Harney County." He was a friend of Theodore Roosevelt, William Howard Taft, Edwin Markham, CES Wood, William Jennings Bryan (to whom he bore a striking resemblance), senators and governors, writers and painters, the famous and unknown, rich and poor. At the cornerstone laying of the Deschute Railway in Bend, tycoon James J. Hill handed Hanley the golden spike and said, "I am building this road to come to see you, Mr. Hanley." And, noted the Burns *Times-Herald* upon Hanley's death, "When Will Rogers stopped here between planes on his fatal flight into the northland last month, the first person he inquired of was 'my old friend, Bill Hanley.'"

In his time Hanley had known well the powerful cattle kings of eastern Oregon, Peter French, John Devine, and the Miller and Lux bosses. He had known and helped hundreds of poor settlers, who came into the Harney Valley broke and out of food. By 1930 he had seen the rise of corporate agriculture and the decline of the small farmer. He was disturbed by the first and bothered by the latter, but his social consciousness had been developed long before.

A liberal in a conservative business, he never forgot his own lean times, and he never let his wealth get in the way of his vision. He was sympathetic to labor, sided with the Indians, espoused women's rights, was nauseated by bigotry of any kind, championed conservation, looked upon World War I as "commercial" in essence, had the populist contempt for the "money lenders," and preferred conciliation to violence.

He expressed his sentiments about women with this observation after watching a woman judge in a New York City courtroom:

"Law is built upon the old idea of a tooth for a tooth and

an eye for an eye, and a life for a life. No one seems to have made evolution enough to dare make a step beyond that old code, till we got women judges."

At a time when the establishment's response to the hungry pressing for jobs and bread was callousness and brutality, Hanley offered a different approach. He was in Huntington, Oregon, on a big cattle drive, when he was told by the town mayor that word had been received that a freight car of unemployed, a contingent of Coxey's Army, on their way to a nationwide protest demonstration in Washington, DC, was coming into town and the men were hungry.

Hanley responded to the situation in the only way he knew: "Called for a few quarters of beef to be boiled up, plenty of flour to be worked up into bread, kettles of prunes put on to cook, and beans put on in the pots. Used hotel kitchens, private kitchens, the baker—everything. Then we collected wash boilers and filled them with coffee.

"The men filled the town, but they showed good will for everybody and respect for the mayor . . . Fed, they moved on."

Reflecting the populist suspicion of powerful finance and the fear of corporate dominance, Hanley translated his feelings into action when he ran for US Senator on the Progressive ticket in 1914. It was his first and last venture into politics but it was not uneventful. He received a noteworthy 10.68 percent of the total state vote and in his own Harney County polled 48.81 percent, besting the Democratic candidate, winner George Chamberlain, by 13 percentage points and the Republican by 33. Neighboring Malheur County gave Hanley almost one-fifth of its vote and far-off Multnomah County (Portland) did almost as well for him.

By the time Ann Shannon Monroe began to "put together" *Feelin' Fine!*, Hanley had come a long way in miles, status, and wealth from his origins. But, as is evident in the book, he had the self-made rich man's romantic, nostalgic and sometimes poignant way of looking back at his early years. He noted: "Seems like I hear someone calling: 'Billy, Billy, the cattle's leavin' the beddin' ground!'"

Inside of one paragraph of her lilting introduction, Ann Shannon Monroe, using the idiom of her hero, sums up his coming to the Harney Valley, his native wisdom, and his career:

"As a boy in the early seventies, William Hanley . . . struck out for himself from his father's ranch in southern Oregon, driving a small herd of cattle across the mountains into this golden land—a blanket for his bed, the mess wagon for his food. Just a boy taking his chances with Nature, trusting her, learning of her, becoming in time first brother to all her native land—this his high school, and this his university . . . 'Riding the range and raising cattle, listening in the stillness as I rode along—that's been life, mostly, as I have lived it,' he says, and again, 'Cattle's led me into lots of nice life.'"

Feelin' Fine! is of many things: Hanley's "boy days," as he described his youth in the Rogue River Valley; the settling of Harney County; the long cattle drives ("Nothing could be marketed until it could walk out 300 miles and over"); the Modoc War, with Hanley sympathizing with the Indians; the folklore and mores of cattlemen and nesters; Hanley's observations on all aspects of life he experienced; and his never-ending awe of and devotion to nature.

Hanley was compared to Will Rogers, and in some ways the comparison was valid, as witness Hanley's appraisal of Congress:

"When you get close to it, it grows on you how much of it is endless treadmill to get no place. Made up of phonograph records. Each fellow has to play his little tune. When you elect a Democrat or Republican, all the difference is between a Victor and a Columbia record."

Rogers was funnier, but Hanley was at least equally introspective and contemplative. He said—and he experienced it: "The mind with all its education doesn't get a vision bigger than it travels over. It can work out theory, but it can't get at the truth of things without living it."

On war he wrote: "You can never kill a condition by killing a man. No one can carry his brains in his hip pocket and in his head at the same time. When he puts his defense in his hip pocket, he weakens his head. You can't hold position with two powers; one or the other must dominate— brains or force. Rely on brains, and brains grow; rely on force, and force grows . . . Power can't be in a soul when the gun dominates . . .

"The wrongness for individuals to settle their troubles with guns and knives is only being repeated on a larger scale when nations use this method. Gains made this way can't stand any longer than the efficiency of the youth raised up to defend them. The great motive power back of building up an appetite for war is the excitement in tragedy . . . the reason is commercialism. It's just bunched herds on stampede."

His religion was in the outdoors and in nature:

"Stayed overnight at the OO, and watched the sun come up out of the ground . . . brought its many colors into my room to give me welcome. What with the big ride yesterday across the desert, and a chicken dinner last night, I had a real church without the annoyance of a preacher giving me his idea of it . . . Feelin' fine!"

He believed in a "General Plan," an accumulated wisdom. "But just what you may mean to the Big Future, none seem to understand. One thing, you know there is no such thing as death—just change. You know that if you watch Nature."

And he wrote: "A reporter wanted to know how old I was. Funny question. Who knows how old he is? Birth is just continuous, like death. When I'm on a nice little horse

William Hanley
Courtesy Oregon Historical Society

out in the fields looking over some well-provided-for cattle, all so happy, eating grass, and good water in abundance, I don't feel any age at all. I'm just contemporary. Sometimes I feel like I'm not fully born yet.

"Only one thing makes age, a lost vision of something in the future that can't get along without you."

People who were riding high ought to be brought back to earth now and then, Hanley thought, and illustrated his sentiment with this incident: "An old saddle horse walked all over me . . . haven't been able to ride for a week. Necessary to have a walking-over once in a while. Feelin' fine!"

He studied people avidly: "Every man carries a plain look of what he is in his face, if you just know how to read it."

He was more fascinated with birds and animals. He believed that if you understand what motivates any living thing, and act toward it out of kindness, you will not be betrayed. With remarkable empathy and clarity of expression he projected pragmatic insights to the ways of ants, bees, cattle, hogs, dogs, and birds.

Eight pages of *Feelin' Fine!* are devoted to cameos of birds Hanley knew on his ranches. He had grain by the sackful spread for the birds and his ranches became feeding stops for wild geese on their flyway patterns. On the Double O, some geese made their appetites known by striking at the cook house door with their wings until food was put out for them. He took particular delight in inviting friends, acquaintances, and strangers to drive to the Double O in the fall to watch the migration of the great flocks of huge white swans.

He loved birds and had contempt for "sportsmen" hunters. Once, when he had some hunters arrested for shooting birds at the Double O, he commented: "They always say wild birds . . . I say wild men."

All his life he had dogs and would not do without them. "No eulogy of a dog can be too strong," he wrote.

He was at ease with all of life. "Watched some ants," he observed. "At every little ant hill the ants will welcome you if you add to their building material . . . You can lay all around them and they'll crawl right over you and won't bite you . . . That's one of the prettiest thoughts, if a nation and everyone would get it, that everything recognizes the superiority of kindness. Even a bee gets the understanding that you feel kind toward him, and he won't sting you . . . Feelin' fine!"

Toward the close of his life he grew increasingly philosophical, and pensively noted: "An awful lot of people fall just before the daylight of their dreams. Many fall the evening before. Trouble with undertaking a big thing—got to check out about the time you get everything going. Only way is to keep open accounts . . ."

His open accounts were a matter of doubt when a heart attack checked him out in 1935 at the age of seventy-four. He had been ill for several years, which had forced him to resign from the State Highway Commission in 1933, relinquish management of his properties, and spend much time in balmier southern California. Against the orders of his physician he traveled to Pendleton for the great Round-Up on the final day, designated as Hanley Day. Entering the stands he was given a rousing ovation, exceeded only by the applause when he left late Saturday afternoon. He was ill and ashen but managed to wave a final farewell. Early the next day his heart called it quits.

Tributes poured in torrents. Every obituary was laden with praise. The one that would likely have given Hanley the most pleasure appeared in his local paper, the Burns *Times-Herald*: "There was a new hand at the ranch of the boss in the sky Monday—Bill Hanley, cattle baron Harney County—riding light with boots, slicker and bed roll; ready to throw in with the big outfit." If left to Bill Hanley to sum up his presence on earth, he might have said, as he once did, looking out over the far valley:

"Each life is only a little spot in time. And there is no death. Nothing can be lost—it only changes.

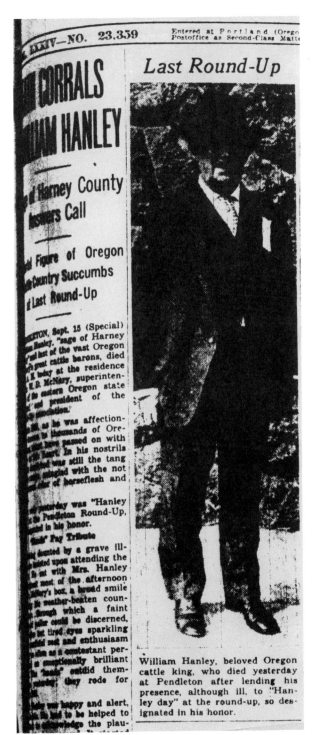

Last Round-Up

CORRALS

WILLIAM HANLEY

Harney County
Answers Call

Figure of Oregon
Country Succumbs
Last Round-Up

PENDLETON, Sept. 15 (Special)
William Hanley, "sage of Harney
county" and last of the vast Oregon
country's great cattle barons, died
early today at the residence
of W. B. McNary, superintendent of the eastern Oregon state
hospital and president of the
Round-Up association."

Just as he was affection-
ately by thousands of Oregonians, he passed on with
full vigor. In his nostrils
there was still the tang
of sage mingled with the not
disagreeable odor of horseflesh and

Yesterday was "Hanley
day" at the Pendleton Round-Up,
designated in his honor.

Rodeo Pay Tribute

Undaunted by a grave ill-
ness that insisted upon attending the
Round-Up with Mrs. Hanley
for most of the afternoon
in McNary's box, a broad smile
on his weather-beaten coun-
tenance through which a faint
pallor could be discerned, and
his tired eyes sparkling
with zest and enthusiasm
as each contestant per-
formed exceptionally brilliant
work outdid them-
selves, they rode for

William was happy and alert,
and had to be helped to
acknowledge the plau-

William Hanley, beloved Oregon
cattle king, who died yesterday
at Pendleton after lending his
presence, although ill, to "Hanley day" at the round-up, so designated in his honor.

Front page announcement of William Hanley's death in the Portland
Oregonian.

"'Will I return?' people ask. It's what's in you that returns.

"It's just another season. The winter has passed, the water has run, the grass is coming . . . Feelin' fine!"

Buried Boodle Of Oregon

If you are big on folklore you will not find it hard to believe that there is some buried loot in Oregon.

I've heard gossip of cached gold in Jordan Valley, near Sparta, outside Port Orford, on the McKenzie Pass, south of Sisters, north of Brothers, east of Westfall, and west of Eastside. Traveling around the state all these years I've heard a hundred rumors, most of which I attribute to sleepy minds listening to an idle wind.

But if you're interested, let me reel off a few tales.

In 1933 a prospector, CL Eubanks, beating the bush along Louse Creek in Douglas County, came across a large manzanita tree on which had been carved the year 1890 and, on the trunk, the initials MLP and LPM and, below, an incomplete message, Go to . . . . . .

The tree stood in the vicinity of a spectacular stagecoach holdup. The bandits had been pursued and killed but the gold was never found. Just before the last brigand died he whispered that the money was hidden in a hole in the ground about a quarter-mile from the scene of the crime.

For years treasure hunters had searched in vain, but with the discovery of the carved manzanita Eubanks was sure he had the right clues. He labored at tracking down the cache one summer and then another but, to the best of common knowledge, he always came away empty-handed.

Somewhere between Pendleton and Stanfield there may be more long-buried loot awaiting a finder. The main clue to this alleged cache comes from the testimony of two old-timers, John Vert and Mrs. Lee Moorhouse, in a small book titled *Reminiscences of Oregon Pioneers*:

> A stage robbery that created a good deal of excitement occurred at or near Prospect Farm in 1880. An employee of Wells Fargo was accused of the crime.
>
> On the day that some very valuable express was sent from Baker City, H. P. Page, who was an official of the company, announced his intention of going to Portland.
>
> As the stage was rumbling along in the dusk over the sagebrush-covered hills, northwest of Pendleton, Page, who was on the box seat beside the driver, decided to have a nap in the boot. A cozy, sheltered place was the boot of the old Concord coach and the mail sacks a sufficiently comfortable bed for the weary traveler.
>
> While the horses were being changed at the barn across Stage Gulch, at Prospect Farm, someone in a shed nearby was busily sorting express papers by the light of a candle. The following morning it was discovered that the place was strewn with burnt matches, torn waybills and other papers.
>
> Some place down the line, the robbery of the valuable express was discovered.
>
> Page was apprehended and brought to Pendleton for trial. The jury took a charitable view of the circumstantial evidence and the defendant was acquitted. The position with the Wells Fargo Express was the last place of trust that Page ever had.

Another story about the robbery, which an old-timer sent me without identifying the source, has it this way: "The weather was cold, Page climbed into the front boot to keep out of the wind and get warm and while there unlocked the box, taking out the gold shipment and dropping it into the bottom of the boot, and destroying the waybills. At Umatilla, which was the end of the division, he waited his

Legend holds that gold from a stage hold up is buried along this sagebrush country road on the way to Westfall.

Phoebe L Friedman

opportunity, secured the shipment of gold dust, and departed by boat for Portland and San Francisco. Some time elapsed before the shipment was missed, and tracers were sent out."

There are still those in Umatilla County who believe Page hid the loot in or near Stage Gulch, intending to return for it later, which he never did.

One of the folk tales of Eastern Oregon—sworn to as history by the true believers—declares that Dead Man's Hill, between Pendleton and La Grande, was the scene of a stage holdup that netted the bandits $6,000 in gold dust. No date is mentioned in the story but, according to the legend, the Carson and San Francisco mints were notified. However, the dust failed to show up. At least it was never reported.

In 1876, $3,000 in gold dust was taken from a stagecoach near Cayuse Station, on the Umatilla Indian Reservation northeast of Pendleton. The loot was supposed to have been cached near the scene of the holdup and, according to the oral tale handed down from parents to children, never recovered.

Every string of crime has a thread of bizarre comedy. In September 1889 a northbound stage was stopped at gunpoint south of Linkville, now Klamath Falls, and just as the unmasked highwayman was ready to take off, up came the southbound stage. Taking logical advantage of the bonus situation he stuck that up, too, and escaped with the plunder from both. For years afterward there were rumors in Klamath County of buried loot.

There is great natural beauty in Horse Thief Meadows of Mount Hood National Forest. And supposedly there is more—a cache of $25,000.

In 1884 a man named Philips showed up in the Hood River Valley and hired a local jack-of-all-trades to help him locate an outlaw's cabin where the booty was said to have been hidden.

According to Philips, the lost loot had been taken in a stagecoach robbery near Walla Walla, Washington, in 1880. The men located the cabin, but if they recovered the gold they were mighty closemouthed about it. Some people think the cache hasn't yet been uncovered.

Somewhere on Laurel Hill, east of Portland, there is, according to an undercurrent of western Cascade foothill legend, still more stolen booty. Some time in the late 1880s or early 1890s two men stuck up a stage and carried off a not-immodest sum. One of the brigands killed his partner and buried the stolen gold and the murdered bandit in the

Rumors of cached loot on Laurel Hill persisted for years.
Courtesy Oregon State

same grave. Upon his deathbed the survivor confessed his crime to his son and sketched directions to the cache. For several summers the son sought the grave. All he could ever locate was a blazed cedar tree which his father said would identify the site. The loot, presumably, is still there, somewhere on Laurel Hill.

In 1857 a miner, whose name history never recorded, appeared in a Corvallis saloon to boast of a rich gold strike. When he realized the folly of his babbling, he stashed his gold dust in a rubber boot near what is now the entrance to the Peavy Arboretum.

There are three versions of what followed. The first is that several men were surprised while digging at the site and fled, carrying what appeared to be a rubber boot. Soon, this version continued, three Corvallis residents became suddenly and unexplainedly prosperous.

A second story is of finding a gun barrel with a bullet lodged midway, leading some citizens to believe that the miner had been robbed and murdered.

Finally, there are those who contend that the rubber boot was never found—and these are the kind of people who keep looking.

Here's another tale to whet your curiosity:

When Fort Grant, south of Medford was in existence, the paymaster was the custodian for money and gold dust given him for safekeeping by prospectors, cattlemen, and others. Ten and twenty-dollar gold pieces were as common as paper money was uncommon, and the paymaster stored the gold pieces and the gold dust in a large iron kettle which he had secreted in the ground.

Who could guess that the paymaster would one day suffer a stroke? Unable to speak, he was handed a pencil and a sheet of paper. He tried to draw a map, but before the diagram was completed he died. Even before he was buried his depositors were prodding the earth all around the camp with an endgate iron. Within a few months the camp was abandoned, but the search went on. For all anyone knows the kettle full of gold is right where the paymaster buried it.

While I'm at it, I might as well retell one more story.

Sometime during the 1860s, so the tale goes, about $20,000 in gold dust and greenbacks was taken during a stage robbery between Boise City and Owyhee County in Idaho.

Suspicion for the holdup fastened on the partner of the miner who did the actual gunwork. The partner was brought to book and sentenced to eight years in the state pen. When the guilty man learned of his partner's arrest, he became fearful that the authorities were on his trail. He was in The Dalles at the time he read the news and instantly took off for the Cascades. After several days he came upon a deserted trapper's cabin and decided to hole up there until the excitement had passed. He dug out a "vault" under a tree stump near the cabin and stuffed the plunder into it.

For several years the outlaw carried on as a hermit. He avoided all strangers and lived off the land, but the imprisonment of his partner increasingly weighed heavy upon him, and there came a day when his conscience could take no more. So he returned to Boise City, where he learned that his partner was still behind bars. Before he could do anything else, he fell seriously ill.

On his deathbed he wrote a full confession of the crime and described the cabin and its immediate surroundings. But life failed him before he could describe—if he ever intended to—where the cabin was located. (Isn't it interesting how many people in these tales breathe their last just in time?)

The partner was pardoned and perhaps was one of the men who set out to find the "lost cabin." Everybody knew it was about a day's horseback ride from The Dalles, but the cabin was never located.

Well, that was a long time ago, and surely the cabin has

fallen to pieces and been swallowed by the woods. But maybe you'll be along that way someday, stretch out for a nap, and lay your head upon a fortune.

Maybe.

The Quest For The Columbia

Ride with the long flow of history as you stand on Astoria's Coxcomb Hill and skim your eyes down the Columbia River to its mouth at the Pacific.

Five years after Columbus first touched a shore of the New World, thinking it to be an island belonging to the East Indies, the mariners of Western Europe began a quest for a shorter trade route to Asia.

There came into concept a mythical river around the northern coast of North America, and this long-sought fantasy was endowed with the romantic name of "North West Passage."

There are times when failure to reach a goal, such as the North West Passage, can yet result in great accomplishments never suspected. Some of the foremost mariners of their times embarked upon voyages to discover the mythical trade route, and along the way found much that was destined to influence, both by land and sea, the exploration of the west coast of North America, including Oregon.

For almost two centuries the vessels of powerful nations scoured the western fringe of the Pacific, almost always within sight of land, but it was not until the spring of 1792 that one of the truly great discoveries was made. It provided the young United States with its first claim to any land on the far side of the continent and proved to be the spearhead of American penetration on the sunset side of the unknown mountains.

The *Columbia Rediviva*, eighty-three feet long, 212 tons

burden, was built in 1773 by James Briggs, at Hobart Landing, North River, Massachusetts, and financed by five Bay State merchants, who subscribed $50,000 to outfit the *Columbia* and a ninety-ton sloop, the *Lady Washington.*

The first captain of the *Lady Washington* was Robert Gray, a Rhode Island man who went to sea early in life and saw fighting in the navy during the Revolutionary War.

The first captain of the *Columbia Rediviva* was John Kendrick, fifteen years older than Gray. Kendrick had a penchant for playing at diplomacy and his personal opportunism was unbounded. Gray took on the characteristics of a Boston trader but remained a staunch company man.

On September 30, 1787, the two vessels departed Boston. Almost eleven months later Gray sailed the *Lady Washington* across the shallow bar of Oregon's Tillamook Bay. He retreated after two days of pleasant trading with the Indians ended abruptly when a quarrel developed, and Gray's cabin boy, a black youth, was killed and several of his sailors wounded. As soon as the tide was favorable, the ship sailed out of Murderer's Harbour, as the crew named it.

Before twelve months had passed Gray and Kendrick swapped commands and Gray pointed the *Columbia Rediviva* for China. He returned to Boston on August 10, 1790, having completely circumnavigated the globe, the first American craft to do so.

Within six weeks Gray and the *Columbia* left Boston again, and the following June, after a quick voyage, reached the northwest coast. The winter of 1791-92 was spent at Adventure Cove in Clayoquot Sound, on the western coast of Vancouver Island, in present British Columbia. On April 2, 1792, the *Columbia* cast off, after Gray's long stay had exhausted the hospitality of the Indians of the Queen Charlotte Islands.

Irked by the increasing enmity of the Indians, who had

taken the lives of three of Gray's men, the captain, sitting in holy judgment, ordered an attack upon a village of two hundred houses.

The village had artistic appeal for Gray's fifth mate, eighteen-year-old John Boit, who observed that every door entered "was in resemblance to an human and beasts head, the passage being through the mouth, besides which there was much more rude carved work about the dwellings, some of which was by no means inelegant." He added, in bitterness, "This fine village, the work of Ages, was in a short time totally destroy'd."

So much for Gray the humanitarian.

The *Columbia* sailed south to the California coast and then turned north. Gray scrutinized the shoreline for river mouths and bays into which he might take his vessel for trade but the weather was foul. Persistent squalls and strong southerly currents kept him spying for safe anchorages, which were disappointingly scarce. Near the reading 46°10′, the thirty-seven-year-old skipper detected signs of a large river, but it was apparent that the outflowing current was too powerful to permit him to enter.

So the *Columbia* continued north until on April 27 it was anchored near Teakwhit Head. There Gray was visited by representatives of Captain George Vancouver, whose *Discovery* had coincidentally sailed into the area.

Vancouver's emissaries asked Gray about the Juan de Fuca Strait, which Vancouver had been seeking. According to legend, a Greek explorer, Juan de Fuca, flying a Spanish flag, claimed to have discovered the Pacific opening of the North West Passage in 1592. He entered, he had supposedly written in a letter, a wide inlet located between 47° and 48° latitude. It was in this vicinity that, about two hundred years later, the strait was, in the annals of white men, officially discovered. The Indians of the area had known about it for millenia.

Not everyone believed the legend of Juan de Fuca. Captain James Cook, the celebrated explorer, was one of the doubters. On March 22, 1778, Cook named a headland facing Vancouver Island across the strait, Cape Flattery, a compliment to the scenery and the weather (he must have been there on one of those rare calm days). For the strait itself he had disdain: "There appeared to be a small opening, which flattered us with the hopes of finding an harbour." With a condescending bow to objectivity, he noted, "It is in this very latitude where we now were, that geographers have placed the pretended Strait of Juan de Fuca. But," he concluded with acid touch, writing off the evidence as far as he was concerned, "we saw nothing like it, nor is there the least probability that any such thing ever existed."

Nine years later, on a fair July day, a more observant British seadog, Charles Barkley, commanding the fur-trading *Imperial Eagle*, sighted the broad inlet. His wife, the first known white woman to look upon the Pacific Northwest, wrote ecstatically in her diary that "to our great astonishment, we arrived off a large opening extending to the eastward, the entrance to which appeared to be about four leagues wide and remained about that width as far as the eye could see, with a clear westerly horizon, which my husband immediately recognized as the long lost strait of Juan de Fuca, and to which he gave the name of the original discoverer, my husband placing it on his chart."

Barkley, however, did not penetrate the waters deeply. So late in April, 1792, here are Vancouver's men asking Gray what he knew about the Strait. Gray had little to offer but he did report that on the way up he had passed the mouth of a large river. When the information was passed on to Vancouver, the Britisher did not do handsprings. A short while earlier he had actually passed the entrance to the Columbia but had misjudged the opening, thinking it to be the Deception Bay that John Meares claimed to have discovered in 1788.

Of the mouth of the Columbia, Vancouver wrote: "The sea had now changed from its natural, to river coloured water, the probable consequence of some streams falling into the bay, or into the ocean to the north of it, through the low land. Not considering this opening worthy of more attention, I continued our pursuit to the N.W. being desirous to embrace the advantages of the prevailing breeze . . ."

So he had missed the river and when he heard what Gray had seen he dismissed the American's report as another piece of misinformation. The sea was full of false tales and Vancouver was too careful a man to go off on wild goose chases.

Almost six months later, Vancouver, who had secured Gray's sketch of the Columbia River's entrance from the Spanish mariner Bodega y Quadra, dispatched his 135-ton *Chatham* upstream, under the command of Lieutenant William R. Broughton.

Overcautious, Broughton anchored in four fathoms of water, almost on the bar. The crew spent a fearful night there, certain the swift and hard surf would smash the boat or that the vessel would go aground and be reduced to pulp.

The next morning Broughton gathered his courage, crossed the bar, and found safe anchorage in a bay on the north bank. Here he was surprised to find a fellow countryman, Captain James Barker, in the small schooner *Jenny*, out of Bristol, doing brisk trade with the Indians.

Broughton explored the Columbia for three weeks. He surveyed the main streams and shores of the broad tidal waters near the river's mouth from the *Chatham*, then took to his longboat and penetrated the river for more than one hundred miles upstream. He named numerous geographic features, including Mt. Hood, that peak to honor Lord Samuel Hood, the British admiral. Broughton observed the Willamette and Sandy rivers more than a dozen years before Lewis and Clark. And, in a moonlight ceremony on October 30, 1792, opposite a sandy point of the Columbia and very

Wreck of a sailing ship. Hundreds of ships have met their doom on the sandbar of the Columbia River near Astoria. The area is a marine graveyard.
Courtesy Astoria Chamber of Commerce

likely near where the town of Corbett now stands, Broughton raised the British flag and claimed all the country drained by the Columbia in the name of King George III. But all the British got out of Broughton's brilliant exploration was a lot of place names.

We return to late April at Teakwhit Head. Vancouver has heard out his men's report of Gray's observations. It was time to find the strait and explore it, he concluded. On the twenty-ninth of April he located the strait and anchored within it. For the next two months he detailed the inland waters, including all contours of Puget Sound. After further exploration along the west coast of Vancouver Island, Vancouver turned south, this time looking for the Columbia.

Mouth of the Columbia River, from an original drawing.

Mouth of the Columbia River. Mountains in the rear are imaginative.
Courtesy Oregon Historical Society

Captain Gray wanted only one thing from Vancouver: assurance that the Britisher was not a trader. Gray had the Yankee propensity of competing with anyone who had the trade and resenting all those aiming to cut in on his business. Assured that Vancouver was solely on a mission of exploration, Gray breathed easy. He turned the *Columbia* south and sailed steady until May 7, when he spotted an inlet which looked like it might have the makings of a comfortable anchorage. He sent a boat ahead to signal the depths and the *Columbia* poised on the bar. Then, when the final signal had been given, the sloop sprinted between the breakers and entered calm water. Impressed with the setting, the ship's officers called it Grays Harbor, and so it is to this day, with the southwestern Washington cities of Aberdeen and Hoquiam fast on its shores.

Trading with the Indians was good the next day but toward evening Gray suspected hostility. His suspicion heightened when his men called out that they saw war canoes approaching, moonlight clearly illuminating the water. Several warning shots were fired, but the canoes continued toward the sloop. Thoroughly alarmed, Gray ordered a broadside on the nearest canoe. The shot landed squarely, killing all of the twenty or so occupants.

Less than forty-eight hours later, when the path was clear, the *Columbia* eased over the bar of the harbor and was once more in the Pacific.

Leaving Grays Harbor, Captain Robert Gray set his course south for 46° 10′, where he thought he had detected the mouth of a large river. This time he was certain, but there was no exhilaration in the discovery. His observations of the broad estuary of the stream which had eluded mariners for so many years were typically terse and business-like. He noted in his log: "At four, A.M., saw the entrance of our desired port bearing east-southeast, distance six leagues; in steering sails and hauled our wind in shore. At eight A.M., being a little to windward of the entrance of the Harbor, bore away, and run in east-north-east between the breakers, having from five to seven fathoms of water."

Fortunately, Gray's fifth mate, John Boit, was of a more imaginative bent. Boit was young, impressionable, his senses alive, his heart innocent. His "Log of the Columbia," which survived most of the ship's official records, provides the clearest picture of the momentous discovery.

On May 12, 1792, Boit wrote ". . . This day saw an appearance of a spacious harbour abreast the Ship, haul'd wind for it, observ'd two sand bars making off, with a passage between them to a fine river . . . The River extended to the N.E., as far as eye could reach, and water fit to drink as far down as the Bars, at the entrance. We directed our course up this noble river in search of a village. Soon after, about 20 Canoes came off, and brought a great lot of Furs, and Salmon, which last they sold two for a

Mural in Oregon's state capitol rotunda at Salem depicts Captain Robert Gray near the mouth of the Columbia River after his landing in 1792.

Courtesy State of Oregon

board Nail . . They appeared to view the Ship with the greatest astonishment and no doubt we was the first civilized people that they ever saw . . . The tide set down the whole time and was rapid, whole trees sometimes came down with the stream. The Indians inform'd us there was 50 villages on the banks of this river."

On May 18, Boit recorded more information of historical moment:

". . . Captain Gray names this river Columbia's, and the North entrance Cape Hancock, and the South Point, Adams. The River, in my opinion, wou'd be a fine place for to set up a Factory. The Indians are very numerous, and appear'd very civil (not even offering to steal) . . . The river abounds with excellent Salmon, and most other River fish, and woods with plenty of Moose, and Deer, the skins of which was brought us in great plenty, and Banks produced a ground nut, which is an excellent substitute for either bread or Potatoes. We found plenty of Oack, Ash, and Walnut trees, and clear ground in plenty, which with little labor made fit to raise such seeds as is necessary for the sustenance of inhabitants."

Boit was convinced that the mouth of the river would be a fine place to set up a factory, or trading post, as John Jacob Astor did nineteen years later, but Gray was not impressed. True, the Indians were eager to barter; they swapped two salmon for a nail, four otter skins for a sheet of copper, took two spikes for a beaver skin and accepted a single spike for less valuable furs. But in the week of trading, Gray took in less than a thousand pelts, of which only 150 were sea otter and 300 were beaver. The remainder was second-class stuff, poor bargaining leverage for a Yankee trader who had to dicker with the sharp Chinese merchants of Canton.

On May 20, the *Columbia*, after a short run up river to Gray's Bar, on the north shore, put out to sea again, Gray's appetite for exploration here having been satiated. The poetic John Boit, who had been delighted with the stay, wrote with light-hearted romanticism, and perhaps with a touch of blushing desire:

". . . The Men, at Columbia's River, are strait limb'd, fine looking fellows, and the Women are very pretty. They are all in a state of Nature, except the females, who wear a leaf Apron (perhaps 'twas a fig leaf. But some of our gentlemen . . . reported that it was not a leaf, but a nice wove mat in resemblance! and so we go—thus, thus—and no war!)."

Boit was happy to leave without bloodshed, to depart with the sweet taste of peace and good fellowship. Gray had kept his cool and the Indians, in their innocence, hadn't felt themselves cheated.

Elsewhere in his log, Boit recorded: "I landed abrest the Ship with Capt. Gray to view the Country, and take possession." But it is plain, as contemporary scholars have demonstrated, that the last three words, written in a different

Astoria in 1811
From Tacoma Edition of Irving's Astoria

ink than Boit used for the preceding words, were inserted later.

There is not a word in the official log of the *Columbia Rediviva* about taking possession of the land drained by the mighty river. Nor is there any suggestion that Gray thought of himself as an empire builder or that he saw the Columbia country in terms of the expanding interests of the United States. Gray could, with the flag waving in Boston on the 4th of July, be as patriotic as the next man, but out here he was all trader and nothing more.

Gray's reluctance to explore the river may have been

Troller off Astoria
Courtesy Astoria Chamber of Commerce

because the Indians coming down the stream to see the strange white men had not enough goods to arouse a fever in the Yankee skipper. If what they brought was the best the river had, he must have reckoned, there was no point wasting valuable time.

So Gray left and the *Columbia* sailed north to Nootka, across Vancouver Island from present Courtenay. Here, at the well-known rendezvous, Gray handed a sketch of the river's entrance to Bodega y Quadra, who later passed it on to Captain Vancouver.

When he had enough cargo, Gray turned the bow of the

Gill-netter in the Columbia River
Courtesy Astoria Chamber of Commerce

Columbia west, for China. At Canton he merchandised his furs and loaded a cargo that would auction at a vast profit in Boston, which he reached on July 29, 1793, after continuing around the world.

The taciturn Robert Gray, veteran of the Revolutionary War, had accomplished much on this last voyage. He had forged the American link of the Northwest-Canton trade, a fur mercantilism built on the slaughter of the sea otter that would start some Massachusetts families on the road to great wealth and prominence. He had cleared up hazy areas on the maps of the Northwest coastline, and he had entered on the maps the hitherto unknown Grays Harbor and the Columbia River. In the long run the discovery of the Columbia, however little and briefly he saw of it, was the most monumental and best-remembered of his successes.

And Sheridan Slept Here Too

The terrible grumble, and rumble, and roar,
Telling the battle was on once more,
And Sheridan twenty miles away.
Thomas B. Read, Sheridan's Ride

One of the most colorful military posts in Oregon history was Fort Hoskins, established in 1856 and named for Lieutenant Charles Hoskins, a complete casualty of the Mexican War ten years earlier.

The only indication of where the post stood is a tavern appropriately named The Fort. It comprises the entire business district of the village of Hoskins and is the social center of this foothill pocket of northwestern Benton County banked on the Luckiamute River.

There is still standing, however, a house that was part of Fort Hoskins. It is seven-tenths of a mile up Pedee Creek Road, which is a mile and three-tenths south of Pedee, a hamlet without post office.

The house on Pedee Creek Road was moved from Hoskins, about five miles to the south, at the turn of the century. By then Fort Hoskins had been abandoned for more than three decades, having been evacuated in the spring of 1865, but the history and legends are still bright.

The location of the fort was selected by Captain Charles Auger of the Fourth Infantry. His choice was opposed by his superior, Brigadier General John Wool, but Augur held fast and the War Department supported him—one of the few times in US military annals that a captain has bested a general.

There had to be a reason, of course, for Fort Hoskins. That was simple: Indians. Until the Civil War there was not a military post in Oregon constructed or maintained for any other reason but to control or supress (and often the two were the same) the children of the first inhabitants of this land.

Indians from all parts of southwestern Oregon had been concentrated at the Siletz Reservation; the fort had the double duty of keeping an eye on the Indians there and serving as protection for farmers in the Willamette Valley.

The ubiquitous Phil Sheridan, who seems to have slept in more places than George Washington, was stationed at Fort Hoskins for a spell and probably completed the construction started by Captain Augur. A lieutenant then, Sheridan also led a party of troopers in scrounging out a kind of rough road—trail might be more accurate—from the fort over the Coast Range to the Siletz country. If you want to follow as much of that route as is feasible today, take the gravel road from Hoskins to Summit, negotiate a paved road to Nashville, and then browse along the quiet pike to Logsden and Siletz.

Sheridan didn't stay at Fort Hoskins until it was decommissioned. In 1861 he was commanding officer at Fort Yamhill, near present Valley Junction. There, after chafing at the bit about missing the big action back East, he finally received his marching orders. Whereupon he rode off, calling to his men, "Boys, I am going into this war to win a captain's spurs or to die with my boots on." He rose to the rank of four-star general, lived until 1888, and died in bed. He had done some heavy fighting against the Indians after arriving in Oregon in 1855, and at Cascade Locks he almost lost his life when a bullet grazed his skull. An inch lower and the town of Sheridan would have been named for

Lieutenant Phil Sheridan
Courtesy Oregon Historical Society

Sheridan House

Ralph Friedman

someone else. The only action he saw while at Fort Hoskins was when he was sent to deal with the Indians at Yaquina Bay. By then Sheridan had learned some tact and was able to effect a settlement without bloodshed.

In its halcyon days Fort Hoskins had a force of about 150 men, but it was less noted for military maneuvering than for high-spirited elegance. The officers spent more time planning dances than leading patrols. To sparkle in the quadrille was greater distinction than to deploy with skill. No tiger in combat could receive the praise heaped upon a lion in the ballroom. Whatever the combat quality of the troops, the post would have furnished consistent news for the society pages of the newspapers of Benton and Polk counties—if the newspapers had society pages.

The house on Pedee Creek is reputed to have been the residence of Sheridan when he was fort commander, and it was from either the balcony or the porch that legend has Sheridan reviewing his troops.

Maybe so, maybe not. All that is certain is that the only building that remains of storied Fort Hoskins is sometimes a gloomy residence in various conditions of repair or disrepair and sometimes a storage shed. If Phil Sheridan came back here to sleep I have the feeling he'd prefer the house as it was more than a hundred years ago.

Letters To The Grave

_____

Part I: Charles Erskine Scott Wood

Valiant trumpeter of our song; camerado and companero of the anguished and the marching; grown scarlet as the vine maple in the autumn of your years: saludo, stalwart soldier, brother of the Indian, caped poet, discourser of Heaven and Earth, Western rider, restless man, sky watcher, puddle walker, white-bearded seer.

I wanted to tell my friends who you were, the CES Wood beyond romanticism, and finally I discovered what I wanted to say in a poem you wrote to an old friend, Mother Bloor, before your passing and sent on by your colleague of love and mind, Sara Bard Field.

Oh, a word or two might have to be changed to fit your manliness, but I have left it as it is, to be my celebration of you, this tribute from a private in the ranks of the anguished, the marching, and the hopeful.

> I saw a gray old oak that stood upon a hill
> And bent and bowed before the storm;
> The howling hurricane that wrenched its limbs
> And whirled them to the ground.
> But always it returned, erect, deep rooted
> In the mother-breast, proud and unconquerable
> And shook its windblown hair in happy laughter.
> And I have seen it guard the lambs in March
> That frisked and sucked, shaking their rapid tails;
> Or, in the August heat, it dropped its cloak of
>   shade
> Upon cud-chewing cows that couched on folded
>   knees
> Or stood with dreamy eyes giving the milk of life
> To bull-headed calves that butted the soft udders.
> O venerable oak, the great Mechanic, Time,
> Has wrought your coat of silver mail.
> The glory of the combat has increased your
>   strength
> And when you fall as every warrior must,
> The lark shall sing your requiem,
> The whispering grass shall soothe your lying down.

Part II: Freda Frauendorf

Scarcely anyone calls it Freda's tree anymore, as the old-timers did. Mr. Martin, my neighbor who died some years ago, gave it that name, and you happily accepted it, and when you passed it by you said, "Hi, Freda."

It is your tree, Freda, that massive chestnut on the corner, the one that motorists sometimes stop in midstreet to admire.

There weren't any houses here and no street when you arrived in 1908, just a trail on which a Montavilla grocer came twice a week on horseback. In this wilderness—all of five miles from downtown Portland—you had to carry water from a well eight blocks away.

You and Walter, your husband, lived in a tent until a house was built, and then you began planting trees. You planted them in your yard until Walter said, "No more. The yard is getting too shady." So you planted a walnut tree out front, and then you started planting trees in the yards of your new neighbors and then in front of their houses.

"Why are you tree crazy?" Walter once asked, and you replied, "Because I was born in the Black Forest."

In 1912, just before the city put in the street, you planted a chestnut switch just three feet high on the corner, a block from your house, because you had run out of space. As it grew, Mr. Martin prophesied it would outlive all the early settlers. It has, and also outlived all your other trees, including that first walnut that toppled before your eyes during the Columbus Day storm.

You were eighty-eight and in a nursing home when I saw you for the last time. You were frail, bony, your white hair thinning, a childlike innocence in your eyes, your face shriveling like a rose that is losing body and color. But when you talked about the chestnut you smiled. "It's hard to believe I lived this long, to see my chestnut grow so big,"

Freda's tree

George Walker

you said. "Every time I passed it I got a special pleasure. I feel I accomplished something."

You did, Freda—more than most of us have or ever will. How glorious that chestnut stands against the rising sun, and how serenely it receives the last rays of day. Coated by rain, bitten by snow, gnawed by winds, it is a tower of stability on this corner. Three generations have chatted under its leafy canopy and hundreds of children have climbed to its iron limbs and every kind of bird that comes this way finds passing shelter here.

You talked at the nursing home that chill day, as we all waited for spring, about baking ducks and stuffing their insides with chestnuts from the tree or sometimes roasting the nuts. "They were pretty good," you remembered.

We've never tried that, content to watch the nuts tumble out of the fountain of leaves and cover all the ground around the huge base of the tree, so far below the tips of the tallest branches that stretch their stubby fingers to the cellar of heaven.

Better to have planted a tree that the Good Lord took care of and just grew by itself, as you said, than to have your name on a hundred public buildings.

I tell my friends it is a sweet chestnut, and leave it at that, but when I walk close enough to touch it I whisper, Hi, Freda, and know that your spirit lives in it.

Part III: Dean Cromwell

It is all there, plainly and completely, the grandeur and the glory, clearly engraved on your gravestone in the quiet burial ground flowing back from the rustic road.

Forty years as track coach at the University of Southern California and, in 1948 (the year you retired), coach of the United States Olympic Track Team.

You were "The Dean" to your peers, and Bill Bowerman, also a maker of champions, called you "the most successful Track Coach in the World for all time."

I found you one day, so unexpectedly, when I paused to look at the little cemetery on my way from Turner to Mehama. Dean Cromwell! What is he doing here?

It is still a good question. It goes to the four corners of the earth and is imbedded most deeply in this, our own, our native land.

You were born in Turner on September 20, 1879 (a year before the University of Southern California was founded); grew up in this small hinterland town of Marion County; married a Marion County girl, Cecelia Gertrude Potter; and, after you had graduated from what became Occidental College in Los Angeles, coached for a year at Willamette University in Salem—though that school says it has no record of you.

So much I learned from your second son, Charles.

You also worked for the telephone company (Portland or Los Angeles or both) and as an automobile salesman (Pierce Arrow) in Los Angeles. Charles is not certain which job came first.

Charles was born in 1908 (the year USC hired you as track coach) and he never lived in Turner nor did he remember you coming back. But there are old press clippings of the Salem papers that tell of your spending parts of some summers in this area.

No Cromwells remain in Turner, and I found no one there who remembers you or any of the Cromwells.

You did not return to Turner when you retired, but you made it clear to your family that when you died, you were to be buried in the Turner cemetery.

Why is it that so many illustrious men and women, having achieved all their fame in a metropolis, want to be laid to rest in the villages of their youth?

In the end is the sweet, still earth of a country cemetery a retreat to innocence? Was all the rest of the world just a place to do business in? Were all the plaudits and trophies nothing more than wisps of smoke that could not be anchored to the soul? In death are the contemporaries more distant than the ancestors?

So here you sleep, among your boyhood chums who grew up to be farmers and shopkeepers and schoolteachers, and if they should awaken for a moment to see the gravestone of the greatest coach in the history of track, all they would probably say is, Dean has come home.

Grave of Dean Cromwell

Ralph Friedman

Part IV: Dr. Marie Equi

Everybody who knew you said you were the most fascinating person they had ever met. And while others stood on the banks of the river, watching the current roll on, you were deep in the stream. And that you were frontpage news.

So where are the books, the poems, the songs, the memorials?

What happened, Doc? Why did history turn its head? For what reason did legend pass you by?

Gone are those who knew the voltage of your name— most at least, all but a few of the many.

They must be dead, all of them, the cowboys and Indians of eastern Oregon who hollered "Here's Doc" when they saw your horse breaking through the cloud of dust. Then they'd be reaching for your bag and later telling each other that there were a lot of men doctors who didn't have your guts or care.

That was around the turn of the century.

And after you moved to Portland to set up practice there, it became the word among the poor that Doc Equi never turned anyone down for lack of money.

A few years ago an old man told me: "She would make house calls whether you could pay or not. She'd even go clear out from downtown Portland to St. Johns in those days, and you know how far that is. She probably went out there by buggy. A lot of doctors didn't like her political ideas, but they all had to admit she was a first class doctor."

That old man is dead now.

Gone, too, is the crippled great-grandmother who remembered you in the last year of her life and said: "Doc was a very warm, outgoing, and generous person, and because she defended working women and working people in all their struggles she could do no wrong."

Who remains to tell the young scribes of the compassion and money you gave to the hungry, the homeless, the women whose husbands had run off, the girls in trouble who could not bring themselves to pious hands and stern tongues for judgment? Who remembers now the falsely imprisoned for whom you hired lawyers?

Does anyone now recall that you were also the most feared and hated woman in the state—or in all of the Pacific Northwest? Yes, the plain people adored you, but the politicians, the civic leaders, and the fat cats would have inscribed your name with burning coals in the pit of hell for all the grief you gave them.

The lumber barons spat at the mention of your name because you had the gall—you, a member of a respected

Marie Equi
Courtesy Oregon Historical Society

profession, and a lady yet!—to visit their camps, tend to the loggers, and expose the filth of their leaky barracks.

The industrialists were sure you were the Devil himself come to plague them when you led the underpaid cannery women and girls in bold demonstrations.

How you were despised by the mighty for your front-line stance in the assault on the citadel of politics for passage of a law limiting the hours of women and child workers.

What scorn was heaped upon you for thundering across the state for women's suffrage!

Who is around to tell how you succored the wounded of the Centralia Massacre and the Everett Massacre and the protestors shot on the good ship *Verona* outbound from Seattle?

That was long, long ago—and almost all the tongues have been stilled by time.

When you organized the trainload of doctors, nurses, and supplies to race from Portland to San Francisco during the fires that followed the earthquake, and gave of yourself day and night in that inferno of the damned, did you ever think that the same government which honored you for your courage and humanitarianism would twelve years later charge you with sedition under the wartime espionage act for unfurling a banner that roared, "Down With The Imperialist War?"

President Wilson cut the three-year sentence to one. You did serve ten months, and you never forgot your fellow prisoners, sending them sewing materials and buying them turkey dinners for Christmas Day until you stopped working.

In what history book is any of this writ?

Gone are the police records to illuminate your fury and your conscience—and every cop then on the force is now dead.

There was that time during the cannery strike when you

were hauled in with the workers. One was a Cherokee woman. When you saw that she was upset you reached out to comfort her. A sergeant knocked you to the floor. Angry, you cried out, "I am going to speak where and when I wish. No man is going to stop me." When you were let out of jail you had been so cuffed up you needed medical treatment.

There was the time you were sent sprawling to the street by a mounted gendarme—who arrested you as you lay with a broken back.

And the time you were pinched for speaking on a downtown street after the mayor had limited free speech in public places to religious matters. (You could beseech for Jesus, but you could not defy authority as He did.) Furious at the policeman who wrenched your arm you stabbed him in the wrist with a hat pin and had to leave town, by arrangement with the police chief, until the furor ebbed, but the $500 you forfeited in bail money would have been given to the poor, to the helpless, to the movement, and that hurt.

You were arrested with Margaret Sanger and with the Jimmy Higginses of labor and with welfare women and once for climbing a telephone pole (with the loan of a pair of linemen's spurs) to speak out against The War To End All Wars. Frustrated, the police called the fire department, but the firemen were from the plain people who admired you, and they took their own sweet time getting there. So, before you spiked your way down to be manacled, you had made your speech.

At fifty-eight you had a heart attack from overwork. You quit your practice and retired to your two-story house on upper Hall Street. Four years later, when, as a reporter observed, "lead whined, buck shot splattered [and] men fell wounded, gasping and cursing," during the general waterfront strike, you pushed yourself out of bed to join the conflict.

When peace came you went home again, and that is

where Julia   Ruuttila, the poet and journalist, saw you in the thirties and forties. Nearing seven decades and five years, Julia remembered of you:

"She had a high commanding presence. She was always sitting propped up in bed in a gaudy brocaded dressing gown and over the high top of the bed there was always a crucifix. She received all of her visitors in bed. It was like being invited into the presence of some Oriental potentate. When she wanted to see you she would call you up on the phone and order you to come to her house. If you weren't there when she called she could accept that. But she wouldn't accept your saying, 'I can't come.' No one ever thought of doing such an awful thing as saying, 'I can't come.' She had done too much for all the working people.

"She had a deep voice, like a man. Her eyes were dark brown and they were almost black when they flashed. I never heard her make a speech in public. I heard her make many speeches when she was in bed; no one else could say a word, she was a non-stop talker. She was a dramatic and flamboyant and wonderful woman. She knew what was a good story and liked to embellish."

Not even the embellishments have made history, as though they were needed. Is not the truth staggering enough?

Tom Burns, the literary master of Skid Road, should have written of you, but he was too busy with his Time Shop and with the enormous library of working-class literature in his basement and in caring for luckless vagrants with cots and meals you helped supply.

Francis Murnane, the longshoreman who looked into the mirror of his soul to find St. Francis of Assisi, and who was always giving his money away to those short of bread and shelter, and who knew so admiringly well of you, should have told the world, or at least the town. But he was busy, too, with his union and all the social issues and the endless

David-Goliath battles to keep Portland worthy of a people's affection. Upon his death the makers and shakers called him the "conscience of the city" and named a few yards of the waterfront green for him.

When you lay dying at St. Vincent's Hospital the longshoremen of Local 8, remembering 1934 and all the money you gave afterward to the Union Welfare Fund, sent you roses, thirteen, the number of your cell at San Quentin. The end came on July 13, 1952, at eighty.

There wasn't a political funeral, as there would have been if you had been struck down in your prime. The people who remembered your prime were dispersed or buried or too old and weary to rouse themselves for one more round of resolves.

And now, who knows? But there will come a time for honoring the people's heroes, even one who spent her last years in bed, robed in a gaudy, brocaded dressing gown, imperiously summoning old friends to sit silently through long embellished speeches.

Someday, Marie, there will be something named after you. What would you like it to be? The kind of a tavern where you sipped beer and broke bread with muckers and gandy dancers? The kind of a hall where you sat with the Wobblies and chastised them because they wouldn't let you, a doctor and a woman, be a member? A clinic for the poor with doors open the clock around? A safe nest for the elderly impoverished? A bookstore where women can bind their wounds and march out to the skirmish ahead? A corner forever dedicated to free speech?

What would you like it to be, Doc? You earned the right to choose.

Part V: Rick Sanders

When we met, I the reporter and you the already legendary wrestler, your first words were: "Don't think of me as a jock."

You said it defensively, almost angrily, and in your aggression I thought you were going to add: "If this is going to be another sports interview, let's skip it."

As though to prove you were more than a jock, you carried in your pocket a science fiction paperback.

But something had to be said about you as a wrestler. You were not only the pride of Portland State University but heralded throughout Oregon for your mastery on the mat. Intercollegiate national champion, all-United States champion, Olympian, second best in world competition. (Only one man denied you the top of the mountain: an agile Japanese you would have traded a hundred other victories to defeat.)

You spoke of him with respect and admiration, and obligingly you recited what were for you the stale facts of your own prowess. Then you turned to what you liked to talk about: the fun of traveling, the comradeship at the pizza joint where you worked as a cook, music, teaching methods, life-styles, the kind of offbeat people that were your friends on campus, your girl friend of the moment, and the war in Vietnam, to which you were strongly opposed.

I tried to turn your mind back to sports. "Pound for pound," I said, "you may be the greatest wrestler Oregon has ever produced." You frowned. "I'm a person," you replied. "Wrestling is just part of me."

I remember you as gentle and witty and straightforward, and without sham, and with a carefreeness that takes life in stride, and doggedly individualistic. You said, "I don't tell people how to behave, and I don't want them to tell me how to act." At times you grinned like a young boy. More than anything else, I have not forgotten that boyish grin.

You wrestled at Munich in the 1972 Olympics and took second place. (That agile Japanese again.)

It wasn't the end of the world, as it had been for the mowed-down Israelis. At twenty-seven you were still some years from your peak, you told yourself; in 1976 you would

Rick Sanders
Courtesy Portland State University

be back at the Olympics, and this time you would make it to the summit. So, carefree, looking for new adventures, you and your girl friend of the moment hitchhiked south through Europe.

In Yugoslavia a truck thundered out of the fog. Did you see it at all? Was there time to scream? Were you sent from fog to darkness without opening your eyes one last time?

Your body arrived in Portland by plane. There were kind words spoken and sincere tears shed at the university. They really loved you, Rick. Then your family buried you on the crest of a cemetery near Eagle Creek, far from the crowds that cheered your triumphs.

I came out to the cemetery once and sat beside your grave and thought of you not as a wrestler or as a soldier killed in a war but as a young-man-about-town who saw the most important part of his life just beginning and with no great faith to die for.

On your stone slab are these words and dates:

Olympic Silver Medal
1968   1972

I think you would, if you could, engrave under this inscription six other words:

There Was Really More To Me

Part VI: Marie Bosworth

Why did you leave us so soon, Marie?

You were the long-stemmed rose no winter would bend or wither. So I thought. When I read of your passing, a little piece of me went out of my life, as it always does when some rare and shining soul departs this bittersweet earth.

Blithe spirit you were, with a will of iron and a heart of compassion and a mind that never ceased probing. You never forgot who you were, and you never tried to be something you were not. You were a lady, in the best establishment sense of the word, and you were, in the best American tradition, a liberal. You would have been at home with the pioneering suffragettes, who dressed properly, spoke the Queen's English, and perservered as winter soldiers.

Marie Bosworth
Courtesy Medford Mail Tribune

You never told me that in centennial 1959 you were chosen Oregon Mother of the Year. I learned that from others. You treated the honor with characteristic modesty, and it did not slow you down one iota from continuing a ceaseless battle for civil rights, civil liberties, disarmament, conservation, and, sometimes above all, the United Nations. For you the only alternative to an ever-arguing council of nations was a short and final debate with nuclear bombs.

No one in town ever saw you garbed in denim. You dressed conservatively, no coarse word came from your mouth, your manners were almost Victorian. That surprised some people in the valley, who could not understand why an outstanding lady, married to a pillar of the community, would provide, one way or another, the only platform in southern Oregon for visiting dissidents, of whatever liberal or radical persuasion.

And when the meetings were over you did not abandon the speakers to the cold town or see them to the bus station. You took them home, to the rustic 1858 house west of Ruch that you shared in love and humor with your husband, Harlan, the World War II colonel who every morning ran up the American flag on the tall pole facing the road.

I have these cameo memories of you at home. Marie working in her yard with flowers and vegetables and fruits, always electrically alive. Marie in the kitchen, humming as she prepared a meal. Marie opening the windows and greeting the sun with outstretched arms. Marie listening, bent forward and intent so as not to miss a word. Marie talking on a social issue, a slender hand gently gesturing and her eyes so very bright.

You were seventy-seven when you left us. I mention your age only because you were, in your enthusiasm for life and in your bonds with the yearnings of humanhood everywhere, young in heart. You were a girl of the frontier, a child of the universe, and a sister to us all.

I did not think winter would bend a rose so soft and tough.

Part VII: An Iowa Farmer

Did you ever think of the kid you picked up outside Spokane and carried in your long black Studebaker (or was it a Buick?) all the way to Portland?

You were a big, solid man, dressed in a cream-colored suit and a Panama hat, the way a touring, retired Iowa farmer might dress, and that's what you were.

"Where are you going?" you asked flatly, the car a hundred yards down the road from where I had stood with my knapsack at my feet. "Portland," I said, climbing in, a little short of breath.

You shifted into first and started slowly. "You live in Portland?" you asked, your eyes ahead. I looked at your face. It rose squarely above broad shoulders and ran from ear to ear like the contour of the prairie. "Chicago," I said.

You let that sink in full, like rain filling the pores of the cornfield until the last glisten of wet has curled its way into the topsoil. "That your home?" you asked then.

"Yes," I said, hoping I would make it to Oregon that day.

Your eyes did not light up, and you did not frown. We were strangers in a distant land, Midwesterners come together in the Far West, I from the factory smoke skies and you from a horizon of cows. You pondered me, steady and careful, the way you drove, and you wondered about me with only less curiosity than you had about the countryside.

"You going away from home?" you asked.

"Away and toward," I said.

That's an odd fella, you must have thought. You meet some queer ones traveling around. You studied me sideways for maybe a couple of minutes.

"What does that mean?" you asked then, your voice sloping slightly above the flatland of your speech.

It was plain enough for me, I thought. I knew my purpose. I had known it the day I left home, with all of two dollars and fifty cents. "I'm going to Portland on the way back to Chicago. You see, I want to touch every state. I've been all over the East already."

"You're pretty young to be doing it alone," you said, the tone sloping back to the flatland.

I had to make a speech then, to show how bright I was at seventeen. "Joseph Conrad," I declared, "once observed that the best time to go to sea is when you're young. Since I couldn't go to sea, I thought I'd see the land."

You had never heard of Conrad, and when I told you who he was you didn't care. Maybe you were wondering how many cows he had milked by hand or how many ears of corn he had shucked. By then we were in Ritzville, and you looked it over with a practiced eye. "Not much of a place," you concluded, "but all a farmer needs is a grain elevator, a bank, and a good store."

You considered the wheatlands closely. "Good country," you approved with a nod or two. "A fella could make it here. Take some work, but a fella could make it."

You weren't the man for it. Not anymore. Not at seventy-five. When your wife died—a year ago, you said—you sold some of your land and rented out the rest and now, with nothing to hold you down, and all alone, you were taking the first long trip of your life. After those cousins of some kind in Portland—the ones that had spent a summer with you nine years before—there was a niece down in Los Angeles, and after that, well, "It's a big country. Let's eat."

We were in Pasco and I was hungry, but I told you I wasn't because I was proud and didn't feel you owed me anything.

"That's a lie," you said, slowly and without malice. "Come on."

At Wallula Gap, where the Columbia split the land wide, you leaned to the right for a better view and made an appraisal. "A lot of water. They could use some of that water back there, in those dry lands up there."

This was before Grand Coulee Dam. Did you ever

return—to see the dam, to see the land irrigated by the waters of the river? Or was that your last trip to the Northwest?

We ate again at The Dalles. By now, comfortable with you, I had shed my pride. It was near sundown when we took to the road again and twilight when we got to Hood River. Then, except for the construction lights at Bonneville Dam, the road was dark. It was not at all the way a national highway—the great Lincoln Highway—should be, twisting tightly, with face-on cliffs lurching up at doorhandle turns, and narrow, with the shoulders dropping off into bottomless pits, or seeming to.

"I wonder maybe if we didn't turn off on a county road," you muttered. Your shoulders stiffened, and the blunt fingers of your broad hands, that had so easily worked with plows and horses, pressed tight around the rim of the steering wheel.

The terror of fog and wind and pitch-darkness gripped both of us. I was afraid because you were. Far from the factory smoke skies and the horizon of cows we were allies now in a strange and terrifying void, imprisoned in a blind machine blindly driven.

You cut your speed to fifteen miles an hour, then ten. I wonder if you ever saw that road by day; it would have sent shudders through you to think you had tried it at night. It is the Columbia River Scenic Highway now, still a deer trail through the cliffs, though an engineering marvel when built. Only fools chance it in winter; in summer it is thronged with city tourists out to see the waterfalls. If we had come two decades or so later there would have been no problem; a water-level road was built then, gradually designed into the Banfield Freeway. (But in winter, in the Columbia Gorge, where fear on the corkscrew smote us to near silence, even that grand road can be an icy hell.)

Slowly we emerged from the terror. A few lights

Ralph Friedman a year after he first saw Oregon.
Ralph Friedman collection

pinpricked the moist curtain of darkness, and after awhile there was a canopy of lights. Then more lights and more lights and Sandy Boulevard—and we passed, without notice, a corner where a third of a century later I would come to wait for the downtown bus, having walked there from my house two blocks away. (I still live there.)

Somewhere near the heart of Portland you let me off, in

front of a large grocery, fruit, and vegetable stand that did not have any doors. That made an impression upon me because I had never seen a food store without doors or a food store open at such late hour, only sixty minutes before midnight.

I think we shook hands. I like to think we did. I had come to like you. I remember you said wearily, "Now I've got to find their house." I wish I could have helped you. I hope you had little trouble.

Where did you go after Los Angeles? Did you return to Iowa? Where are you buried?

Me? I've been here and there—every continent except Antarctica. I've lived in a lot of places, and the funny thing is that I've lived in Portland longer than any other place. Who would have foreseen that, the day I came here with you?

You were seventy-five then, and that was a long time ago. If you lived to be a hundred, or even a hundred and ten, you have been dead for years, and, in my measuring of time, many years.

I've often mused on you, as one recalls another in a shared experience. Both of us, the farmer and the city boy, the stolid, gray old man and the blonde, skinny youngster, coming together to the land of Oregon. I wonder if you ever gave it a second thought.

Rider Of The Pony Express

Oregon had a Pony Express, too, and in Billy Byars, who started his run in 1856, it had as daring a rider as Bill Cody.

Byars was born seven years before William F. Cody, who began riding the mail three years earlier in age (Cody was fourteen) and four years later in date (1860) and was employed as a pony express rider for far less time than the two years served by Byars.

Apart from the fact that both of them were named William and both carried the mail through hazardous country, the two had little in common. Byars remained quiet, prosaic, and Oregon-put to the end of his days. Having no Ned Buntline to turn him into a derring-do paladin of the Wild West, he is only a minor footnote in local history. Buffalo Bill, molded by swiftly written penny thrillers, became a loud and spectacular showman, an international traveler, and one of the biggest liars in a land that replaced the American bison with purple prose, better known as bull fertilizer.

Byars operated out of his "home station" on a high prairie surrounded by oak-covered hills about three miles north of present Oakland. The Oakland post office, which occupied one of the two rooms in the house of Hull Tower, must have been quite an important one. It was the terminus of four mail routes. One went west to Scottsburg and the coast; one north via Yoncalla to Corvallis; one "northerly" over the Coastfork Road to Eugene; and one "southerly" via Winchester and Roseburg to Yreka, California.

Old Town Oakland
Courtesy Douglas County Museum

All lines were weekly routes. The postman traveled on horseback, with an additional packhorse when necessary. The mail day was Friday, between 10:00 am and 2:00 pm. All the mail that had reached Oakland was dumped into the middle of the room and sorted into four main piles, each representing a mail route. Local mail was tossed into a fifth pile. Each carrier then loaded his take into one or more mailbags, packed the sacks on his horse or horses, and took off. The post office was quiet for another week.

Byars worked the southerly road, from Oakland to Yreka. It took him six days to cover the 150 miles. He made one round trip every two weeks, giving himself a day's rest at the end of each leg. When night fell he would lay over at a post office or settler's house. At some places both were the same.

Canyonville as Byars knew it in its early days.
Courtesy Douglas County Museum

There were then fourteen post offices on Byars' route: Winchester, Roseburg, Round Prairie, Myrtle Creek, North Canyonville, Galesville, Leland, Gold River, Dardanelles, Jacksonville, Phoenix, Ashland, Henley, and Yreka.

More than a quarter of a century would pass before any of the still existing villages were incorporated. Some have completely disappeared. Few of the hamlets were more than rude spots on the trail. Ashland, for example (then called Ashland Mills) consisted of a single mill and a single house. The mill also served as the post office; the house was also "a small wayside stopping place."

In those days, Byars noted in one of his letters, travelers generally carried their own beds (probably he meant sleeping rolls) and all they received at the makeshift inns were meals.

Jacksonville was the largest town, the only community of any significance. The postmaster, Hoffman, was the father-in-law of the legendary autocratic banker, CC Beekman, then humbly plodding alongside his packhorses on the trail to Yreka, where he delivered "express freight" to California miners.

Byars vividly described the Jacksonville scene of 1856: "I frequently saw the miners and other citizens lined up for a block waiting for their turn to ask for the mail. Mining was carried on right through the streets of the town."

Jacksonville was wide open. "Everything that was wicked was permitted anywhere in the town where space could be secured. Nearly every man carried a revolver and a knife, and it was considered a greater crime to steal a horse than kill a man."

Byars' route took him across deep and rocky creeks and rivers, up and down harsh and slippery hills and mountains, through thickets untouched by blade, across glades stained red by the blood of both Indians and whites. Rain could be a constant companion; he ran into snowdrifts and blizzards; and there were nights "dark as Egypt."

On the trail he came across nettled bears, runaway teams, overturned wagons, corpses fresh and not so fresh—the bodies of Indians riddled like pincushions, and settlers and teamsters mowed down in retaliation.

Responding in desperation and blazing anger to atrocities inflicted upon them as though they were lower on God's ladder than rabbits, the Rogues sacked homes, put the torch to barns, drove off stock, shot down homesteaders, ambushed caravans, and took on whites in pitched encounters. Much of this kind of warfare was new to the Indians, but they learned fast.

A few miles west of Wolf Creek, wrote Byars, "the famous battle of Hungry Hill was fought—where the Indians in a two-day battle completely defeated the volunteers and regulars. There were about five hundred whites, but the number of Indians was unknown." It may have been the last great Indian victory in Oregon.

William H Byars
Courtesy Douglaas County Museum

Homes between North Canyonville and Dardanelles, near present Gold Hill, were built like fortresses. Giving a specific example, Byars described one dwelling as "surrounded by a stockade, which was constructed by digging a trench four or five feet deep around the house, generally in a square, and then setting timbers twenty or thirty feet long upright so as to make bullet-proof walls and then tamp them solid with earth, and cutting loopholes through for the purpose of firing on an approaching foe. Generally there were small bastions at each corner with loop holes so that the sides could be protected. "In fact," added Byars, "a majority of all the houses in Southern Oregon were so protected."

In 1858 the mail contract was sold to the Oregon & California Stage Company, "who put on a daily stage line and had the mail service increased to a daily line. The Oregon and California Railroad as fast as it was built relieved the stage line and took over the mail route. This was not fully completed until about 1885."

William Henry Byars gave up the job of pony express rider in the latter part of 1858 to attend Columbia College in Eugene. Thereafter, in chronological order, he taught school for a year, spent a year at Willamette University, worked for three years in the Idaho mines, soldiered for a year in the First Oregon Cavalry, graduated from the first class of Wilbur Academy, and was school superintendent of Douglas County.

At the age of twenty-nine he married Emma Slocum Reed. Less than two years later he was appointed surveyor of Douglas County. Switching occupations in his full and varied life, Byars purchased the Roseburg *Plain Dealer* and for ten years was its publisher and editor. After his election as state printer he moved to Salem, where with another man he bought the *Oregon Statesman* and served as its editor.

For four years he was US Surveyor General and mapped vast areas of the Pacific Northwest. He left to become

William H Byars with his three sisters. Left to right: Mrs. Elizabeth
Stout, Mrs. Mary Hamilton, and Mrs. Rebecca McKee.

Courtesy Ray L Stout

commandant of the Soldiers Home at Roseburg. Then he was newspaper publisher again, city engineer of Salem, US deputy surveyor and finally, supervisor of the Goldendale, Washington sewer system.

Billy Byars was still a distinguished-looking man with a flourishing beard when he died April 22, 1922, at the age of eighty-three.

In his life span he had seen messages carried by oxteam, horse, stagecoach, telegraph, railroad, telephone, motor carrier, and plane. He had mapped more townships and counties in Oregon than anyone else; he had seen cities rise from the seeds of tents and log cabins; he had witnessed trails widen to roads; and he had watched the change from the tallow candle in a lonely hut to tall hotels lighted by electricity.

A rich and varied life—but when he summed up his days, with eight decades spread before him, what he remembered with greatest relish were those two years as a pony express rider, when the country was new, death challenged every step, and the only really important thing was getting the mail through.

A Grasshopper Called Kilts

Late in the nineteenth century, a plateau in the eastern panhandle of Jefferson County was called Donnybrook—as obvious a bit of historical explanation as Pistol River, so named because an early settler lost his shooting iron in that coastal stream.

The best description of the region's social development was given by Phil Brogan, the sage of Central Oregon, who was brought to the plateau in 1897, when he was a year old and who spent his boyhood there. In 1943, still full of fertile memory, he wrote in the Bend *Bulletin*:

"It was in the community's range epoch that a group of Celts, celebrating some undetermined occasion at a sheep cabin in Calf Gulch, just over the ridge from Axehandle, did the thing in true Donnybrook style. There was no fair, but one fine fight. Joe Brannon heard of the party and, with typical Irish wit, called the locality Donnybrook. And gradually that name spread to the community, and the county school, below Axehandle Spring, was named Donnybrook School. For many years the community was known as Donnybrook far and wide. Then came the homesteading era. Across Currant Creek and near the shadow of Coyote Mountain, Jesse Kilts homesteaded. Eventually, as homesteaders moved in, a post office was obtained, and postal officials named the community after the postmaster. Since then the community, Axehandle of pioneer days and Donnybrook of the ranch era, has been known, at least to Uncle Sam, as Kilts."

LOCATION OF PROPOSED POST OFFICE

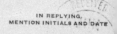

DIVISION OF RURAL MAILS

Post Office Department

IN REPLYING,
MENTION INITIALS AND DATE

FOURTH ASSISTANT POSTMASTER GENERAL

Mr. ~~Floyd C.~~ Kilts,

Washington

December 9, 1913.

~~Ashwood~~, Oregon.

SIR: With reference to the proposed establishment of a post office at the point named below, and
in order that the office, if established, may be accurately represented upon the post-route maps, it is
requested that you furnish accurately the information called for below and prepare a sketch according to instructions on opposite side of paper, which should be returned to this Division as soon as
possible.   Respectfully,

FOURTH ASSISTANT POSTMASTER GENERAL.

 # 5409

Proposed Post Office, _____Kilts_____
(Name)

~~Crook~~ *Jefferson*
(County)

Oregon
(State)

The name proposed for the post office is _____Kilts_____

If the town, village, or site of the post office be known by another name than that of the post office, state that other name

here : _____none_____

The post office would be situated in the _____N W_____ quarter of section No. _____5_____, in Township _____10 S_____
(N. or S.)

Range _____18 E_____, of the _____Willamette_____ principal meridian, County of _____~~Crook~~ Jefferson_____

State of _____Oregon_____

The name of the nearest river is _____, and the post-office building would be at a

distance of _____ on the _____ side of it.
(N., S., E., or W.)

The name of the nearest creek is _____Little Muddy_____, and the post-office building would be at a

distance of _____3/4 mile_____ on the _____W_____ side of it.
(N., S., E., or W.)

The name of the nearest office on the same route as this proposed post office is _____Ashwood_____

and its distance is _____12_____ miles, by the traveled road, in a _____W_____ direction from the site of this proposed office.
(N., S., E., or W.)

The name of the nearest office on the same route, on the other side, is _____

and its distance is _____ miles, in a _____ direction from the site of this proposed office.
(N., S., E., or W.)

The name of the nearest office not on the same route as this proposed post office is _____Antelope_____

and its distance is _____18_____ miles, by the traveled road, in a _____N_____ direction from the site of this proposed office.
(N., S., E., or W.)

The post-office building would be on the _____ side of the _____ Railroad,
(N., S., E., or W.)

and at a distance of _____ from the track. The railroad station name is _____

The post office would be _____6 miles_____, air-line distance, _____N_____ from the nearest point of my
county boundary.   (N., S., E., or W.)

Signature of Applicant for Postmaster : _____Floyd C. Kilts_____

1263   5—6001   Date : _____Dec 20 '13_____

First application for post office of Kilts

Courtesy The National Archives

I couldn't find anyone who could tell me where the Donnybrook School was, or had been, sited. Nor were there any signs of the original ranch houses of Axehandle and Donnybrook. Trying to pin down Kilts was as exasperating as chasing a butterfly without a net.

Kilts was never a town. It had no store, wayside inn, or any other commercial business. There was never a sign that said Kilts. You wouldn't have known if you were there. There was only a post office—but where did it stand?

With the sympathetic aid of Roberta Symons, the then postmaster and storekeeper of Ashwood, and a packet of documents sent by the National Archives and Records, the way Kilts hopped about began to take shape.

On December 20, 1913, homesteader Floyd C. Kilts applied to open a post office, twelve miles east of Ashwood and eighteen miles south of Antelope, in his home three-quarters of a mile west of Little Muddy Creek. He stated that the post office would be "six miles air line distance from the nearest point of my county boundary," but maps of that period show Kilts' home to be south of the Wasco County Line. (The fact that Jefferson County was then part of Crook County has no bearing on the matter. Anyway, by the time the post office was approved, Jefferson County lines had been drawn. The county, established December 12, 1914, retained the northern boundaries of Crook County, which then became placed south of Jefferson County.)

Floyd Kilts, however, was not the first postmaster. That honor went to Ruth A. Kilts, who was appointed September 15, 1914. Five months later Jesse Kilts took over the job and held it until September 14, 1917, when the post office was discontinued.

Came 1923 and Margaret A. Grant put in an application for a proposed post office in her house. She wanted to call it Mount Coyote, but Kilts was kept. The new site was two and a quarter miles west of the old one, according to her application—and three miles south, too, though all indications are that her home was practically on a straight line from the Kilts house. Like Floyd Kilts, Margaret Grant placed Kilts north from the nearest point of her county boundary.

At that time there were three patrons within a mile of the post office, so you can see how densely populated the country was. Anyway, Mrs. Albertine H. Hawley became the postmaster, though Margaret Grant had done the spadework.

In 1926 the post office was moved again, this time two miles air line distance west to the Dan Crowley home. There is the usual stickiness with figures. Margaret Grant had stated that Ashwood was nine miles away; Dan Crowley puts the distance, after a move of at least two miles toward Ashwood, at eight and a half miles. For Margaret Grant, Antelope was twenty miles off, but Dan Crowley, after crossing out seventeen miles, gives the mileage at sixteen, which still does not jibe with Grant's computation. However, Crowley placed the post office, in his home, *south* of the nearest county line, which is correct. But again there is a discrepancy: his home would be four miles farther north than Grant's—though, in reality, there is not half a mile difference in that direction.

The post office of Kilts stayed at this site until 1934, when Mrs. Gertrude Finnell became postmaster and moved the office to her home, "about two and a quarter miles" air line distance southeast of the Crowley place. And she lists the post office as being six miles air line distance *north* of the county line, falling back into the Kilts-Grant error.

In October of 1935, Dorothy A. Lowrey applied for the postmaster position, declaring, "No one to take care of the P.O. at present sight—Parties moved." She added: "The proposed Kilts P.O. is the original P.O. sight where the post office of Kilts was first established."

The last surviving farmstead that housed a post office at Kilts.
Ralph Friedman

It may be that Lowrey, in choosing "sight" over the proper "site," was trying to give Washington a picture of the situation. Otherwise, her spelling is perfect. (By this time there are no patrons of the post office living within a mile of it.)

If the post office was transferred to the original location, why did Dorothy Lowrey place the site in the northeast corner of Section 6, whereas Floyd Kilts had the post office listed in the northeast quarter of Section 5 of the same township and range? Other inconsistencies appear—and again Lowrey has the post office north, instead of south, of the nearest county line—but that was the way things were then.

Well, now you have an idea of where Kilts stood. And in this brief account is mirrored the life of so many Oregon homesteader "towns."

Directions: From Antelope, on Oregon 218, drive 4 miles east to Ashwood Jct. Turn south. 12.5 miles, Mitchell-Horse Heaven Jct.

From Willowdale, on US 97, drive south 2 miles to Ashwood Jct. 13.4 miles, Ashwood. North, 6.5 miles, Mitchell-Horse Heaven Jct.

Turn east at Mitchell-Horse Heaven Jct. A house 0.4 mile down the road, on the left, or north side, was the post office when Dan Crowley was postmaster. All other houses that were post offices have been torn down or burned.

Journey Through Darkness

The night sky was dark as an uncharted sea. "It may be a good omen," he said to his wife. "Heaven grant it be your shield," she replied.

"I don't know when it will be safe to return," he said slowly. "You understand . . ."

"Yes, we've talked about it enough. Pray that peace ride with you."

A mist covered Wagner Creek. He could not see it, or the grove, or the barn, or the fences, or the grazing cattle, or his mare, which had brought him from Illinois.

"All that labor, almost three years of it," he sighed and turned to his son. "You will care for the farm, Welborn, and be your mother's strong arm. I don't enjoy placing a burden upon you, but you're a man now."

"Almost twenty," Welborn nodded.

John Beeson shook his head. "I don't like running away. I don't like it, Ann."

"I don't like you dead, John."

"God save our civilized souls." His tone was soft but bitter.

Welborn looked at his watch. "Near midnight. We'd best be getting on, Father." He touched his mother. "I'll be back tomorrow."

John Beeson took Ann's hand, and they walked together to the door and out to where two horses were saddled. "Farewell, Ann," he whispered as they embraced. She was fighting back tears; he could see that. It was the last he saw of her. When he looked back at the gate she was lost in the mist.

I must remember this day, he thought. He lifted a finger and wrote in the air: May 24, 1856.

As they rode silently through the darkness they were glad the mist had turned to rain. It would muffle the sounds of the hoofbeats. Welborn had been to Jacksonville that morning and had listened to ugly talk of what the Volunteers would do to his father. Some had said they planned to camp near the Beeson house and seize his father in the middle of the night. Tomorrow might have been too late to leave.

John Beeson had felt the enmity growing against him for weeks. It had climaxed yesterday, when he had been called to an "Indignation Meeting" at the school house and charged with writing and talking against what everyone called the Indian War. Several resolutions denouncing him had been passed, and they would be printed in the Table Rock *Sentinel.* His son had told him: "I am afraid, Father, you will have to leave this country, public opinion is so strong against you. Some would about as leave kill you, as kill any Indian, just because you have spoken the truth out boldly against the rascality of this Indian War, or rather, this butchery of the Indians." After Welborn had returned from Jacksonville with word of what he had heard from the Indian-haters, all the talk the small family had done about the possibility of the father having to leave had quickly come to a head.

John Beeson mused in his saddle as the horses followed the trail north. This Rogue River Valley—was there any place on earth more beautiful? Could God have been more generous to his children than to give them this sweet, fertile land of rich pastures, cool waters, and wooded hills? Why should not all share it in tranquility?

He was now almost fifty-three years old, at an age when most men had settled down for good to reap the fruits of their labor, and here he was fleeing from home. It did not seem fair, but if conscience had its own rewards, it also incurred its own penalties.

"Shh!" hissed Welborn. They reined in their horses and listened intently. "What?" John gasped. Welborn's reply slipped out in a breath of relief. "Only the wind." They rode on.

It's been a long road getting here and now a swift departure, John Beeson thought. And Ann, sweet Ann . . .

He had been twenty-four when he and Ann, both English-born, had married in Woolsthorne. Three years later they had journeyed to the New World and lived in Ithaca, New York for a few years. He had been a baker and confectioner by trade but had always wanted to farm, so they moved to Illinois, where land was available. Welborn was born in La Salle County in 1836. Father and son had seldom been apart a day.

As though Welborn was reading his father's mind, he leaned toward John and softly asked, "Do you remember those days in the underground railroad, when we hid fugitive slaves being shepherded to Canada? You were always in trouble, and for good reason."

"Aye," John nodded, "for God's good reason."

"I remember," said Welborn in a low voice, "that once, when you saw a wagon come by with a fugitive slave hidden in it you left your plow and said, 'Oh, when will the laws of the United States become humane enough to abolish slavery?'"

"Yes," replied John as softly. "Slavery is an evil. So is the way the Indians are treated. No one can justly call God 'Father,' who refuses the claim of every man as 'Brother.'"

There was no sky now, only rain. It fell ahead of them, as though making tracks for the horses to follow. It had rained, too, when the Beesons left Illinois.

All through 1852 they had talked of Oregon. In the spring of '53 they started west, on a journey that was to explain the bigotry of Oregon, as he wrote years later:

"The majority of the first emigrations to Oregon were from Missouri, and among them it was customary to speak of the Indian as a Buck, of the woman as a Squaw, until at length, in the general acceptance of these terms, they ceased to recognize the rights of humanity in those to whom they were so applied. By a very natural and easy transition, from being spoken of as brutes, they came to be thought of as game to be shot, or as vermin to be destroyed. This shows the force of association, and the wrong of speaking in derogatory terms of those whom we regard as our inferiors."

At the end of August 1853 the family arrived in the Rogue River Valley. Six days later they located on Wagner Creek, between Ashland Mills and Jacksonville.

The Rogue River Wars, which were to reduce the various bands of the Rogues from nine thousand to two thousand, had already started. To John Beeson it was quickly clear that the whites were the aggressors. They had come to Oregon primarily for economic gain, and it was the same motive which impelled them to clear the Indians off their ancient lands.

As he and Welborn wound through the darkling woods, he reflected on what greed and cruelty had been done in the name of patriotism and religion!

First, some settlers had attacked the Indians. Then they had created a war hysteria, sending other settlers into panic and thus creating the condition to justify a force of "Volunteers." The federal government had been called on in the most urgent way to supply funds for "defense," and any reluctance on the part of Washington was met with cries that the administration was abandoning its citizens.

Jacksonville miners, idled by lack of water during the dry season and low on beans and bacon, tided themselves over until water was plentiful again by joining the Volunteers and collecting payment from the federal treasury. Farmers met the lean times by charging severalfold the value of the stock and feed supplied to the government. Broken-down mules were listed as in top condition and horses secreted in wooded pastures were marked as killed or stolen, and inflated bills were presented with straight face to the authorities. Merchants whose businesses had dwindled when cash was low filled their shelves with fresh orders and pinned swollen price tags on the goods to be paid for by Washington.

Politicians pursued the war fever until they ran in front of it and posed as its leaders; to have done otherwise would have meant finish to their careers and ambitions. Newspapers furiously beat the war drums in their editorials and inflamed reporting. The clergy, finding their churches fullest when they most zealously defended the Volunteers, and fearing the wrath of their parishoners if they opposed the conflict, gave their blessings (and those of the Lord) to the most heinous of white indignities.

Everyone profited except the nonconformists who raised their voices in behalf of the Rogues. Major General John E. Wool, commander of the Military Department of the Pacific, who refused to actively involve the regular army in the wars against the Rogues, was branded as unpatriotic because he asserted that the Volunteers were murdering innocent Indians. Joel Palmer, superintendent of Indian Affairs for Oregon, was vituperatively denounced for seeking to restrain the most hotheaded and bloodthirsty settlers from massacring the Rogues and for trying to protect them on their way to reservations. (Later, the politicians, the businessmen, and the clergy forced his removal from office.)

"Father!" Welborn whispered hoarsely. John pulled the reins tight, sidling his horse to the edge of the trace. He sat tense, his ears reaching out for sound. All he heard was the rain.

"Welborn?" he asked.

"Yonder," the son replied. "Something brushing against the trees. Perhaps it was a deer. Weren't you listening?"

"I've been deep in thought," the father said, and they signaled their horses to move on.

There were others besides General Wool and Joel Palmer who held sympathy for the Indians. He must remember them, and in print he did, writing later that throughout the territory, "there were also several clergymen, and many citizens, whose hearts yearned within them at the shameful impositions and unmerited sufferings they were compelled to witness. And even among those who were actually engaged in hostile measures, there were men who refused to participate in the work of death. Some of them even fell down and wept at the sight of such barbarities. There were scores of men who, after enlisting under an idea of duty and patriotism, became convinced of the injustice of the war and left the service in disgust."

But few had the boldness to speak out and the silence of many others was of no comfort to the Indians undergoing systematic extermination. In attempting to present his case, Beeson had met with closed lips, cowardice, and wrath from editors, churchmen, business leaders, and farmers.

By what right could the whites say that their religion and culture were superior to those of the Indians? Why could they not both be good, each for their own people?

By what Divine commission had the whites sought to destroy the Indians? How could they act contrary to the Golden Rule and still call themselves Christians?

And peace—what mockery of it! The more liberal of the Pharisees argues, "We must whip them first, and then the treaty will be kept."

The sounds ahead of them were not that of rain, and John froze in the saddle. So did Welborn. The sounds drew nearer, a voice was heard. John and Welborn shushed their mounts behind a big tree, pulled their slickers tighter around them, and peered around the fir. They could not recognize any of the four men who rode by. It was too dark for that, and the rain was falling too thickly to make out the brief phrases that reached their ears.

"I thought I heard them say 'Beeson,'" John said.

"I don't know, Father," Welborn replied, "but we must keep going."

John Beeson was afraid and angry. "What is my crime, that I should be a fugitive from home?" he asked himself. "Have I transgressed the laws, or violated the Constitution? Have I done anything contrary to justice and truth, or which the feelings of humanity have not clearly indicated?"

He might have done better. He knew that. But he had tried, and his conscience was clear.

His fellow citizens had not understood him, suspicious of his motives and believing—or telling themselves they believed—that he was a traitor in their midst. Not one of the letters he had written during the last winter for Oregon and California newspapers had appeared in print. They had all been suppressed by the postal agents or refused by the editors.

He had tried—in every way he knew. As a sudden downpour leveled out to a long drumbeat of rain he remembered the time he had learned of a widely circulated plan to slaughter a group of Indians. The date? The date? October first. Yes, that was it. He would have to get the dates right when he wrote a book on his life in the valley.

He had tried to dissuade the organizers of the attack, but to no avail. A week later he attended a Methodist quarterly meeting in Jacksonville, to plead that the God-fearing people rally to prevent the aggression. When he came home that night he told Ann and Welborn what had happened, as he later recalled in print:

"I arose, and spoke with all the feeling, and all the power

I had, in the behalf of these poor Indians. I entreated that Assembly, who had gathered themselves together in the name of Christ—whose whole life and ministry was a living Gospel of Love—to put on the spirit and the power of Christ. I begged them, by every principle of humanity and justice, to inflict no wrong upon the helpless. I drew in strong colors the scenes that would inevitably follow such an attack as was meditated. I thought if there was a soul, or a heart in them, I would find it, even if it could be reached through nothing but their own selfishness. I pictured our burning houses, our murdered wives and children, our silent and desolate homes, and all the wrong that would inevitably flow into that crimson torrent they were about to open. In conclusion, I strongly urged them, as citizens and Christians, to raise a voice of remonstrance, or to call on the Authorities for the administration of justice, and thus avert the impending calamity.

"No voice responded to the appeal, and the meeting closed; for no one had independence enough to speak his thought."

If only the clergy had stood firm! Later, he remembered, too, that a man in that assembly who had taken part in the atrocities solemnly declared that he had been led into it by the preachers.

He was not so naive, John Beeson told himself as the night dragged on, to think that the Indians were blameless, but they had been driven to their cruelty by white atrocities. What he wanted (as he tried to tell everyone whose ear he could catch) was peace—so the Indians would not be provoked to strike back in fury at the whites. Could not the settlers understand that he cared for their safety as much as he did for the Indians?

There did not have to be blood spilled between white people and red people. It was not written in the stars that war between them was inevitable. William Penn and the

Quakers had demonstrated that both races, respecting each other's ways, could live in harmony.

At fourteen John had converted to the Methodist religion and vowed "to be good and useful in the world." Well, he had tried. He was still a Methodist, although he had found himself leaning more and more toward the Quakers. The people of the valley, especially those who disliked him, thought he acted more like a Quaker than a Methodist and called him, often in derision, "Friend Beeson."

The black of night slowly cracked in the east to a sodden blue. The men rode on, the rain still falling. Weary, they scarcely noticed the creeping turn to gray until a rooster crowed, a dog barked, and they could see through a clearing a flickering light in a cabin.

It was half-past seven when father and son reached Fort Lane, a regular army post. For the first time since they started they felt safe.

Lieutenant Underwood, a tall, husky young man with calm eyes, came out to greet them, and they went to breakfast with him. "I've heard about you and your work," he said to John Beeson, smiling softly. "It's a gory situation. How can I help you?"

"I am bound for Salem and Portland," John replied. "But I fear that those who would do me harm may yet be waiting ahead. If I can get through the canyon I should be without further difficulty."

Lieutenant Underwood promised an escort of dragoons through the dangerous passage and bade John rest a while before starting out. Then the officer departed the room, leaving father and son alone.

I must remember him, Welborn thought, looking intently at his father. God knows when we will meet again.

This was the portrait Welborn impressed on his mind: a wiry, medium-size man with lean cheeks, a strong chin, and hair turning gray. His nose was strong, too, and his eyes firm. His hands were those of a farmer, fingers blunt and veins running into his knuckles. Altogether his face looked like the picture of a Roman senator Welborn had seen in some book—or a preacher. In fact, he looked more like a preacher than did the ministers of Jacksonville.

At nine o'clock Welborn said, "I must be getting home, Father." "Yes," John replied. "Mother will be waiting."

They shook hands, each trying to find words to say and each finding none. Welborn mounted and for a moment sat motionless. John watched him, understanding. Then Welborn gently slapped his mount and before John could call out a last farewell, his son was riding through the gate of the stockade. Five hours later Welborn was home.

John Beeson and the dragoons flanking him spent the night at Evan's Ferry. The house, protected by log pickets, had been built to withstand Indian attacks and was considered a stout fort. Early the next morning the men started north again, passing many Volunteers encamped on the road. None made a move toward Beeson, and the Regulars avoiding friendly recognition, seemed to regard the Volunteers with contempt.

At noon the party halted. "I'll be all right from here," Beeson told the sergeant. "I think I've got beyond the circle of excitement."

"Then safe traveling," the sergeant said. "We've got to be back by nightfall."

For seven days Beeson traveled alone, until he reached Salem. There he sought to see the governor but George Curry, who considered Beeson a dangerous radical, would have none of the visitor. For Curry the Indians were savages, and that was all there was to it.

Portland was scarcely more hospitable to Beeson's views. War fever had extended up and down the state. He went by ship to San Francisco, where he found greater tolerance but not the concern needed to arouse the populace to the defense of the Indians, constantly under siege and their traditional modes of life already smashed. Sad of heart, but his commitment still resolute, he left for New York.

The intellectual ferment and social consciousness of the nation was then in the East. Here Beeson found a history of other voices that had protested the abuse and slaughter of the Indians. They ran counter to the romanticism of the "Winning of the West." The Mountain Men and the fur companies were seen not as heroic but as brigands who had destroyed the furclad animals, frightened the buffalo from their traditional grounds, violated federal laws which expressly forbade trapping and hunting on Indian lands, and drove the Indians from their ancestral homes.

As far back as 1832 a writer in *New-England Magazine* had denounced the fur trade invasion of the West, which after a few years had left but "few fur-bearing animals this side" of the Rockies.

"What right have we to fit our armed expeditions, and enter the long occupied country of the natives, to destroy their game, not for subsistence, but for their skins?" he asked rhetorically. "They are a contented people, and do not want our aid to make them happier. We prate of civilizing and Christianizing the savages. What have we done for their benefit? We have carried among them rum, powder and ball, small-pox, starvation, and misery."

Beeson was finally among men and women more sympathetic to his views than were his Rogue River Valley neighbors, who had passed resolutions charging that his letters to Eastern newspapers "were the product of a low and depraved intellect."

He plunged into writing and speaking on behalf of justice for the American Indian. He appealed for funds for the education of the Indians; advocated setting aside land for all tribes and protection of these lands from aggression; called for withdrawal of all troops from Indian territories, leaving the Indians to govern their own lives; demanded reform of the Indian Bureau, which he called corrupt to the bone; pleaded for Indian representation in Congress; and strongly urged full protection of Indian rights, as guaranteed to whites by the Constitution. The robbery or murder of an Indian by a white, he argued, should be punishable as "though the crime was committed on an American citizen."

In 1857 his small book, *A Plea For the Indians,* now a rare collector's item, was privately published. (Only one edition came off the press.) The contents and purpose are outlined in the preface:

> To the earnest and benevolent minds in our favored land, the Author addresses the following pages. He does not profess to write a book of history, strictly considered as such, but merely a statement from memory, of matters with which he became aquainted during a journey across the Plains, and three years residence in Oregon Territory.
>
> He is induced to work by the hope that a more thorough knowledge of the wrong to which the Indian is subject, may awaken attention to the necessity of some remedy, so that Emigrants across the Plain may go in safety, the Frontier settlers live in peace, and the Red Man's race be preserved from annihilation.

He had dedicated himself to the cause of the Indian, Beeson noted on the first page of his book, because "while every other class of suffering humanity has its specific organizations for relief," the Indian had been short of friends "from the very moment the White Man set foot upon our shores."

Beeson's energetic crusade for the Indians won him the support of the Abolitionists, who often joined him on the platform in the meetings he organized in church and public halls throughout the major cities of the East.

Among Beeson's fellow speechmakers at Boston's famed

Anna Ballard

A

PLEA FOR THE INDIANS;

WITH

FACTS AND FEATURES

OF

THE LATE WAR IN OREGON.

BY

JOHN BEESON.

"Not claim hereditary—not the trust
Of frank election— * * *
Not even the high, anointing hand of Heaven,
Can authorize oppression, give a law
For lawless power, wed faith to violation,
On reason build misrule, or justly bind
Allegiance to injustice. Tyranny
Absolves all faith; and who invades *my* right,
Howe'er his own commence, can never be
But a Usurper."

NEW YORK:
PUBLISHED BY JOHN BEESON,
No. 15 LAIGHT STREET.
FOR SALE BY ALL BOOKSELLERS.
1857.

Title page of John Beeson's book, in the rare books collection of the
Oregon Historical Society

PREFACE.

To the earnest and benevolent minds in our favored land, the Author addresses the following pages. He does not profess to write a book of History, strictly considered as such, but merely a statement from memory, of matters with which he became acquainted during a journey across the Plains, and three years' residence in Oregon Territory.

He is induced to the work by the hope that a more thorough knowledge of the wrongs to which the Indian is subject, may awaken attention to the necessity of devising some efficient remedy, so that Emigrants across the Plains may go in safety, the Frontier Settlers live in peace, and the Red Man's Race be preserved from annihilation.

J. B.

New York, May, 1857.

Preface of *A Plea for the Indians*

Faneuil Hall on October 9, 1859, were some noted Massachusetts reformers, including two distinguished orators. One was Edward Everett, who four years later was the principal speaker at the Gettysburg battlefield when Abraham Lincoln briefly addressed the memorial throng. The other was Wendell Phillips, a supporter of another friend of the Indians, John Brown.

A week after the Faneuil Hall meeting, John Brown seized the arsenal at Harpers Ferry. The Abolitionists, realizing this made Civil War certain, turned their attention from the Indians. They continued to be sympathetic to Beeson but their first priority was the destruction of slavery.

Beeson saw things differently. To him, the havoc reaped upon the Indians had set the immoral tone for the establishment of slavery. Slavery, he contended, was the logical "extension of the unneighborly, unChristian and destructive practice which for generations has been operating against the Aborigines." And since slavery had its foundation and rationale in the wrongs done the Indians, he concluded, "their redress is of right and necessity the first step in the order of national reform and of self preservation."

Almost completely abandoned by the Abolitionists, Beeson carried on. Once again, as he had when he came to New York from Oregon, he spoke through the printed word. In February 1860, he issued *The Calument*, aimed to be an Indian Rights Journal and the voice of the new National Indian Aid Association. It was powerfully written but poorly financed and did not live to a second edition.

Obsessed, Beeson knocked on every door that carried the possibility of hope and tugged at the sleeve of every federal office-holder he could corner. An overburdened Abraham Lincoln warily but kindly received Beeson several times at the White House, read each letter Beeson sent to him, and called him "Father Beeson." In November 1862, responding to accusations by Beeson that there was wholesale "robbery and fraud" in three Western superintendencies of the Indian Bureau, Lincoln ordered an investigation.

Lincoln and Beeson met for the last time in 1864. Nine years later Beeson recalled in a letter to the commissioner of Indian Affairs what Lincoln had then told him: "My aged Friend. I have heard your arguments time and again. I have said little but thought much, and you may rest assured that as soon as the pressing matters of this war is settled the Indians shall have my first care and I will not rest untill Justice is done to their and your Sattisfaction."

Beeson's final letter to Lincoln prophesied: "If you are firm in Justice toward the Indians, Your sunshine on earth will grow brighter and never set, but if you fail to be prompt in Justice, Your sun will go down to rise no more."

Apart from Lincoln, the only national political leader to give Beeson sincere encouragement was Senator Thaddeus Stevens, the lion-hearted, uncompromising foe of slavery. Stevens introduced Beeson to other influential legislators and arranged for an audience with Congress. Heartened, Beeson addressed a memorial to the Senate, proposing that a special committee be selected to probe "the treatment of the Indians in general" and "the Sioux in particular." Nothing came of it.

Never discouraged to the point of giving up, Beeson joined forces with every ally near and far. Before his work was done he had linked his efforts with those of the Indian Rights Association, Women's National Indian Association, Universal Peace Union, churches, and educational groups. Like anyone standing on the frontier of a social crusade, he gave much of himself, so much that he lived as close to poverty as he did to his convictions.

For a time he subsisted on the money he brought with him; when it ran out he supported himself and his labors through collections taken at his talks. Somehow he managed to make it through the Civil War, but by then he had only enough money for passage home to Oregon.

The animosity that had hounded Beeson before he fled the Rogue River Valley in 1856 was largely absent when he returned. Some of his old enemies were dead or had moved away, and thousands of new people had moved into the vale. More important, the Indians were no longer a "threat." They were now on reservations, their lands occupied by whites.

For nearly three years Beeson practiced "rigid economy and persistent labor" on his farm, all the while reading at night of the continuing indignities suffered by the Indians in almost every part of the nation. After the death of Ann, his wife, he no longer felt a strong pull to keep him fixed to the homestead and he returned East to again take up the battle that had long dominated his life.

Still intensely close in heart to his son, he spoke his thoughts in letters to Welborn. "The vindictive feeling against the Modocs and the other Indians is terrible," he once wrote. "I can scarcely find a man who does not have more prejudice than reason on the subject, hence my work is an uphill business, but I believe the tide will turn."

He tried to turn the tide through a seemingly endless stream of letters to government officials, requesting their aid in his obtaining a position that would have him deal with Indians. He sought to be appointed commissioner of Indian Affairs and failed. He asked that he be named a special commissioner to the Indians and received no response. He would have been an Indian agent but was turned down. Someone who might institute reforms which did not alter the status quo was acceptable to the power structure but not a reformer who had fought the establishment and insisted on far-reaching changes. What was involved here was the obvious difference between the pragmatist who would not rock the boat and the true believer who would and, as factual then as today, the true believer was shunted aside.

By the mid-1870s Beeson was deep in phrenology. He proposed the government use that "science" to determine which applicants for the position of Indian agent "have the requisite amount of benevolence, conscientiousness, and intellect."

For a time he studied medicine in New York under the tutelage of a physician and was regarded as a "practical doctor." His therapeutic methods included hot packs, cold packs, massage, diet, rest, hydrotherapy (as practised by the Indians), encouragement, and faith. He never gave or prescribed medicine. Living today he would probably associate himself with naturopathy.

He had gone beyond the Methodist Church and the Society of Friends to "the doctrine of modern Spiritualism." There is on record no explanation for this. Perhaps, identifying closer to the Indians, as he suffered one defeat after another in their cause, he sought something that would parallel what he considered the divine mysticism of Indian religion. In a way, a coming to spiritualism may have been his own personal Ghost Dance—the hallucinatory ritual of some Western tribes to revive the unfettered past so as to break the shackles of the present.

Complex as his life became, the one central theme in John Beeson's existence remained the constant struggle for Indian rights. He spoke earnestly to President Grant, who listened attentively and actually did modify a policy which Beeson strenuously opposed—to concentrate all tribes on a few reservations. Still, not enough reservations were created to satisfy the reformer, who believed that each tribe should have its own land.

He joined together with prominent New York women, including Mrs. John Jacob Astor, in sending petitions to Congress seeking appropriations for Indian education. He spoke wherever he was invited, and sometimes invited himself. He warned, too late, of rivers of blood to be spilled because of the barbaric violations by whites of treaty provisions. In 1879, after the major Indian tribes had been shattered, he wrote President Hayes: "War is certain, while the unchecked love of gain prompts the Whites, and the love of family and home prompts the Indians, and the Government does not restrain the one nor protect the other.

"Hence," he concluded, in proposing a solution, "the necessity for the immediate appointment of a peace commission, composed of such persons as can command the respect of the Whites and the confidence of the Indians, for which women, with men are indispensable."

He pushed his peace commission plan for more than ten years, starting in the 1870s. In 1885 he specifically explained its purpose: to ask both Indians and whites two questions: First, "What do you want which you do not have?" Second, "What do you have which you do not want?" But the inquiries had to be carried on and the program derived from the replies carried out, he cautioned, "with a full recognition that the Indians were included in the declaration 'That all men are endowed by their maker with the right to life, liberty and the pursute of happiness.'" Once again he had flaunted the noble words of the founding fathers in the faces of their successors.

Nothing came of his peace commission proposal, but he continued the good fight until he was too tired to go on. He was eighty-four, bent and white-haired, when for the second and last time he returned to the Rogue River Valley, to live with Welborn and the son's family on the old farmstead.

Few people noted his presence. Fewer knew of his work. Scarcely anyone paid him homage. To most he was simply another aged pioneer.

He lived quietly, writing an occasional letter to further the cause, and exchanging experiences of extrasensory perception with fellow spiritualists.

The cock had just begun to crow, and the black of night in the eastern sky crack into patches of dark blue, as the mist turned into rain on the third Sunday of April 1889

JOHN BEESON

Born in England Sept 15 1803

Died Apr 21 1889

A Pioneer and man of Peace

Gravestone of John Beeson

Jennie Deardorff

when John Beeson passed away. One month and three days later would have marked a full thirty-three years since he had fled for his life and, in the fleeing, launched a career of devotion and heartbreak in behalf of the American Indian.

An hour before noon on the following day, April 22, his neighbors came together to tender their last respects. They had been invited by the Southern Oregon Spiritual Association, whose members buried John Beeson in Stearns Cemetery outside Talent. There, in the same plot, he was reunited with Ann.

On the rather simple marker, at home in a thick growth of old-fashioned myrtle, is the inscription: "A pioneer and man of peace." There should have been added: "and noble struggle."

Only A Barn Now

One lovely summer day in Lebanon I strolled into the office of the weekly *Express* and asked the editor if he knew anything about the Rock Hill School.

His smile expressed a helpful manner. "Sure. It used to be a rural school, no different than a lot of others that were in the county."

"I think I'd like to take a look at it," I said. "Can you tell me how to get there?"

"No problem," he replied, somewhat amused, "but you won't find anything interesting. It isn't a school anymore. It's only a barn now."

That whetted my curiosity, so armed with his directions, off we started. The directions were good but not precise; twice we had to inquire along the way. Each time we were looked at oddly when we stated that we wanted to photograph the old Rock Hill School. "Nothing there," asserted a man. "Just a building setting on a hill," declared a woman.

As friend wife was picture-taking, a farmer driving by halted to ask if we were from a magazine or something. "I don't understand what anybody would see in it," he said, bemused. "It's just a place to store hay."

"That reminds me of what an Arizona cowboy said about the Grand Canyon: a long way to spit down," I remarked. The farmer didn't grasp the analogy and continued toward Lebanon.

I didn't try to gather information on the old school house, which looked as though it had been built in the last century.

Former Rock Hill School

Marcia Workentine

It was enough for me that it survived, if not as a place of learning then as a storage bin for food.

Of all the country schools I have seen in Oregon, this had the most inspiring location. From the knoll the teacher could visually reach out in all directions to see the kids coming: the ones on foot and the ones on horse and the ones buggied by their parents. The teacher could ring the bell, and the peal be heard down the slopes and in the draws, echoed by the hillocks across the wavy plain. You could stand here at dusk, those many years ago, and watch the lamps go on one by one in the farmhouses that dotted the choppy vale, until the darkness was rent by a flickering arc of yellow glows. You could tell by the lights where the houses stood, the same way ships at sea can be seen at night. When there was a social, as there must have been, you could hear the tinkle of bells and the beat of hooves and the songs of expectations that warmed the ridge.

Think, as you see the wheatlands that engulf the school, of all the colors mixed by the chemistry of the seasons: the greening of spring, the yellow and gold of harvest, the brown patterns of autumn, the black of the plowed loam, the strange sharp white of snow under clear skies, the bleak grey snow beneath buttermilk clouds, and the mystic lunar designs of bright amber nights when the sleds came out and every slope was a toboggan ride.

What stories we could hear if we listened! But if we are deaf to the winds that swirl about us, how can we hear the wind that sleeps?

The Gentleman Cowpoke

This story was written a long time ago, about a man who has been dead for many years. It has appeared in several publications. I include it in this book because I think Billy Sweetpasture deserves more lasting fame than an ephemeral magazine or newspaper article and because, traveling around the back country of Oregon, I have met a few other fellows like him. Maybe, in his own way, Billy is a type the historians and Western novelists haven't gotten around to yet.

Let's call him Billy Sweetpasture. That isn't his right name, but it will do for the occasion. Applying the correct handle to Billy might land me in a heap of trouble with Mrs. Sweetpasture. I don't think so; when we parted she was sweet as pumpkin pie, but you can never be sure about women who want their men perfect.

Billy is a cowpoke, and he doesn't like anybody to put an ex in front of it. He's seen his eighty-eighth birthday, so he'll settle for being called an old cowpoke. "It's all I know," he sighed once. "Been on a horse about all my life."

At five he was jumping ponies over fences; at thirteen he participated in his first cattle drive; at fourteen he strapped his bedroll and frying pan on a packhorse, mounted his sorrel, and left home to start a cowpunching career that actively lasted more than half a century.

Billy has been "retired" for some years now, but he's still on a horse. "Just pushin' cattle around fer friends," he says. "Keeps time from pilin' up on ya."

Some years ago I had a long talk with Billy in the tavern of an out-of-the-way cowtown, and subsequently wrote an article about him for a magazine. I came away with a warm feeling for the venerable plainsman. He was a man to admire: open, modest, and direct. He had perspective—plenty of that. When I lamented that I had three high mountain passes to cross in the snowstorm then raging and that I didn't own a single tire chain, Billy snorted quietly: "Hell, I've been caught in worse weather than this, on a horse, and without whiskey."

Once having seen Billy, it is hard to forget him. Ramrod straight, wearing dignity as comfortably as his Stetson, his long, bony nose protruding far out above his white handlebar mustache, and clear, blue eyes observing with humorous curiosity and sympathy the world around him, he is the unblemished portrait of the old-time range rider. When he talked of stampedes, long drives to market, the hungry clattering of cowboys coming to town, and the last days of the frontier, the scenes came alive, simply and vividly. And when he spoke of great grazing grounds, once abundant with wildlife and rich grass and now desert barren of even squirrels, there was in his voice a sadness for the land which those who have not been intimate with it will never know.

Last summer, traveling through the big country of the open sky, I swung seventy miles out of my way to pay my respects to Billy. After registering at a local hotel, I set out to find him, but he was always a step ahead of me. At the first tavern I was told he had gone on to the next. At the second, he had moved on to the third. At the third, he had departed for a hotel which had a television set in the lobby. At the hotel, he had decided to visit a friend.

The next day I drove to a hidden valley, where Billy had spent some of his early years. When I returned to town, toward evening, the pursuit was renewed. It extended to Billy's house, which was dark; to the movie theater, where

Billy had walked out in the middle of a Western; and to all the places I had tried the night before. For a man who wasn't too far from ninety he had set a brisk pace.

The following morning I arose early, determined to catch Billy at home before he started his day's rounds. The phone rang as I was shaving. "This is Mrs. Billy Sweetpasture," announced a very formal voice with a sharp cutting edge. "I understand you've been looking for Billy. If you can be here in an hour, he'll be home."

The Sweetpastures live in a small frame house set back in a corner of town. I was there fifty minutes after the phone call and was greeted by Mrs. Sweetpasture, a large, energetic woman of fifty-eight. Billy had married her twenty-five years ago, when he was sixty-three. "You always fall for one, don't ya?" he had remarked with a twinkle, the first time I met him. At sixty-four he was a father.

It soon became evident, as I sipped the coffee Mrs. Sweetpasture had placed before me, that Billy would not be home for at least half an hour. He had left shortly after dawn to help a rancher friend. Mrs. Sweetpasture wanted to be alone with me; she had something very important to say, and she lost little time in going at it.

"I read your story," she began. "Everybody in town read it. I was never so humiliated in all my life. And I was angry, sir, very angry. I don't mind telling you that. If you had been here when the article appeared, I think Billy's friends would have run you out of town."

Imprudently, I smiled. "It's not funny!" She snapped, with an unequivocal glare. "Our anger has cooled, but I can tell you, sir, that what you wrote was fiction, not fact. Every word of it."

"Fiction?"

"Unadulterated fiction." She leaned amply over the table. "Who did you talk to about Billy? Just who told you all those inventions?"

"Billy," I said.

"Billy never saw you!"

I pointed to a picture on the wall. "Is that him?" She nodded curtly, her eyes tight and hostile. "He's the man," I said.

"Billy never told you any of that make-believe!"

"What make-believe?" I asked. "I'm afraid you've got me confused."

"All of it," she replied sharply. "You made Billy out to speak ungrammatically, and he doesn't. He speaks perfect English. He never said 'ain't' in all his life. I know, I'm married to him. I've lived with him for twenty-five years, and I've never heard him use that uncouth word. You put rough edges on him that just aren't there. He's a gentleman. He never said a harsh word to anyone in all his life. He's the most courteous and considerate man I've ever met. He just hasn't got it in him to swear, or cuss, or speak bluntly. If you had been brought up in range country, you'd know that all the old cowmen were perfect gentlemen."

She paused on a note of triumph, but the pause was brief. "And you make him out to be a tall story teller, to put it mildly," she continued unmildly. "Billy could never have told you some of those fantastic things you put in your story. He always speaks the truth. He has never made anything up as long as I have known him."

"Like what?" I asked.

"Like that dance-hall girl wearing black garters. Where," she demanded, "did you get that preposterous lie? And who gave you her name?"

"Look," I said, "Billy had been a cowboy a long time before he met you."

She folded her heavy arms and planted them squarely on the table. "I know that man like a book."

"Didn't you ask him if he had talked to me?" I inquired softly.

"Didn't have to! I know that man."

"And Billy didn't say anything?"

"As I told you, sir, he's a gentleman. He wouldn't embarrass anyone, not even in private."

I squirmed a look at the front door. "Oughtn't Billy be coming home soon?"

She turned to a clock perched on a wall shelf. "Soon. I just want to tell you this: I'm a writer myself, sir; I've written many essays and short stories, and some of my poetry has been printed in the town paper. It covers the whole county. I've thought of writing a book about Billy. I know reporters, too. I worked in the office of a newspaper. Let me remind you, sir, that destroying a man's life just for the sake of a few pieces of silver is not an honorable thing. I hope you derived great satisfaction from the sale of that malicious article."

"I might have," I replied weakly, "if I had been paid. But the magazine folded."

"Poetic justice," she grumbled with grim satisfaction.

At this point the door opened and in came Billy Sweetpasture himself, dressed in tight Levis and the brim of his Stetson pulled up. I arose, put out my hand, and said, "Sure been a while since we palavered, huh Billy?"

"Sure has," he agreed heartily, with a firm handshake. Mrs. Sweetpasture blinked her eyes. Billy lowered himself with a hint of effort into a straight-back chair staring at an old-fashioned, pot-bellied stove and laid his hat on the floor. "How ya been? Come fer another story?"

"Your wife tells me you were doing a little buckaroo work this morning," I said. "How's the riding?"

"There isn't a man in the country more graceful on a horse," Mrs. Sweetpasture interjected. "Billy rides as well as he ever did."

"Ain't so," muttered Billy. "I get a little lame in the back sometimes."

The Gentleman Cowpoke

"You're as good a horseman as any around," Mrs. Sweetpasture insisted.

"Ain't not," Billy retorted. "Too damn old. I just ride fer the hell of it an' to help out some fellers."

Mrs. Sweetpasture's face fell, but a moment later she was back in the conversation. Being a literary woman she sought to turn the casual talk into an interview, so that I might get the true story of her gentleman Billy. Not only did she intrude upon our comments with questions to Billy but she answered questions I put to him, and often supplied lengthy background for unimportant remarks.

Billy shifted uneasily in his chair, gestured with his shoulders for me to ignore her, and several times tried to stare her into silence. But like a brook at springtime she rolled merrily on. Finally Billy kicked a stove leg with a dusty boot and snapped at her: "You just sit there and shut up!" As she paled in shock, he grumbled: "Damn women. Yakety-yak all the time." Then he apologized for her with a smile, and we continued talking.

Another cup of coffee and Mrs. Sweetpasture was back in the thick of things. Billy and I had been mulling over some tales of the plains he had told me several years ago when Mrs. Sweetpasture suggested to her husband: "Tell him about the time those four Indians tried to scalp you and you only had four bullets in your gun and you shot them dead with a bullet apiece."

Billy frowned. "What you talkin' about?" he said irritably to the stove. "I never carried a gun an' I never had no trouble with Injuns."

Mrs. Sweetpasture's eyes narrowed and she sucked in a deep breath. Then, regaining her calm, she said to Billy, "Well, tell him about the time they wrapped kids who acted bad in green hides."

"Green hides?" repeated Billy, raising his eyebrows.

"Certainly," said Mrs. Sweetpasture. "You remember. Tell him."

"Never heard of it," mumbled Billy.

"Why!" exclaimed Mrs. Sweetpasture, "I've sat here many a night, sitting right where I am and you sitting right where you are, and listened to those stories."

"You read it somewhere," growled Billy, turning his head away. "I never seen such things."

"But you told them to me!" his wife protested.

Billy twisted sheepishly. "You're imaginin' things," he muttered.

Mrs. Sweetpasture looked long and straight at him, then at me. The look she gave me was softer and more sympathetic than the one she had for him.

Billy picked up his Stetson, arose with a little grunt, said he had to get back to his friend's ranch, and parted with: "If you're stayin' tonight, set down to a feed with us. If you're leavin', look us up soon's ya come back. Like to have ya stay a spell."

After Billy left, Mrs. Sweetpasture couldn't be nice enough. She presented me with several jars of preserves, wanted me to meet her friends, and asked me to send her anything I wrote.

"It's been a real pleasure to talk to a famous writer," she glowed, walking with me to my car.

Still, even with that laurel shining bright, let's stick to the name of Sweetpasture. Ladies who want their men perfect have short memories.

A Crime In Time
- or -
Tune In Next Week
For More Of The Same

More than a century and a quarter ago, with radio and television still a long way off, melodrama (today's soap opera) was broadcast by way of the printed word.

Oregon newspapers were full of the kind of stuff that runs in the more uninhibited TV series of our day. You can take one newspaper feature and, properly fleshed out, work up at least a year's programs of five-times-a-week TV melodrama suds.

If the newspapers didn't have the original stories to report (or invent), they borrowed from anyone around. Of course they didn't part with any of their own money for reproduction rights. It is likely the unwitting lenders had probably never heard of the easy-take borrowers.

Here is a case in point—two would be one too many for this kind of book. The February 24, 1864, issue of the long-defunct Portland *Daily Union* carried a front page opus titled "A Story of Crime," which it lifted from the October 1863 issue of, of all places, the *American Presbyterian and Theological Review*. It had been written by a Professor Wines and had been headed, "The Sources of Crime."

Now, if you will turn off your television sets, here is the lathery tale:

Mr. Gould relates the story of a fallen woman, whom he encountered in one of our penitentiary hospitals, which casts a terrific light upon the tendency of licentiousness to produce crime. She had been a woman of exquisite beauty and elegant culture. Her father, a wealthy merchant in New York, failed in business and gave up everything to his creditors. She was reduced to the necessity of learning the trade of a dressmaker to earn her daily bread. She became proficient in the business, and her taste and skill commanded liberal wages, which enabled her to provide an ample wardrobe for herself. She had been intensely devoted to the glitter and gaiety of fashionable life, and hope, which springs eternal in the human breast, whispered that a fortunate marriage might yet restore her to the charmed circles whose delights she had once tasted, and which she longed to reenter. She used every effort, by the charms of person, dress, voice, and manners, to attract the notice and win the love of eligible young men. At length she thought she had succeeded in her object; but the young man whose affections she dreamed she had won proved to be a cold-hearted villain, who was in pursuit only of amusement and gratification for the passing hour. One evening he invited her to ride. Driving into the country he alighted at a house of refreshment in the neighborhood of the city. He offered her a glass of wine, which she drank. The liquor had been drugged. A profound stupor ensued, and she awoke the following morning to find herself ruined.

With returning consciousness the whole magnitude of the injury burst upon her. She instantly resolved upon revenge, and the plan for its accomplishment flashed upon her mind with the suddenness and rapidity of lightening. She betrayed no emotion. She uttered no reproaches. She treated what had happened as a harmless jest, and blandly invited a continuance of the intimacy.

The young man exulted in the ease and completeness of his victory; but from that moment she became the evil genius of his life. Professing the tenderest and most unselfish affection, she drew money from him continually, with which she hired sharpers to furnish him with provocatives to drinking, gambling and debauchery. At every rally of his better nature, by skillful alternation of persuasion, banter and menace, she choked the rising impulse of virtue, chained him to the car of dissipation, and confirmed him in his career of vice.

Full well did she know whither all this would lead him; nor was she disappointed in her malignant expectation. Drunkenness clouded his understanding; debauchery ruined his health; and gambling reduced him to poverty. Not until this point, the goal of all her prayers and efforts, had been reached, when poverty and disease had done their work and he was unable to procure a wretched bed or a scanty meal, except through charity, did she wreak upon him the full measure of her vengeance. Then it was her daily delight to visit him, to load him with reproaches, and to reveal to him, in bitter exultation, the whole scheme, so cunningly devised and so steadily pursued, by which she had wrought his ruin. And when the closing scene drew near, she sat by his bedside, and mingled her execrations with the shrieks exhorted by his dying agonies.

Nor was her vengeance even yet satisfied. Her warfare was against the whole sex, whom she regarded as accursed; and her insatiate vengeance cried out for still other victims. Wherever she could fasten her fangs on a young man of genteel family, whose unclouded prospects foretokened a brilliant career, she never relaxed her hold. She studied, with an earnestness sharpened by experience, every point in his character—his tastes, his passions, his hopes, his fears, whatever attracted and whatever repelled him; and then, with an almost unerring sagacity, adapting the means to the end, she seldom failed in her domestic purposes. She claimed in this manner to have hunted down thirty-two young men, involving them in disgrace, crime, and ruin. Some of them had ended their days in prison, and others, hopelessly fallen, were on the road to the drunkard's and felon's grave.

When asked whether all her sisters in infamy felt the same hatred to mankind, she replied that she thought the feeling to be general, if not universal among them; adding that when a woman had once fallen she desired to revenge herself, not only on her seducer, but on all his sex; that no game was followed with greater relish than that of involving all who came within their toils in crime and its consequent punishment; that most of them could number at least two or three victims whom they had ruined, and that many of these victims went to the length of the actual commission of crime.

For all its hyperbolic caricaturing, soap opera is a reflection of the way some people live, at least in part, and of the way others see the world beyond the arc of their experience. "The Sources of Crime" was probably amusing or outrageous to male readers of the Portland *Daily Union*, but it must have struck home to some female readers who, if they had personally not been betrayed, were aware that some of their sisters had been, and quietly cheered for vengeance.

Reading the Oregon newspapers of more than 125 years ago, it doesn't seem that behavior and response are so different from today. One gets the feeling that only the names and places have changed—sometimes they almost seem the same.

Welcome to soap opera—only five years and ten days after Oregon gained statehood.

The Patron Of Lake County

No one during their lifetime stamped their character more indelibly upon any part of Oregon than Dr. Bernard Daly did upon Lake County.

Three-quarters of a century after his passing he is still alive in memory, through a scholarship fund which has enabled hundreds of Lake County youths to attend college.

The inscription upon his tombstone, taken from Daly's last will, is testimony to his concern and fraternity with Lake County students. Eroded by long years of wind and rain so that it is difficult to decipher, the legend on his gravemarker in a Lakeview cemetery reads:

"It is my earnest desire to help, aid and assist worthy and ambitious young men and women of my beloved County of Lake to acquire a good education, so that they may be the better fitted and qualified to appreciate and help to preserve the laws and constitution of this free country, defend its flag, and by their conduct as good citizens reflect honor on Lake County and the State of Oregon."

Bernard Daly was twenty-nine and one year out of medical school when he came to Lake County as a horse-and-buggy doctor in 1887. He had traveled a long road to reach this raw land. Born in Mayo County, Ireland, he emigrated with his parents to the United States when he was five and settled in Alabama, where he grew up. In 1886 he received a degree from Ohio Northern University and the next year graduated from the medical department of the University of Louisville.

Burial marker of Dr. Bernard Daly

Phoebe L Friedman

During his thirty-three years in Lake County, Bernard Daly remained a doctor to the end, and his faith to his profession produced legends which are still handed down from parent to child.

In reporting Daly's death, the *Lake County Examiner* wrote:

"Many were the fearful night rides he was called upon to make, and numerous instances are related where he seemed to be possessed of almost superhuman endurance during his younger days. No instance is known where he refused to answer a call although he might have just returned from a long tiresome trip extending over several days and nights. His record as a physician in relieving the suffering and answering the call of the afflicted is doubtless without parallel in the annals of the Northwest if not in the whole world."

On Christmas day of 1894 Daly was relaxing at his home in Lakeview when a haggard rider pounded at his door to gasp out a message that a fire at the Silver Lake dance the night before had killed dozens of persons and severely burned many more. Daly aroused a friend, Willard Duncan, and at 4 P.M. the two left by buckboard for Silver Lake. At Paisley they took to horseback, pushing on to Silver Lake through snow so high it often reached the bellies of their horses. Arriving at 6 A.M., after fourteen hours of gruelling travel, Daly promptly went to the assistance of Silver Lake's only physician, Dr. Thompson, who had been southward bound when another rider had overhauled him at Summer Lake. The two medics worked until the last of the injured had been cared for. Then, near exhaustion, Daly rested a few hours before starting the long drive back to Lakeview and his patients there.

Daly was more than a country doctor and the operator of the only hospital in Lakeview. He owned property all around town and turned a neat profit on every deal. He established the Bank of Lakeview in 1898 and was its president until his death. He was on the Lakeview school board for almost thirty years and was instrumental in building the town's high school. He was elected to the Lakeview town council every time he ran. He served on the board of regents of Oregon Agricultural College, now Oregon State University.

Oh, there is more. For twelve years he was Lake County Judge, acting with eminent distinction. "When he took the county reins," as the *Lake County Examiner* put it, "finances were in the red, but twelve years later the treasury

Dr. Bernard Daly

showed a healthy balance and meantime he had replaced the old one-story frame courthouse with a magnificent three-story red brick structure topped by a giant tower with a four-faced clock and high chimes."

He was elected Lake County Judge in 1902, twelve years before he was admitted to the state bar and appointed as the first circuit judge of the fourteenth judicial district, created that year to serve Lake County.

There is no halting the record of Bernard Daly. He was organizer and president of the Lake County Land and Livestock Company, which owned the extensive 7T Ranch at Plush. It made money, of course. There was a saying in

Lake County that whatever Daly touched turned to gold. And for twelve years he was president of the Lake County Agricultural Society.

He was elected to both branches of the Oregon legislature; he was a born winner, Lake County people said, until, in 1900, he ran for Congress. He won the Democratic nomination but was defeated by Thomas H. Tongue of Washington County. It was a Republican era. A Democrat hadn't been elected to Congress since 1878 and he had served only one term. There would not be another Democrat elected to Congress until 1924, after Daly's death. Ironically, the way the state was divided then, Daly ran for Congress from the First District, from which no Democrat had ever been elected to go to Washington until 1974!

Before he was thirty-five, Daly began to find ways of making money apart from medicine. A story of how he became a banker was told in 1961 by OK Burrell, professor of finance at the University of Oregon and from 1923 to 1927 a teacher of commercial subjects at Lakeview High School. In the *Oregon Business Review*, published by the Bureau of Business Research at the University, Burrell wrote a series of "Footnotes to History; Banking in the Far West," and one of these concerned Daly's start as a banker:

"In most of these early banks, private bankers did not suddenly become bankers. It is quite probable that sometimes men became bankers without planning to do so. In Lakeview, for example, Bernard Daly was a pioneer doctor who early in his career found it convenient and profitable to lend his surplus funds to businessmen and ranchers at high interest rates. At some point friends and associates began to entrust their funds to his care, which is merely another way of saying he began to accept deposits."

Not all of his transactions brought him praise. Some left him with bitter enemies. There is the tale of the rancher who approached Daly for a loan and was told that the lending capital of the bank Daly headed was committed for the moment but that if the rancher returned the next day, Daly might be able to help him with his own funds. After the rancher left, Daly borrowed the necessary sum from his own bank, at the standard rate of interest. The next day he loaned the money to the rancher at a much higher interest.

Daly never married, and for those who seek romance and intrigue there are tales of a liaison with a local teacher. Daly's buggy, parked outside her home until late, quite late, in the evening, was a subject of town gossip. She is supposed to have been at his side when he died and talk persists that he left her a sizeable sum of money.

In his will, signed December 27, 1919, Daly expressed his gratitude to Lake County. The terms provided for the bulk of his estate to be invested and managed as the Bernard Daly Educational Fund for the purpose of benefiting the young people of Lake County through college scholarships.

He was seriously ill when he signed the will. Nine days later, while headed for San Francisco and a hospital there, he died aboard the train as it reached Livermore, so close to San Francisco and so far from his beloved sagebrush hills.

Most of Lake County mourned. The old remembered him as he was in the flower of his manhood: handsome, bright-eyed, with a full mustache; a strong, striking figure with an Irishman's tenacity. The young could only see him as he was the month before: a silver-haired, distinguished-looking man who dressed conservatively, as befitting a broker of power.

The will was contested by Daly's relatives but they did not prevail and the terms of the will remained although, later, parts dealing with investment were altered, with judicial consent, to permit greater returns.

In 1922 the first list of Daly Fund students (nineteen young women and men) was named. In 1974 the fifty-third annual list had close to the same number, with about four-fifths being from Lakeview and the remainder from Paisley.

Seventy years after the Daly Fund went into effect, more than a thousand Lake County high school graduates had been rewarded scholarships. Most, especially in earlier years, would never have been able to attend college on their own.

Bernard Daly would be pleased. "It's the debt I owe Lake County," he would say.

The Ghost Of Alec's Butte

I never pass it without chill running through my bones. I never think of it but wonder what really happened there. Once I climbed it and cried to the wind, "Where? Where are the bones?" And the wind echoed, "Where? Where?"

There is a legend in Yamhill County, known now only to a few keen students of local history, that on a misty night the ghost of frontiersman Alec Carson, who met his sudden and bloody death on this low, sloping hill, two miles north of Carlton, walks the wooded ridge, vowing revenge to the wind, and the wind replies with wails of remorse.

The legend has two versions. Some points are in agreement, and they are these:

Alexander Carson, better known as Alec Carson and sometimes Alec Essen, was twenty-nine, a free trapper and a gunsmith, when he joined the Astor Overland Expedition in 1811. After undergoing numerous adventures and hardships, he arrived at Fort Astoria on February 15, 1812.

For twenty months Carson served with the Astor hunting and trapping parties and became known to every trapper in the area. After the sale of Fort Astoria to the North West Company in the autumn of 1813, Carson again took up the life of a free trapper, bound to no one. He wandered the Pacific Northwest, trapping and selling furs, first to the North West Company and then to the Hudson's Bay Company, and each year returning to the Yamhill Valley, where he had built a cabin.

Now the legend splits. One rendering is that Carson

Alec's Butte from Yamhill-Carlton Cemetery
Ralph Friedman

quarreled with a local Indian band and sought concealment
on a large oak limb when he saw that he was being pursued.
The Indians could not find him until he sneezed. Then he
was killed and his body left to the wolves. The bits of him
that remained were found by white travelers and buried on
the knoll without mark or identification.

The other telling is more specific, detailed, and fanciful. It
dates his killing as 1836, a year later than the first version.

According to the latter tale, Carson fell sick while
trapping and spent April or May at the home of a settler in
what later became Fairfield, south of St. Paul. With Carson

were his Tualatin Indian helper, Boney, Boney's wife, and their teenage son.

When Carson regained enough strength to move on, he and the Boney family started north. That night they reached the top of a rise in the undulating valley. Here on the butte were camped other Indians.

During the night Boney forced his son to shoot Carson. The other Indians plundered Carson's property. Click-kowin, a part Tillamook who had helped plot the slaying, did not live long enough to enjoy his new possessions. He was slain soon thereafter by Waanikapah, chief of the Tualatins, whose name appears on early documents as Nefalitin.

In this patch of odd yarns, the seams are too weak to conceal flaws and loose ends, which is why I offer this more as folklore than history.

Both versions agree that the killing took place on the small, softly sloped hill where, in a dim legend of Yamhill County, a ghost walks the wooded ridge of Alec's Butte.

Grizzly Gone

There ought to be a good old tall story to tell about Grizzly, out in the wide open spaces of Jefferson County, but there isn't. A town shouldn't die without having some good yarns to survive it, but Grizzly did. The folks who had some whoppers to enliven a gabfest either left them behind in clapboard shacks for packrats to cart off or took the tales to their new homes, where the stories were misplaced or died of loneliness.

You go to a place like Grizzly just because there still might be someone around who can fetch back the past with an hour of talking. But there is no Grizzly at Grizzly.

In the autumn of 1971 the post office fell to the wrecker's bar, and a bit of history was chipped away to a pile of weary, fragile, sunbaked boards and rusty nails. A year later the entire pile had been removed, perhaps by souvenir hunters.

It might surprise and perhaps grieve and anger you to know how much of Oregon history is being snatched away by those who prize the artifacts of nostalgia as decorative conversation pieces. All over the state, especially in central Oregon, pioneer houses and barns and rail fences are torn down for the lumber to put into bars, dens, and what have you. Sometimes the owners aren't even asked permission.

Like a good many other post offices on the rabbit-brush plains, Grizzly evolved through name changes, fires, and relocations. A soul could have six addresses in twenty years without leaving the homestead. When the farmers left, as many did, the post office folded.

The first post office around here started up in 1872 as Willow Creek—or Willoughby. No one seems to know. (Nor does anyone care.) Seven years later it was out of business. Most of the people it was serving had loaded their wagons, said something like "So long, it's been good to know you," and plodded on to the next Garden of Eden.

For two years there wasn't any mail station hereabouts. Then Harley Belknap opened one on the Henry Cleek ranch near Willow Creek. It was a good place for a post office because stagecoaches paused here for a change of horses, and what was lacking in quantity of mail was made up for in the gossip of the drivers and passengers.

You can hear Henry Cleek urging the driver to get along because he was behind schedule, while Harley Belknap was trying to get him to stay a mite longer. "Tell it again, Fred. Just one more time. I want to have it right so I can pass it on to the folks. The Harringtons will be interested, you betcha. Their boy has got his eye fixed on a schoolmarm too."

Less than two years after it opened, the Cleek post office was discontinued and the business turned over to Hay Creek, about fifteen miles to the north. Once again the people around Willow Creek were without a mail station. But the situation was solved when a post office was opened at a ranch house called the Edmonds place. It stayed there until about 1890, when it was moved to the Grizzly General Store, two or three miles east of the Cleek spread. And now the letters and packages and newspapers and magazines were delivered to Grizzly, Oregon.

Grizzly took its name from 6025-feet Grizzly Mountain, a prominent butte about four miles to the southeast, and across the line in Crook County. A farmer would point there as he joshed his children, "Grizzly bears live there." They didn't. The butte was so-called because of its grizzled color.

A trace of Grizzly, 1991

William Hall

At the turn of the century about 150 families lived in the area and did their trading at the Grizzly General Store. By 1970 no more than fifteen persons were residents of Grizzly. The post office had stayed on until the early summer of 1948. In its last few years it was more of an oversight than an urgency.

We came to the emptiness of Grizzly after the remains of the town along "main street" had been removed. Apart from a nearby ranch dwelling there was only one other house in the vicinity.

Half a mile down a dirt road from the stagecoach pike that ran from Shaniko to Prineville, the old, abandoned house (said to have been built about 1890) was part of a homesteader print that included a weathered barn, a gaunt windmill, and a sagging rail fence. It was a scene out of a past that none of us who weren't there can really comprehend: bleak and rich, genuine and unreal, trick photo and something you could touch. It was at once eerie, warming, depressing, and poignant. In short, it was an Oregon of yesterday that today is swift erasing.

We passed through a creaky gate, trudged up a hillock, hiked across the baked, thirsty wheatfield cracking for lack of water, and less than a quarter of a mile from the road we came to the ghost of pioneer Grizzly—the burial ground.

When Grizzly was still alive the cemetery was enclosed by a lovingly cared-for picket fence brightly painted, and the markers were upright. Now the fence was a shambles, and some of the markers were toppled or had been moved so that they lay headless in the parch of drying wild lupines and lumpy bunchgrass.

That's all there was of Grizzly. That's all, but more, at least, than a dozen other settlements in that part of central Oregon which have totally disappeared in face and name.

The Boys Of Winter

From the east a county road slides by undisturbed meadows, passing the school and the church as it slopes to the crossroads four miles from Oregon 99W.

From the west, shimmering down from Green Peak, the highest hill on the skyline, a row of Douglas firs interspersed with oaks, maples, and ash spreads shade over neat patches of cropland that flows down to the hamlet.

From the south the road dips off roller coaster terrain that uncoils at the village of Alpine, two miles away.

From the north the road that fans out from Corvallis and Philomath hums off a prairie to reach the pocket of Bellfountain. This is the semi-suburban path to the junction that contains only the turn-of-the-century community church, the country school, a small store, a rural oil distributorship, and a few houses, scattered as though they had been tossed into the air with the intention of throwing them far, but stopped in flight by the wind and thudded to earth.

Bellfountain dozes in a hollow that lazily reaches out to peaceful fields and rolling hills. The only sounds come from the school when the children are arriving or leaving, or at outside play when the weather is permissible. Then the sounds, bent against the sleeping calm of the hamlet, seem as a set of wind chimes, tinkling and gurgling in a rippling pattern.

Across the road from the grocery store, in a burnished frame house he had occupied for forty-six years, the old man

Bellfountain and church in 1903

Source unknown

arched in his rocking chair that had at least a decade ago
rubbed the pattern off the linoleum, and exclaimed: "That
was a most wonderful day!"

Above the rocking chair, clasped to the wallpaper that
had yellowed when he was still seeing Nellie home from
Aunt Dinah's quilting party, hung an oval-framed photo of a
handsome young blade. Now moving toward ninety on that
winter afternoon in early 1973, his face was a wrinkled
parchment, a geography of age.

"It was the biggest thing that ever happened to
Bellfountain," he enthused. That had been thirty-six years
ago, but he talked as though it had happened only yesterday.

"Just imagine!" cried John Vivian Bain, who nobody in
town knew as John and who most everyone called Vivan,
omitting the "i" of his middle name. "The state basketball
championship! And we beat that big school in Portland to
do it!"

J V Bain

Courtesy Veryle Rickard

The village was still named Dusty when Vivan Bain migrated to this crevice in Benton County in the autumn of 1901. It had been Dusty since a post office was established on December 6, 1895. On July 31, 1902 the name was changed to Bellfountain through the persuasion, it is said, of a man from Bellefontaine, the seat of Logan County, Ohio, and best known for being the first city in America, in 1891, to have concrete pavement. The post office was discontinued January 17, 1905 and has not since been renewed.

"All of the family came here on what they called a tourist train," said Bain. "My folks bought a farm of fifty-five acres right out here, on the other side of the telephone company. We didn't have much luck with farming so we took to different jobs. Done anything and everything the people asked us to do. First job was slashing down seven acres, mostly timber, on the hill here. There was lots of work, the farmers hired a lot of people."

In 1907 he married his country girl, Erma. They were inseparable until death took her in 1964. Friends and family dreaded his living alone; if nothing else, he could go to a retirement home. But he was obstinate. "I'm a Bellfountain man," he declared, and settled down in his little house.

Vivan Bain, small and frail, eased back into the rocking chair and said, contented, "This is the best place in the world to get along with people. I got the best neighbors on earth." Then he fell into reminiscing. He recalled when the village on Muddy Creek had a daily stage to Corvallis and the nearest railroad point was Sims, on a branch line of the Portland, Eugene & Eastern RR. And with a smile that churned the dirt road lines that stenciled his face he said softly: "When I was a young man Bellfountain was a lot bigger than it is now. It had a general store where you could buy almost anything, a blacksmith shop, the Fraternal Union and the Woodmen of the World, the church, the school, and there was the Grange, where everything went on."

Across the blacktopped county road from the school stands the fishscale, slatted, bell-towered Bellfountain church, where people have prayed, socialized, pondered solemnly, wept and rejoiced for almost a century. But it was at the Grange where the folks came to dance.

"Those Saturday dances were something," Vivan Bain

Store of Woodcock & Taylor, Bellfountain, in 1905
Source unknown

remembered. "Lovely times, wonderful times. We had an orchestra for every dance—four or five of us. I played for many a dance—played violin and mandolin. No trouble, no drunks. We wouldn't stand for anything like that."

There was theater, too, and J.V. Bain was also part of that. For instance, he played in an "original drama, in four acts," *The Spy of Gettysburg*, at the Grange Hall, on Friday evening, March 18, 1910. His role was that of Cyril Blackburn, "the black sheep of a noble Virginia family."

The poster advertising the program stated, in a postscript, "Pie Social immediately after the drama. All ladies requested to bring pies. Purchasers of pies will have admission refunded."

Bellfountain town band, circa 1905

Source unknown

Everyone who lived in or around Bellfountain in the first four decades of the twentieth century remembered it with Norman Rockwell nostalgia. Edith Larkin, clerk of the Bellfountain School for thirty-two years, came at the age of three to the village in 1898 from a farmstead just across the line in Lane County, and in her eighties recalled the warm feeling of the Bellfountain of her youth. "It was a world to itself," she reminisced in her apartment at the Senior Center in Monroe on a glazed autumn afternoon in 1979. "No, we weren't big but we felt we had everything we needed. There were two rooming houses with feed and barns, so some people stayed instead of rushing through. And when the telephone office came in, that made us feel important. And we thought our roads were grand when they were graveled."

Kenneth Litchfield, a Willamette University graduate who served as high school principal and athletic coach from 1929 to 1936, recalled more than forty years after he left Bellfountain the friendliness of the villagers: "There wasn't a house in the community that we hadn't eaten dinner in."

Burton "Bill" Lemmon, who succeeded Litchfield, had his own nostalgia: "Our house was adjacent to the school yard and frequently my dozen chickens would follow me to school, or they might meet me on the way home. We had a battery car radio to keep in touch with the outer world. People would keep track of one another by lamps in the windows."

"Maybe we were backwoodsy," said Mable Larkin, her mind reaching back to the 1930s. "Electricity hadn't yet come to the village or the farm homes. But life was tranquil."

Her daughter, Dorothy Silver, added: "We had the only radio in our area, a big Atwater Kent. At night we would put it on the front porch and turn it on high so that everybody could listen."

Lynn Hinton, a member of the state championship basketball squad, recalled, "People got together evenings. In the winter people visited each other every night. Not like today, where you don't even know who's next door."

Only the school had electricity. "It had one of the first generating plants in this farm country," remembered Homer Hull, who was born in 1920, had started school six years later, and who had stayed with it through the twelfth grade. "That was a little four-cylinder Kohler. I think the lights were thirty-two volts direct current. It was almost a novelty at the time it was put in because there weren't very many schools with electric lights then."

The school was the pride of the village. It had been so before there was a post office called Dusty. The first school, a log cabin, was across the road from the present site. No records are on file prior to 1895, when the one-room school had thirty-four pupils and was taught for four months a year by Isabel Gray, whose salary was forty dollars a month. After two years she departed for greener pastures and marriage. The school term was then lengthened to eight months and the teacher, W. W. Brostow, was paid fifty dollars a month. Eventually he moved on, another wandering schoolmaster.

The present school building was erected in 1908 and the old schoolhouse sold to the Woodmen of the World for a lodge hall. It was moved to a lot across from the store, near where J. V. Bain later lived, and in time torn down. In 1913 the high school celebrated its first four year graduating class of three students.

Homer Hull remembered that when he started school, in 1926, the grade school and the high school consisted of two rooms and the gymnasium. The gymnasium, where the Oregon state high school basketball champions practiced and played their home games, was built in 1912, said Edith Larkin, and at first had only a dirt floor. A wood floor was added some years later. "Then," noted Homer Hull, "the gym was one of the most modern in Benton County," leaving the visitors to wonder how primitive the less modern facility must have been.

In addition to basketball and volleyball the gym was also used for plays, parties, church bazaars, and social gatherings. "I must mention," said Edith Larkin, "that there were no dances and skating in the school gym; prohibited by the school board, and everyone was encouraged to wear tennis shoes." The school also put on the village Christmas program, which was held at the church.

Through this gym on game nights rang the strains of the school song, composed by two local women:

> Hail! historic old Bellfountain
> At the foot of Green Peak Mountain,
> We're the students you can count on,
> Rah! Rah! for our school.

We believe in education,
'Tis the bulwark of our nation
We're the best school in creation,
Rah! Rah! for our school
Onward, upward, forward ever,
This shall be our chief endeavor,
May Bellfountain flourish ever,
Rah! Rah! for our school.

There is another stanza, but few former students remember even the first and the song is not sung today. "We're a little more sophisticated now," said a parent wryly.

Out of this backwash school came several doctors, including Edward Bennett, who served as local physician for more than half-a-century, a few dietitians, a number of teachers, a mayor of Albany, a county judge, and a professor of speech at Duke University. And a dedication to learning. Kenneth Litchfield remembered with satisfaction his stay at the school from 1929 to 1936: "Those were the depression years, but we never had a single dropout in the seven years that I taught there."

J. V. Bain became custodian of the school in the early 1930s. "I'd been doing interior work—paperlaying and painting and being a carpenter and after I became custodian I continued my interior work, working in the school at morning and night and at the other work during the day. My being custodian gave me a chance to know the boys and be close to them.

"I can tell you the names of all the boys, I think." And he recited them.

Bellfountain High School in its championship year had nineteen boys and ten girls. Eight of the boys comprised the basketball squad. They were: Richard (Bunny) Kessler, Clifford Larkin, the brothers Frank and Stanley Buckingham, Harrison (Harry) Wallace, these were the starters; and John Key, Lynn Hinton, and Norman Humphrey. Of the five boys in the senior class, four were starters; only Larkin was an underclassman.

Bellfountain School Song

Kessler and Wallace were the only boys not from farms. Harry's father worked in the woods or in the mill and Kessler lived right in Bellfountain.

No buses took the students to school. "Sometimes we walked, sometimes we rode bicycles, sometimes people took us," recalled Lynn Hinton.

"I ran the mile and a half to school with Clifford," said Larkin's sister, Dorothy Silver.

"I walked two miles to school each way," said Stanley Buckingham. "Rain or shine. Two miles there and two miles back." So did his brother Frank.

With little to do for youthful recreation, it seemed logical for the father of the family to nail a hoop to a barn wall and for their boys to shoot baskets—with whatever ball they had. "I started playing basketball as soon as I could pick up a ball," recalled Lynn Hinton. "I was pretty young," said Cliff Larkin. "Just a little kid."

Legend has it that the boys started playing together in the fifth grade, because it was then Kenneth Litchfield came to Bellfountain to teach and coach. But not everyone remembers it that way. Two of the first-stringers were certain the boys began playing as a unit in the third grade; two others insisted it was the fourth grade. Whichever, over the years the coordination of the players became exquisitely honed. "We developed a sixth sense for each other," said Larkin.

Practice was part of physical education; the boys seldom stayed after school. "After the last class I went home and did my chores," said Lynn Hinton. "We had sheep and some cows and chickens to look after." The Buckingham brothers pitched hay and milked cows. "None of the boys practiced together when they got home," said Dorothy Silver. "And basketball wasn't an all-consuming topic at home." Nor did the boys practice together or play during the weekends. "Chores," said Clifford Larkin. In summer they put the game aside to work at home.

There was no football at Bellfountain so basketball was played in the autumn and winter and part of spring. Baseball was a lost cause: too few interested boys, too few bats and balls and gloves, too much inclement weather. In 1937 the baseball team played only four games, losing three.

The twenty-nine high school students in 1936–37 were divided into four grades, and the basketball players were active in three of the classes, there being no freshman on the squad. Bunny Kessler was student body president and took the lead in three school plays. Frank Buckingham, reported the school annual (the first ever at Bellfountain, and probably the last), "has been in two plays and reached his supreme dramatic height as 'Bluebeard' in *Hobgoblin House*." Stanley Buckingham appeared in two plays, was business manager of the annual, and valedictorian of the senior class. Lynn Hinton, a sophomore, had the highest grade point in the school.

The faculty consisted of Burton Lemmon, principal and coach, and Elizabeth Gabler. Lemmon, fresh from Willamette University, taught mathematics, history, geometry, typing, and mechanical drawing and supervised the three elementary teachers. Gabler, who matriculated at Oregon State College, taught English, science, sociology, and sewing. Both left at the end of the school year, Lemmon to a better teaching position, Gabler to take up housekeeping.

There were the usual high school romances. John Key and Louise Davis went on to Oregon College of Education at Monmouth and were there married. Prior to Key, Louise dated Bunny Kessler, whom his friends called Bun. After Key's death, Louise married Clifford Larkin, making her the sister-in-law of Dorothy Larkin Silver. John Key's sister married Norman Humphrey and Harrison Wallace was wed to Treva Bloor. Thus, half the championship basketball squad married Bellfountain girls.

"The boys from somewhere in Benton County," as a

Portland sports writer called them, lived as clean as the mist which eventide rinsed down Green Peak Mountain. "None of them drank or smoked," said Dorothy Silver. "They regarded their bodies as sacred to the game and they followed good habits." Her brother, Cliff Larkin, agreed: "Basketball and Ken Litchfield had a lot to do with all our lives. He was strict about smoking and drinking. I don't think that any of us has ever smoked and, as far as I know, some of us just have an occasional social drink." Kenneth Litchfield noted: "The kids on the team took care of themselves, they went to bed early and trained hard; they all became good citizens and never got into any trouble."

Nor did the players strut and show off. "They were not conceited, any of them," remembered Homer Hull. "If they had been of that nature they never would have won the state championship. It was a teamwork thing from start to finish and they knew it had to be and there wasn't any glory seekers on the team, that's for sure. They were treated by the other students in just an ordinary way." Vivan Bain could not speak of the boys without becoming ecstatic: "They were nice, just about the best. They just worshipped Kenneth Litchfield."

From the fifth grade on, Litchfield knit his future whiz kids into a cohesive, unselfish unit. When they entered High the community knew that something special was being molded at the school in the foothills. It was only a matter of time. They had become convinced of that when the eighth graders had defeated the JV team of Philomath High, 42 to 10.

"Bellfountain turned out en masse to see the games," Mabel Larkin reminisced. "We wouldn't have missed them."

"When the boys played in Bellfountain," Vivan Bain remembered, "the gym was packed. Everybody was so proud of the boys. Why, people from miles away would say they were Bellfountain people."

In 1936 Oregon high schools were divided into two categories, A and B, with A comprised of the larger schools, but there was only one state tournament, made up of sixteen teams. The four Class B schools that made it to state were bracketed together, with the winner entering the Class A semi-finals.

Bellfountain won the 1936 B championship, defeating Myrtle Creek for the title. During the regular season the Bells had committed as few as a single foul in their games; against Myrtle Creek they did not foul even once, setting a state tournament record.

In the semi-finals, Bellfountain lost to Corvallis in a game Litchfield thought could have been won. Rebounding, the Bells defeated Mac-Hi of Pendleton for third place.

At the end of the school year Litchfield left Bellfountain to become principal of a bigger school at Shedd. From there he studied law and went on to become a prominent attorney in Lincoln County, where he had been born. He was succeeded as principal and coach by Burton "Bill" Lemmon, another Willamette graduate.

"It was a very interesting job, with none of the problems of the average high school today," Lemmon recalled. "About the most severe student problem was a little tiff between a girl and her boy friend at a student body meeting."

He was somewhat surprised to find out in the past no time had been taken off from class for pep rallies. He liked the idea and kept it that way.

Lemmon was handed an eight-member squad of four seniors, one junior and three sophomores that comprised forty-two per cent of the male high school enrollment. The starting team averaged about five feet nine and 160 pounds, with Kessler the tallest and heaviest at six feet and 180 pounds. Hinton was also six feet but he saw little action.

Kessler was the acknowledged star. If there was one

player the Bells could not do without, most people agreed, it was he. Litchfield said of Bunny: "Kessler had awfully long arms, and he could really jump. Even when he was outjumped we still got the ball half the time."

Vivan Bain, the ardent fan, remembered with excitement: "Kessler could jump higher than anyone I ever saw. He was the big scorer and the best rebounder." "But," said Lynn Hinton, "Harry Wallace was just as important, because he was the floor general."

Basketball was a slower game then, which may or may not have helped the Boys of Bellfountain. There was still a center jump after every basket and free throw(s), the set shot was prevalent, the jump shot was rare and looked upon as showboating, and dunking was far in the future. Within these confines, Bellfountain perfected the fast break.

Lemmon, who had been an all-state high school cager at Tacoma, Washington, knew good fortune when he spotted it and he did not tamper with the team's strength or change Litchfield's format. The team, in his words, "made very few mistakes. Bad passes were rare, the shooting averages were unusually high. Four of the five were excellent shooters. What produced such a sensational team? Ken Litchfield deserves much credit for this. The boys just went out and did the job, with a little strategy that I helped them with. We practiced for about an hour and a half. They couldn't work too long as there were farm chores to perform. And never on Saturday or Sunday."

Every school supporter in the Bellfountain area, which numbered about three hundred persons, knew that, as an old timer put it, "They were Ken's boys." Dorothy Silver was more explicit: "Lemmon contributed nothing. The boys had Litchfield's style down pat; he was the only coach they knew." Litchfield, never arrogant, appreciatively accepted the bows Lemmon took in his direction.

Before the season started the boys were divided as to their

prospects. "I knew we would win the state championship after we took third place," recalled Stanley Buckingham. A few others also shared this certitude. Some dared not dream that high. "I never thought we would take state," said Frank Buckingham.

For John Vivan Bain there was no doubt. "I knew it!" he exulted. "I told everyone: This is the year!"

In its regular season of eighteen games the Bells lost only twice, by two points to Corvallis and two points to St. Mary's of Eugene, whom it had previously beaten decisively. The team defeated both Salem High and the Willamette University frosh twice. It trounced schools its size and up to three times as large: Harrisburg by 57 points, Shedd by 47 and later by 52, Monroe twice by 21, Alsea by 44 and 34.

"There was an exhilaration all through the basketball games," remembered Dorothy Silver, "because we knew our team was good. With each victory there was always the anticipation of going to the state tournament. And it built into a crescendo of excitement."

Having successfully completed its season, the Bells moved on to the Benton County tournament. There they defeated Alsea and Monroe (each again) and advanced to the district tournament. Here Bellfountain began by whipping Shedd by 35 points. Its next opponent was Coburg, which the starters handled so well that Lemmon inserted his substitutes. Coburg surged back in fury. When the score had considerably narrowed the starters were returned and closed the game with a four point victory. In the district championship game the Bells were more cautious and came home with an 11 point triumph over Thurston. The next move was State, held at Willamette University in Salem.

In the waning days of the winter of 1936–37, the gloom that lay across America covered western Oregon, too. Everything could be bought for a song, but there were few singers. A five room house with full basement, at S.E. 34th

Ave. and Clinton St., in Portland, was put on sale at $1,950—the full price!—but potential buyers were scant. In Corvallis, hamburger was marketed at ten cents a pound; in Harrisburg a cafe advertised a juicy hamburger for only a nickel; a hamburger steak at a respectable Eugene restaurant was on the menu at twenty-five cents—and people walked the streets hungry. In Albany, a pound of coffee had a price tag of fifteen cents—but in many houses not a single family member was employed and in some homes it took hard digging to scrape up a dollar.

Bellfountain did not escape the gloom of the Great Depression but the people in the area survived on what they grew, what they received in barter, and what cash work they could scrounge. As winter edged toward spring the most frequent talk, apart from Hard Times, was of the state tournament. On the morning of Wednesday, March 17, as Amelia Earhart was taking off from Oakland on a planned round-the-world flight and the Portland City Council voted to experiment with a strange new gadget called a parking meter, a dribble of cars moved out of the village area on gravel roads, bound for Bellfountain's first game in the tourney.

At 1 pm the ball was tossed up and the Bells fell swiftly upon their opponents, Amity. When the score reached 20 to 3 the Bells substituted. At 34 to 28 the Boys from Bellfountain turned serious again and closed with nine straight points to win 43 to 28. Kessler hit 9 of 12 shots from the floor, most from under the hoop, and ended with 20 points.

At 3 pm the following afternoon Bellfountain took on Chiloquin for the B title. Once again the Bells stormed to an early lead, surging ahead 16 to 5 at the quarter and 24 to 9 at the half. Kessler was everywhere, scoring at will. By the end of the third quarter the Bells had widened their lead to 32 to 13 before Lemmon cleared his bench. When the game was over the score read: Bellfountain 39, Chiloquin 21.

Now that Bellfountain was in the semi-finals the dribble of cars to Salem bloated into a soggy caravan. "Just about all the people in the territory were there," recalled Vivan Bain.

A few stayed home, Edith Larkin among them. "There was one or two there in Bellfountain that had radios and those of us who remained behind gathered in around the radios and listened to the game."

Both those who went to Salem and those who stayed behind were confident of success, a sentiment few others in Oregon shared. A poll of sportswriters covering the tournament expected the championship to come down to the game between the two Portland entries, Franklin and Lincoln. Each, declared general opinion, was superior to the Corvallis team which had taken state the year before. Bellfountain was matched against Franklin in the game set for 7:30 pm on Friday, March 19.

Franklin, the Portland league champion, was tough and aggressive, playing more in the contemporary style than the center jump, pre-jump shot era. (Years later, Larkin was to complain of what he saw on the court: "I don't like this rough stuff. We weren't allowed to play that way.")

In the quarter-finals, Franklin was credited by the sports journalists with having "talked" Eugene into defeat with a steady stream of face-to-face jibes. Against Bellfountain Franklin tried the same tactics and for a quarter the psychology worked, the score being tied at 4–4. Franklin stopped taunting Kessler when he made a short basket and turned upon Wallace. But the Bells' captain drilled a long shot, working his impaired left arm as a rod. When the half ended Bellfountain was in front 16 to 9.

During the last four minutes of the second quarter, the entire third period and the first minute of the final quarter, Franklin did not score a single point, so tight was the defense of the Bells and so thorough their ball control. Bellfountain 39—Franklin 13.

Now the Bells stood just below the pinnacle. Barring its path to the peak was Lincoln of Portland, a powerful team representing a student body of some fifteen hundred. It had swept through the tournament and felt certain it would lay low the "giant killers of Benton County." But sentiment was on the side of the Bells. "The whole state of Oregon was rooting for Bellfountain that night," said Vivan Bain, his face flushed.

The game began at 8:30 pm on Saturday, March 20, with Bunny Kessler giving away significant height as he jumped at the tipoff. As usual, Bellfountain started quickly, passing as though the ball was propelled by a rifle, fast-breaking and giving Lincoln no time to adjust. At the end of the first quarter Bellfountain led, 9 to 4. In the second period the Bells were even more dominant and went to their dressing room with a 20 to 8 lead.

Lynn Hinton, who had not played a single second in the first two quarters vividly recalled the half-time period more than forty years later: "Coach Lemmon gave each of his players a sniff of ammonia. When the bottle was extended to Kessler the cork fell off and he got a far larger dose than had been anticipated. The team had no doctor and was a little scared. But Kessler came out of it fine and when he went back on the floor he was just as fresh as when he started."

In the second half Bellfountain outscored Lincoln 15 to 13 and won the game 35 to 21. The Bells had no more field goals than Lincoln but sank 15 of 17 free throws, with Kessler going 9 out of 9. Bellfountain fouled Lincoln only four times.

Following the game, Kessler and Wallace were named to the state tournament team and Stanley Buckingham made the second team. Larkin, Kessler, Wallace and Stan Buckingham were selected on the all-state B team. Kessler received the trophy for the outstanding sportsman of the

The state championship basketball team. *Left to right, back row:* Coach Bill Lemmon, Stanley Buckingham, Harrison Wallace, Richard Kessler, Frank Buckingham, Clifford Larkin, Norman Humphrey. *Left to right, kneeling:* Lynn Hinton, John Key.

Courtesy Clifford Larkin

tourney. The year before, the trophy had been given to Harry Wallace.

It was the last game—and year—in school basketball for the seniors and the last year nationally of the center jump.

In 1938 an A school and a B school again clashed for the state basketball championship, with Baker, the A team, defeating Amity, the B team. Soon after, the B teams had their own tourney.

The Boys from Bellfountain accepted their honors, showered, dressed, and joined the caravan home. When the cars approached the village every horn was pressed hard and not before or since has Bellfountain known such din.

"Even if you hadn't listened on the radio, you'd have known we had won by all the honking," said Vivan Bain, with a grin that carried him twenty years closer to the portrait of the young man on the wall. "It was a great occasion to bring in the spring. But the noise was soon over and everyone went home sober."

Tongue in cheek, Don Upjohn of the Salem *Capital Journal* wrote: "The folks back home were in a kind of tough spot when their lads won. Because when the boys returned home the mayor couldn't meet 'em on the steps of the city hall and present them with the keys to the city for the simple reason there ain't no mayor, there ain't no city hall, there ain't no keys and, in fact, there ain't no city."

There was no dearth of news to be reported by the Sunday papers in Oregon on March 21, 1937. Scotland Yard was investigating a suspected plot against the life of King George VI, Amelia Earhart had cracked up her $80,000 "laboratory plane" and her world flight plans during an attempted takeoff from Hawaii to Howland Island, the United Auto Workers were threatening a general strike "unless the brutal eviction of sit-down strikers and the ruthless clubbing of workers by Detroit police is immediately stopped," and a military court of inquiry began hearings on the causes of an explosion of a heating system which took the lives of 455 children and teachers at the New London, Texas consolidated school, reputedly the richest in the world.

But in Oregon the big news was local: the large boldprint banner of the *Oregon Statesman* of Salem read: BELLFOUNTAIN IS STATE HOOP CHAMPION.

A sub-headline told more: History Made When First of B Teams Captures Championship. The head revealed more awesome information: Small Benton Town is Hoop Capitol Today.

Paul Hauser, who wrote the front page article, was poetry

on fire as he poured out his molten impressions of the stunning event:

"Jim Corbett beat John L. Sullivan in 1892, Centre College licked Harvard in 1921 and David beat Goliath several years ago but last night Bellfountain beat Lincoln to become the basketball champion of the state of Oregon.

"Bellfountain, a town which has no post office, no electric lights and is little more than a crossroads in the Benton County hills has the state basketball champions, as fine a bunch of ballhandlers that ever made an opposing team look sick.

"Bellfountain spotted Lincoln the tip-off advantage by six inches, spotted them height everywhere else and then went out and beat the socks off Lincoln.

"Even towering height around the basket and a zone defense that had stopped three other teams couldn't dampen the effect of Bellfountain's swift and accurate passing into the scoring zone.

"Lincoln couldn't figure an offense that whipped lightning passes right under its nose and then up and in. Lincoln couldn't figure a defense that not only checked them way out of scoring range but which intercepted their passes and tied them up on their breaks into the foul circle.

"It was the same combination which beat Franklin the night before: Wallace to handle the ball in the back court and whip it in for almost certain shots, Kessler to take them under the basket, Stan Buckingham to break around, in and under, Larkin to pot them from the corners . . ."

After the homecoming "the people probably had a big feast because they were always having something like that," said Edith Larkin. The more impressionable Vivan Bain had a clearer memory: "The community put on a big celebration. It was the biggest feed you ever saw. And there was lots of speeches."

Through the spring of 1937 Bellfountain had its day in

the sun. "The championship was so newsworthy that there was even a small blurb in a New York paper about it," said Dorothy Silver. Edith Larkin was more expansive: "Bellfountain was world-wide known at that time. Some people came here to see what it looked like." The high school annual stated: "It is difficult for us to write about our own team since so much has been written about our Champs in the papers even to the Atlantic Coast. Great fame was brought to our school, our team, and our community."

After the celebration of the honking and the big feast, the village returned to its routine pace. "We were proud of our boys but life went on just the same," noted Edith Larkin. "The boys weren't any different after they won the championship," noted Dorothy Silver. "They were students like all the others and they continued to do their chores."

After the 1937 school year Bill Lemmon left Bellfountain to coach at Eatonville, Washington, "a basketball hot house," he called it. After three years he went on to Clover Park, where he stayed five years and where one of his players later coached Lemmon's sons at the same school. From Clover Park, Lemmon moved on to Stadium High in Tacoma, where in 1931 he had been a member of the Washington state champions. The best any of his Stadium teams could do in his twelve years of coaching there was third: "I kept hoping I'd find another Bellfountain team," he recalled ruefully. "I never did." The year following his departure the team won the state championship. Thus did history come full circle: the Bellfountain team Lemmon inherited won the Oregon championship and the team he developed at Stadium gained the Washington title for the coach who followed Lemmon.

"Bellfountain ranks at the top in my educational and sport experiences," said Lemmon more than forty years later, but after he left Bellfountain he did not correspond with any of

the Bells, nor did they seek him out. Though he had helped
them in some tough spots, the boys owed their allegiance to
Ken Litchfield, and Lemmon knew it.

The 1937–38 team, with Larkin sidelined with injuries,
had a rather mediocre season. Thereafter the high school
was discontinued and the students transported to Monroe,
where Hinton, Humphrey, and Key completed their last
year.

"We hated to see the high school leave us," said Vivan
Bain, his parched, latticed face growing older yet for a
moment as he slumped into his rocking chair. "But it had to
be."

A campaign was begun to move the basketball trophies to
Monroe High but instant indignation squelched the intended
expropriation. "Over my dead body!" bristled Vivan Bain.
"We weren't going to allow it," said Edith Larkin. "That's
all we have left and they're still there. We built a case
around them."

The slightly tarnished two-foot trophy, about a dozen
other smaller trophies, the bracket of the 1937 state
tournament, and the scorebook of a 1937 game are still in
the reliquary, modestly sited in the fifth and sixth grade
room. No one knows what happened to the key. Principal
Pat O'Mealey said, "We go in through the back, which is
held on with screws."

After high school, some of the players went on to college.
Only one graduated, Stanley Buckingham, with a B.S. at
Oregon State. An unidentified clipping saved by Dorothy
Silver reported: "Not one of the Bellfountain state champs
has crashed a college yearling or varsity lineup as yet, and it
looks as if none will. Dick Kessler was all set for Oregon
State but he fell down scholastically.

"It was a great team, that Bellfountain outfit," the clipping
continued, "but it was a great team because the boys
worked together so beautifully and every man always knew
just where every other was."

(The closest any of the Bells came to college basketball was Cliff Larkin, whose sister, Dorothy, married Morris Silver, a star player at Oregon State.)

Lynn Hinton sought education in another way. On October 9, 1939 he enlisted in the Navy. "It seemed like the big thing to do," he recalled. For ten months he was stationed on the battleship *Arizona*, in the Pacific. Fourteen months after he left the *Arizona* the big seawagon was destroyed at Pearl Harbor. For the rest of the war Hinton served on the east coast.

All of the boys but Kessler served in the armed forces during World War II. Of the seven, six survived; Johnny Key was killed off Okinawa. None had a cushy job. Stanley Buckingham spent four years in the infantry. Frank Buckingham served four years in the Air Force, reaching as far as Australia and New Guinea. Cliff Larkin, a tank commander, sweated out two years in a German prison after his tank was shot out from under him in northern Africa.

In 1946, after war's end, the Boys of '37 came together to play the Monroe High team and, displaying touches of their old magic, won handily.

Two of the boys, the Buckinghams, took advantage of a government homestead offer to veterans and turned to farming, Stan near Tulelake, California and Frank near Pasco, Washington. Harrison Wallace became a contract logger out of Corvallis and Norman Humphrey worked at farming and logging at Bellfountain before, decades later, moving to Monroe. Lynn Hinton was employed by Bell Telephone in Portland as an installer and put down roots in Sherwood, a Portland suburb. Cliff Larkin "farmed, drove log truck and worked for OSU." He joined the Sheriff's Posse and cared for the horses. Kessler, who made Corvallis his home base, drove truck for a gravel company.

"Well," said Homer Hull, reviewing the post-school lives of the championship Bells, "they've been really far above average. You take that seven of 'em, they've made quite a

mark in the world, I feel. Not one got divorced, that's
something. Seems like there was one or two that had a little
tough luck but they're quite successful, above average."

The fire of the great victory did not cool suddenly.
Bellfountain put up no banners or statues to proclaim or
memorialize its rage in history but the flame was kept alive.
"For years," said Vivan Bain, glowing and lifting himself an
inch from his rocking chair, "the big talk in Bellfountain
was the state championship. There was nothing like it since
that year. The old timers still talk about it and the
newcomers are told. Everybody that moves in here learns
everything that ever happened in Bellfountain. But," he
added, "we never let it go to our head."

In 1962, a quarter-century after they had reached their

The boys of Bellfountain at their 25th reunion, in the same formation
of the 1937 photo. Missing is John Key, who was killed in World War
II.

Courtesy Clifford Larkin

Mt. Everest, the surviving seven came together at Eugene, during the state basketball tournament. They had dinner and then were taken to McArthur Court, where they received a standing ovation from the more than 10,000 spectators.

"I wish I had been there," said Vivan Bain. "I'd have cheered along with everybody else. The boys deserved it."

Nor was Bain around when the seven gathered once more at Bellfountain on March 6, 1977 for the fortieth anniversary banquet held in the school gymnasium. Organized by the Bellfountain Church Christian Women's Club, the driving spirit of the reunion was mill owner Ralph Hull, reputedly the wealthiest man of the area and the patriarch of Bellfountain basketball nostalgia.

Dorothy Silver recalled: "The gymnasium was full. About two hundred people were there. Litchfield was there. And Lemmon. One whole length of the gym was tabled with the most delicious feed, all donated by the community."

That day the Bells played a basketball game of sorts, taking on Monroe High in four two-minute quarters. Dorothy Silver remembered two years later: "Until they ran out of steam the boys had the Monroe team baffled. If it weren't for their looks—some seemed so old—you would have thought they had been playing together since high school. The old plays seemed to click as though they hadn't forgotten a thing and they were as coordinated as ever. But time ran out on them and Monroe won." The final score was 16 to 14. Not bad for men approaching sixty.

All the players remained interested in sports after they left school, retreating from the playing areas to television. At seventy they were as enthusiastic as ever, and sometimes they wondered, or were asked, how the Bells of '37 would match up against a contemporary Oregon premium high school team.

Most felt they would acquit themselves, primarily because of their airtight defense, excellent conditioning, teamwork and quickness. But Lynn Hinton offered a firm dissent: "We

The cheerleaders 40 years later. *Left to right:* Treva Bloor Wallace, Julia Holder, Vivian Bloor Black.

Courtesy Clifford Larkin

were such a small team by today's standards that a team with our height would be run over."

None of the seven regretted having gone to a small school. "Had we gone to a larger school most of us would not have made the team," said Stan Buckingham. "Playing together since we were little kids developed the highest example of team work."

Frank Buckingham had another reason for being glad to have attended Bellfountain. "There was more personal attention and a chance for medium students to excel."

As the boys matured the magic of Bellfountain lost its spell, as would be expected. Some said they returned "once

The Bellfountain Bells in 1977, at their 40th reunion. The formation is the same as in the photos of 1937 and 1962.

Courtesy Clifford Larkin

in a while," others rarely. The three starters residing in Corvallis—Kessler, Wallace and Larkin—maintained infrequent contact with each other but time had lessened the camaraderie of the others. "We don't even send each other Christmas cards," said Lynn Hinton. "We should keep in touch more than we do, but that's life. I should send cards to my old Navy buddies, but I don't. That's life."

For all the players the winning of the state championship was one of the great peaks of their lives. "My only real claim to fame," said Stan Buckingham. "The highlight of my life," said Lynn Hinton. "It was the most outstanding thing I was associated with, even though I was a spectator," he laughed. "Every so often, some one brings it up, in a

J V Bain

Phoebe L Friedman

newspaper or someone I'm around, and the memories come back in a flood." Clifford Larkin equated the championship with coming home from the war.

For those who attended high school in Bellfountain during

the glory days of the Bells, "the championship," said Dorothy Silver, "is a life long memory."

For Vivan Bain, thirty-six years after the cardiac week of '37, it was still high noon. His geometric face, the geography of age, rose in ridges and his eyes glistened as he angled forward in his rocking chair by the purring oil stove to bring back the triumph of the village:

"The whole confounded county was just plumb crazy at that time. Why, wherever I went around the state and people heard I was from Bellfountain, they asked a lot of questions. Why, it was famous then to be a Bellfountain man!"

Postscript: John Vivian Bain died February 28, 1976. Few people come to Bellfountain out of curiosity now. In 1990 Pat O'Mealey, the grade school principal, noted: "Maybe some people drive past the school to look at it but nobody comes in. But I have run into people as far away as La Grande who are familiar with the story." The gymnasium is still the same as it was in 1937, with a wood burning stove and a single tier of wooden bleachers enclosing the court. Back of the school is a playground, that looks like a delightful cow pasture with a shed and swings. Behind the playground stands a charming old barn.

The Quotable Oregon

Searching for a book I needed I came across a text I had forgotten I possessed. It is called *America the Quotable* and is filled with quotes that cover every state.

Naturally, I turned to the Oregon pages—four out of five hundred.

There are no immortal quotes here, and there are some errors. For instance, this is taken from a book, *The Pacific States of America* by Neal R. Peirce and published in 1972:

> Moving westerly from the Cascades, one comes immediately on the Willamette Valley, the heartland of Oregon. The valley stretches 180 miles south from Portland and some 60 miles across, abutting the Coast Range on the west; within it is Oregon's breadbasket and some of its great timber stands.

Well, the Willamette Valley doesn't extend 180 miles south from Portland—certainly not as the crow flies—and the breadbasket—and meat platter—of Oregon is east of the Cascades.

Peirce again: "If any West Coast city could be said to have a monopoly on propriety and an anxiousness to 'keep things as they are', it is Portland, a town of quiet old wealth, discreet culture, and cautious politics."

Maybe so, but a lot of people in Portland would say things have changed since 1972.

In 1968 Robert Kennedy said of Oregon: "The state is like one giant suburb." (Maybe that's because we don't have rust belts or tobacco roads.)

Twenty-seven years before, Philip Wylie had written in his then-famous *Generation of Vipers*: "Oregon is only an idea. It is in no scientific way a reality."

John Gunther had some trenchant things to say about Oregon in his well-researched *Inside USA*, published in 1947:

> In the early 20s—largely because so many Southerners had moved in—Oregon was, in fact, strange as it may seem, the strongest Ku Klux Klan state in the Union outside the solid South, and hangovers of this still show. Agitation against the nisei was fiercer in Oregon than anywhere else in the West; the Portland police department for years maintained a 'red squad' like that in Los Angeles. Portland was considered one of the main Nazi centers in the country by the FBI, and I heard more and more bitter anti-Negro talk than in any other northern city.

It is nice to report now that the situation has considerably changed, though acts of bigotry appear to be on the rise.

Writing in the February 25, 1974 issue of the *New Yorker*, EJ Kahn Jr. had words we would rather hear:

> That the state of Oregon, with two million people, or roughly one percent of the national population, should have got the jump on most of the rest of the country in perceiving an energy crisis does not especially surprise Oregonians. In the last seven years, they have become accustomed to all sorts of innovative and bizaare goings-on. They have laws so progressive that, by comparison, many other states look doddering.

Having absorbed the quotes on Oregon from the text, I set down some of my own quotes, taken in quick snatches from some of my writings. Here goes:

> Oregon is either—take what you choose— the most conservative liberal or the most liberal conservative state in the Union.

□ ■ □

The best way to appreciate Oregon is to move away from it for a while.

□ ■ □

We Portlanders feel we have plenty to complain about, but after visiting other cities in the USA we can't wait to get back to Portland.

□ ■ □

It rains more in a lot of other places than it does in Portland, but no city in all America so identifies with rain. It is omnipresent in the mind. Here it can be dry for fifty days in a row, and the minute a few drops fall, someone is sure to say, "There it goes again."

□ ■ □

One of the reasons people in the Portland area have a sense of frustration that is so evident a part of their personality is the teasing presence of Mount Hood. At least half the time you can't see it, because of rain or fog. You are absolutely sure it must be there—or there!—or right there!—but you can't see it, so you really can't be sure.

□ ■ □

In Portland, if it's below freezing four days in a row, it's a catastrophe. If the temperature rises above 100 degrees four days in a row, it's also catastrophic.

□ ■ □

Here's an example of how Portland is provincial. In Los Angeles, if you aspire to be a professional dancer and you are working as a waitress to make ends meet, the people around you know you as a dancer. In Portland, given the same situation, you are known as a waitress.

□ ■ □

There is a compelling reason for little great literature having been written on Oregon. Apart from the settling of the land by the pioneers, nothing really great happened here. The Civil War scarcely touched the state, no large "Indian war" was fought on our soil, no great labor struggles took place here, cattle drives were, in the main, minor compared to some other states, no massive campaigns for civil rights or civil liberties were waged in Oregon. The dynamism of events that provoke creativity were elsewhere; on the whole, our history has been pretty sedate.

□ ■ □

The Oregonian is a natural gardener. Let me give you an example. Once, after three days of almost constant rain, the heavens suddenly dried up. Ten minutes later my neighbor was out with her pruning shears.

□ ■ □

In some other cities in which I have lived, gardenering is a middle class pursuit. In Portland—as well as in Salem, Albany, Roseburg, and Medford, among others—

gardenering is an act of faith, carried on by people of all classes. I live in a workingclass neighborhood and we all put in a lot of work on our lawns, flower beds, trees, shrubs, hedges, and the rest.

□ ■ □

One of the reasons that Oregon has had so few crooked politicians is that there isn't much to steal. Another—and more important— reason is the number of people looking over the shoulders of the politicians and their appointees. On the state level alone there must be a hundred boards, commissions, committees and what not, each a zealous watchdog of the public weal.

□ ■ □

Changes are everywhere. The grocery store-gas pump is making a comeback; twenty-four-hour food stores are all over the state; the most prominent institution in many a town is the senior citizens organization.

□ ■ □

Isolation in Oregon is a myth. The rancher who tells you that he is far away from the world has an expensive TV dish that brings him news from every corner of the earth. The same with uniqueness. Every county road burg claims it's unique, and all for the same reasons.

□ ■ □

Timothy Davenport was correct when he stated that Oregon came closer to being a slave

state than did Kansas. Only the adroit
diplomacy of George Williams turned sentiment against slavery. In a rather racist way,
Williams argued that slavery was non-
economical and would work against the
ambitions of Oregon agriculture. A John
Brown would have skinned the hide off
George Williams. But the Oregon pioneer
would not tolerate a man who opposed slavery
on moral grounds.

□ ■ □

A prominent legislator told me that the
biggest political division in the state was
between the peoples of eastern and western
Oregon. "Tell me," I replied. "With whom has
the impoverished senior citizen of Baker more
in common—a banker in Baker or a poor
senior citizen in Coos Bay? Does the mill
worker in Harney County feel closer to the
absentee owner or to another mill worker in
Roseburg?"

□ ■ □

The innovativeness of Oregon politics and
legislation can be traced to the sharp class
divisions of the pioneers. There gathered here,
inside of a decade, former slaveholders of the
Deep South and Southern farmers who hated
the slaveholders because slavery had given the
former a strong competitive edge; sophisticated
New England merchants and backwoods
Missouri lawyers; Illinois storekeepers and
Ohio preachers; Tennessee cabinet makers and
Pennsylvania bankers. The leadership was

almost equally apportioned among the sons of the industrial revolution, traditional agriculturalists, mercantilists, and financial and transportation activists—the hardest-driving and most successful belonging to several of the categories. The groups were too diverse to form a viable coalition or political machine and by the time alliances were being solidified, they were submerged by new emigrants. Out of this welter of competing interests came the need to enact political means to neutralize antagonisms and to prevent any single group from holding almighty power. In the end the rich won out, as they always had, but the others had gained the right to strike back.

□ ■ □

Oregonians pride themselves on their history but, in reality, we comprise as historically illiterate a state as I know. Not only does the state do a horrible job in preserving its physical history, most of its citizens know precious little of its history. How many people can tell you anything about Bill Hanley, Captain Jack, Captain John, John Beeson, Os West, Marie Equi, Bill Brown and/or Frances Fuller Victor, to name but a few of the noteworthy?

□ ■ □

The Oregon native brags that his latchstring is always out while he is posting a No Trespassing sign at the head of his driveway and a No Soliciting card looks down upon the welcome mat at the foot of his doorstep.

□ ■ □

In Oregon, if you don't like the state, you move to another county.

□ ■ □

Two of the main sources of Oregon income are strange ingredients to the economy. The leading cash crop is marijuana. Oregon could amply finance its impoverished school districts by legalizing and taxing marijuana—and then carrying on a strong education campaign against its use, a la cigarettes. The state has no general sales tax; its northern neighbor, Washington, does, and a rather substantial one. Washington residents near Oregon pour across the state line to shop in Oregon stores. If Washington ever repealed its sales tax a lot of Oregon merchants along the Columbia River would have to close their doors or, at the least, lay off most of their employees.

□ ■ □

The descendants of the pioneers—people who came to Oregon prior to statehood in 1859—are much more tolerant and good-humored in evaluating the records of their ancestors than are the johnny-come-latelys (especially the Californians!), who are some-times rigid and humorless. The newcomers see the pioneers as super-heroic and every event as super-dramatic; the descendants view their ancestors as ordinary people living in a difficult, but interesting time. (The descendants see themselves as also living in a difficult time.) If you want a distorted impression of

Oregon history, spend an hour listening to an overheated recital by one of the five-year-here patriots.

I've often been asked which part of Oregon I like best. I always reply, "The place I just left or the next place I'm coming to."

Now, reader, compose your own quotes. Who knows, you may be cited in a later edition of *America the Quotable.*

McCoy Was For Real

Come, put up your horses: come, feed them some
*   hay:*
Come, sit here beside me for as long as you stay.
"Old Smokey" (Tennessee Folk Song)

There are still scores of tintype hamlets within a few miles off a main road, all of them looking like photos in a nineteenth century hamlet.

McCoy, a mile west of Oregon 99W, is one of them. Few people driving north toward McMinnville or south toward Corvallis turn off to see McCoy. For one thing, it isn't on most Oregon maps; for another, there isn't anything striking about it. It's just a spot on the landscape that interests only those of us who find charm in a vignette that is old, serene, and folksy.

When the railroad came through Polk County it cut across the land of Isaac McCoy. He was willing to give the line right-of-way, asking only that the station built on his property be called McCoyville. The company officials thought the title too cumbersome and shortened it to McCoy. Isaac, always a man ready to reason, accepted that as a just compromise.

By 1915 McCoy had grown to a population of 130 and was the market center for a cluster of dairy, livestock, clover seed, small grain, poultry, fruit, and berry farms. All through Polk and its contiguous counties, the area was noted for its high-grade sheep.

The town then had a combined elementary and high

This is McCoy

Marcia Workentine

school, a Presbyterian church, a Grange, and two lodges, IOOF and Rebekah. Farmers from miles around would come to McCoy to shop, pray, dance, politic, hold meetings, get married, and bury their dead.

There isn't a school in McCoy today. Or a church. The lodges are gone. So is the Grange. The young, what few there are around, go dancing and get hitched elsewhere. Those who pass away are buried in other cemeteries.

All that exists now is a musty country store building reputedly put up in 1886 (the IOOF met upstairs), a grain elevator, a powerhouse abandoned decades ago, and a few houses and barns almost as old as the village.

Spring Valley Presbyterian Church
Marcia Workentine

There is a trace of folklore here about a "fierce gun battle" on the steps of the store in the 1890s, but the old-timers who would know have departed for other scenes. I once tried to prove, by showing up the contradictions in the tale, that the shootout really didn't take place, but my friends were true believers. Somehow it gives us a sense of importance to identify with the smoke and thunder of the Old West, while it demeans us to be contemporary with the violence on the streets of our neighborhoods.

There was real violence here, in early June of 1887, when Oscar Kelty, son of a farmer in neighboring Bethel, shot to death his wife, Clara, at the home of her parents, a mile southeast of town. Later a posse rode down to Dallas and lynched Kelty. His body lies in the Bethel Cemetery, a little more than two miles from McCoy. Near him sleeps Isaac McCoy.

You would think that McCoy would be the proper place to escape the madding crowd, but it doesn't always work out that way. One of the storekeepers I knew vowed he would stay for life, having found the real McCoy of his dreams, but after several Oregon winters, one rain too many sent him back to California.

Flat on the plain, beyond the last westward wave of the Eola Hills, McCoy is about halfway between Perrydale and Lincoln, two other hamlets long past their prime. In those thirteen miles are some soft and hazy momentos of another Oregon.

Perrydale, founded about 1870, is down to a grade school, a church, and a century-old baroque frame house. There is no indication of the flour mill and warehouse of the dawning years of this century or of the other church that stood here then.

Between McCoy and the early Willamette River landing of Lincoln, traveling westward, are Bethel Academy, one of Oregon's pioneer secondary schools, and now a church; Bethel Cemetery, with gravestones dating back to the 1850s; a homesteader house, with widow's porch and three chimneys; and the Spring Valley Presbyterian Church and cemetery, at what was once the settlement of Zena. Down the road a piece, and clearly seen from the church, is the bell-towered Zena School, now a residence, with the bell gone.

Just a few decades ago there were few fairer sights in all Oregon than the gossamer vale below the hill upon which the Spring Valley Presbyterian Church stands. But the vale is now suburbanized, and each new house diminishes the magic. Still, not all the loveliness has disappeared, and one can be alone on the knoll for hours. As for the church, it was built in 1859, the year its bell was brought 'round the Horn. Thankfully, the structure has not been altered.

Some day—and too soon, I suppose—the store at McCoy will be torn down and then there won't be a hamlet anymore. Bethel Academy is of the past and so is Zena. But so long as the store stands and is in business (as it sometimes is), I keep returning to McCoy, just to keep within my grasp a vision of a horse-and-buggy Oregon.

A Race For Berlin

When my Oregon For the Curious tour group, which I led or taught or whatever, for Portland Community College, arrived at Waterloo on one of our regular off-the-beaten-path expeditions, I announced, "From here we'll go to Berlin."

It was the custom for the car in which I rode to lead the caravan. It was more than custom; it was ironclad rule. But on this occasion the madhatter spirit seized one of our drivers, whom we shall call Mary Smith (and may the Mary Smiths of Oregon and elsewhere forgive me), and I watched astounded as she and her passengers tore off for Berlin.

The rest of us did not find Mary that late afternoon. She returned to Portland about three hours later than we did. "I couldn't find Berlin," she moaned in exasperation. "It's on the map, but none of us saw the town."

You can get lost if you use the official highway map of Oregon in looking for some settlements. I can name more than a score of mappoints where there isn't a store or a filling station and, in several cases, not even a house. (At one mappoint there is, at the time of this writing, only a watering trough for cattle.) Berlin is a metropolis compared to some of these nothing places; it actually has a couple of houses and a church. But there are a lot of churches and houses on country pikes and Mary raced on, trying one spinoff road after another and, in her anxiety, searching several of them twice.

Like some other hamlets that have faded away, the most

This is Berlin

Marcia Workentine

interesting thing about Berlin is how it got its name. It came about in an odd way. Horse races were held near the home of JW Burrell, an open-hearted man of means. He fed spectators for free and so lavishly that soon he started worrying about going broke, with folks coming from as far as Albany for the feasts as for the races. So he began to charge for his meals and after a while, he was in the restaurant business.

What had been a quiet home bustled into Burrell's Inn. When the post office was established the locals wanted to name it Burrell's Inn, since the home was to be the post office. The department officials back in Washington thought it not fitting and, after some palavering, a compromise was reached: Berlin. About all the town ever had, apart from the inn and the church, was a store and a school, and the last two are gone.

Return to the map. What do you see in the nothing places? Gunter is just a vacant spot on a lonely road. What is at Klondike but the ghost of a long-abandoned store and a few windswept houses? Harney has been dead so long that nobody really knows where any of the former buildings stood. Kellogg is but a single farm dwelling. Only a covered bridge remains of what was Wendling. And when you come to the former Berlin Union Church, you are smack in the middle of the town that started as Burrell's Inn. Mary Smith knows that now, and you are forewarned not to look for more.

Lane Of Oregon

As the muffled procession somberly passed through the heart of Portland a washerwoman pointed to the coffin on the caisson. "Who's that?" she wondered.

"Don't you read the papers?" asked a seamstress.

"I don't have time," said the washerwoman.

"Why, it's the little doctor," the seamstress replied. "Our little doctor. He come out on that dark street in the middle of the night to care for my old man. And didn't take our money. Said we was too poor, to use money for rent, bless him."

"I've owed him money for five years," the washerwoman said. "I think it's only right to pay up. But where? To who?"

A man in a business suit standing at their elbows broke into the conversation. "It's all right. Doc burned his records. He didn't want any of his patients to be badgered for payment of debts. I know. I was his friend."

As the caisson rolled slowly on under a bright spring sun, a Yakima Indian who had traveled from his reservation lifted his face to the sky and pressed his fists against his chest. "Goodbye, friend," he whispered. "Goodbye, brother."

A middle-aged policeman sent to keep the sidewalk throngs from spilling into the street bit his lip and said over his shoulder, "There goes the most honest mayor Portland ever had."

A Pullman porter standing erect at a light pole moaned as tears salted his mouth. "Jesus, they crucified you again. I wonder who will remember you."

General Joseph Lane
Courtesy Douglas County Museum

His teenage son was puzzled. "He is remembered. There's a county named for him."

The porter's moan turned to indignation. "That's for Joseph Lane, his grandfather. Joe Lane was a bad old segregationist, a Confederate lover, a hater of Abraham Lincoln. Harry Lane," and he pointed to the passing caisson, "was the strongest voice for equality we had in Oregon. There wasn't an ounce of racial discrimination in that man."

"I seen his face. I really seen his face!" a newsboy cried to his buddy. "At the Masonic Temple. They weren't lettin' people in but I told 'em I knew Doc, he was my friend, he always talked to me, he talked to all the kids. They let me in, I seen his face, I told 'im goodbye."

A longshoreman holding his cap muttered tersely, "The bastards killed him."

As the funeral procession moved slowly to the grave, the thousands who lined the route swelled by the minute. George Norris was impressed. The Senator from Nebraska later remembered that "the streets were crowded and packed with the saddened faces of those who knew best his life's work. Their admiration for him seemed to be unbounded, the sorrow that was manifested cannot be measured. Men and women came from all over the state of Oregon to attend the funeral. In the few minutes I had to mingle with the crowd I talked with three different people who came a hundred and fifty miles to be present on this occasion. Not one of them had ever seen Senator Lane. They knew him by reputation only. They knew that he always stood for what in his own heart he believed to be right, and that during his whole life, he had always been fighting an uphill battle for those who were oppressed. They knew that when attended his funeral, they would not be able to gain admission to the temple where the services were held. They knew that in all likelihood, they would not be able to even look upon the face of the man whom they honored and loved. They knew that all they could do would be to stand on the sidewalk, and with bowed heads watch the procession as it passed by. They knew that no gain could come to them in a material or financial way by making the sacrifices to make the trip, but they wanted to do something to show their love and admiration for the man who had lived and died for humanity's cause. They were satisfied to be permitted to visit the last resting place of the man in whom they had unbounded confidence, and for whose memory they had unmeasured love."

Not all in Portland that twenty-ninth day of May 1917 were as reverent to the deceased. In an exclusive men's club, a group of power brokers toasted Lane's death. An insurance executive leaned out of a window to rhetorically ask, "Why are they honoring that damn anti-American?" A contractor spat on the sidewalk. "Good riddance," he sneered. A banker decried, "He was bad for business, with all that baloney about the little people."

Standing alone, Charles Erskine Scott Wood, the close companion of Lane, who had come to a disagreement with him over the most important issue in their contemporary lives, shook his gray beard and asked himself, "Was he right?"

Wood, the grandest of Oregonians, had been Lane's campaign manager in the arduous and successful race for a US Senate seat in 1912, the peak year of populism in Oregon. At the funeral procession a dirt farmer from Malheur County, who had driven all day and all night to Portland, told a logger from Coos County, "Doctor Lane came out all alone in that muddy old automobile. He came right up to the house and we started talkin' like we'd knowed each other for ten years." The logger nodded with a smile clouded by moist eyes. "He came to my logging camp, too. Ate with us. Talked sense. Got every vote." "Wasn't he a downright simple fella?" exclaimed the farmer. "Genuine," said the logger.

Harry Lane
Courtesy Oregon Historical Society

Harry Lane had come to the Senate as a nominal Democrat but he had always been independent in mind and spirit. His best friends in the Senate were two nominal Republicans of the same free-wheeling, philosophical bent, Norris of Nebraska and La Follette of Wisconsin. After his death the Portland *Evening Telegram* summed up Lane's life in six headline words: "LANE TOOK ORDERS ONLY FROM LANE."

Like Norris, Lane was unassuming. Requested to submit biographical material to the Congressional Directory, Lane sent in only one line: "Harry Lane, Democrat. Term expires March 3, 1919."

As a senator, Lane continued his populist views. He did not, as a colleague recalled, "look forward as a candidate and backward when elected," nor was he the kind of senator who spent the first five years of his term serving the moneyed interests and the sixth reaching out to the people. His political agenda was anathema to the Oregon Establishment; one utility executive wrote to another that the mistake began when the people elected Lane to a second term as mayor.

Lane supported a graduated income tax, taking the Senate floor to charge that "the aristocrats of the big interests" had successfully lobbied Congress to permit the rich to conceal their income tax returns.

Pursuing his motto that justice be done "without fear or favor," Lane declared: "The plain people are open to inspection; the one-eyed Irish woman who takes in washing for a living; the old colored woman who goes on crutches to do scrubbing around these walls; it is on their behalf that we are pressing this bill, and the day will come when they ask for the accounting."

In the Senate, Lane worked hard in the fields of child labor, pure food, Indian affairs, and fisheries. In the words of Senator Gronna, Lane "believed that the natural resources should belong to the people, and that any law enacted which would deny this right was not a good law." He proposed limiting the profits of the munition makers and he was one of eight senators to support a measure that would ban the armed forces from collecting debts for private companies. He supported a measure to liberalize the immigration laws "not only for those persecuted abroad by lawless mobs because of their religious or political beliefs, but also for minorities discriminated against by the established governments of foreign nations." Often disregarding party lines, he was steadfast in support of labor and the masses of the people. He opposed the expenditure of public funds to finance the Reserve Officers' Training Corps (ROTC) in the nation's colleges and universities. The young men inculcated with militaristic thinking would, he argued, pose a threat to labor. He was staunchly against sending troops to interfere in industrial and labor disputes. And he advocated sending old men to the battlefield, "including public officials, if you please, members of this body and of the other House of Congress," and to spare the nation's youth in the first battles.

Above all, Lane championed civil liberties. For him the Constitution of the United States was sacred. When the "respectable citizens" of Portland tried to run anarchist Emma Goldman out of the city, Mayor Harry Lane protected her right to speak. As mayor he had broken the political and religious barriers that barred some applicants from municipal employment, and in the Senate he would not swerve from his beliefs.

Throughout it all, Lane and his wife, the former Lola Bailey, whom he had courted at her home on Portland's near southeast side, lived a simple life. They would have no part of Washington society and dressed as plainly as the humblest government office workers. They did not attend church and shrugged off comments that their lifestyle could injure Harry's senatorial prestige. Lane came to Washington without a car and rode the streetcars, often with his great friend, George Norris, and sometimes with two other of Lane's favorite senators, Bob La Follette and Asle Gronna.

One morning on the streetcar, Gronna informed the others that the yacht of JP Morgan had anchored in the Potomac River. Norris, the quiet plainsman, laconically commented, "I'm glad to see the government has moved to Washington at last." Lane laughed uproariously when he recounted Norris's words to his daughter.

The super-financier and metaphor of immense wealth and unbridled power in America was John Pierpont Morgan, whose family had made a killing in the Civil War by selling defective rifles to the Union Army. Morgan became Lane's symbol of financial plutocracy and social immorality. When Lane heard of Morgan's death he remarked, "I'll bet St. Peter met him at the pearly gates with a baseball bat."

Lane was both amused and irritated by the antics, stuffiness, and incessant speechifying of some of his senate colleagues. He told George Norris that his experience as superintendent of the Oregon Insane Asylum had prepared him to adapt to Congress. Once, when he thought matters had become ridiculous, he strolled up and down the aisle with a petition authorizing the turning loose of twelve Gila monsters in the Senate. When some perplexed senators challenged this odd request, Lane replied tongue-in-cheek that the bite of the Gila monster reputedly rendered the bitten speechless.

In his droll, understated manner, Lane could present his views with a clarity that, as a colleague described, "shed rays of sunlight" upon a subject.

A tribute Lane did not live to hear was made by a Southern conservative, Senator James K. Vardaman of Mississippi:

"I was impressed with the unique fact that he was

endeavoring always to serve others, rather than himself. When a public question came up for consideration . . . all he desired to know was: Is it right—is it best for the Nation—best for the great silent, slow-thinking multitude whose interest legislators are especially commissioned to protect. His love for the lowly was a divine passion. When he determined upon a course of duty he never faltered . . . He was strong enough to stand alone, which is the acid test of true greatness."

Woodrow Wilson had been reelected president in 1916, millions of voters assumed, on a pledge to keep this nation out of war. Wilson had never given that pledge but he made no effort to deny the public assumption. Indeed, according to historians Charles A. and Mary R. Beard, as far back as February, 1916 "the President was contemplating war and sounded out his party in Congress to see whether his project was acceptable."

Lane had campaigned for Wilson in 1912 and had supported Wilson again in 1916 because "he kept us out of war." But in 1916, when Wilson called upon Congress to appropriate immense sums of money for armaments, Lane balked and joined with several other senators in opposition.

Wilson's plan included a post-war strategy which would, in essence, have curtailed the spoils of victory envisaged by England and France, but the rulers of England and France knew exactly what the war was about and would not even listen to Wilson until defeat stared them in the face. Wilson, for his part, hesitated to involve this nation directly into the war until Germany renewed its submarine attacks in 1917. (Biographer Albert Lief, in his *Democracy's Norris*, echoed other historians in declaring, "In December, 1917, the Bolsheviks threw open the archives in Petrograd and indelicately disclosed the Allies' secret treaties. The holy cause was somewhat tarnished.")

In March 1917, Wilson requested Congress for authority

to arm American merchant ships. By an overwhelming majority the House quickly supported the president but the situation in the Senate was far different. There twelve senators filibustered the bill to a standstill and for their efforts were branded by interventionists as "Iscariots" and "traitors," and denounced by Wilson as "a little group of willful men, representing no opinion but their own, [that] have rendered the great government of the United States helpless and contemptible."

Wilson was wrong. He had lost his ability to listen to the people. The senators who opposed the arming of merchant ships spoke for a sizable segment—the majority in some areas—of the nation. As future senator Richard L. Neuburger observed in his biography of George Norris, polls taken throughout the midwest in the spring of 1917 showed overwhelming anti-war sentiment. In Minneapolis the vote was 8,000 to 300 for peace and in Sheboygan, Wisconsin the citizens were more decisive, 4,082 to 17.

Lane was severely criticized in the Oregon press for being one of the filibusters though he had not lifted his voice. He was, however, one of the fourteen senators opposed to Wilson's plan.

Lane sought to explain that he would have voted to arm the merchant ships if ammunition were not included in the cargoes. The transport of munitions, he declared, was an act of war and would lead to a great spillage of blood. And for what? Certainly not for anything in the interest of the nation.

Harry Lane had entered the Senate in relatively good health. For the first year he was fairly robust and physically active. He seemed to thrive on the long hours he spent serving his constituents. For him there was no such folly as overwork when it came to helping the people. Then, as the Portland *Evening Telegram* stated after his death, "The disease which finally carried him off was rapidly working its insiduous way and unknown to him was sapping his vigor and force." But that was only half the story.

Lane had come as close to adoration of Woodrow Wilson as political worship in a democratic society is possible. Even when he disagreed with Wilson his devotion to the president remained binding. Lane trusted Wilson to keep America out of war. When Wilson asked Congress to grant him authority to initiate a policy of "armed neutrality," Lane was shocked. The disillusionment, his fight for principle, and the abuse heaped upon him contributed greatly to the deterioration of his health and the loss of spirit.

Lane was accustomed to criticism. It was part of political life, but what he heard and read now was beyond all bounds of fair play. To be branded a traitor was reckless enough but to have all his family and ancestors marked as radicals was sheer madness. Guilt by blood extended back at least three generations and included Joseph Lane, the state's first territorial governor and one of Oregon's first US Senators.

The newspapers, with the Portland *Oregonian* leading the pack, tore into Lane as fierce as famished wolves. Worse yet, they did not print his statements, leaving its readers small opportunity to learn Lane's side. A Portland friend wrote Lane that most of the people with whom he discussed the vote "insist that you did exactly right. It is the newspapers that are doing most of the kicking."

Elsewhere in the nation the press was as venomous. The New York *Times*, which boasted of its fairness, said of the senators opposed to Wilson's "armed neutrality," "The odium of treasonable purpose will rest upon their names forever." The New York *Sun* called the senators "A gang of moral perverts" and the New York *World* tarnished them as "delinquents and dastards." The Cleveland *Press* went a step further and suggested execution at sunrise.

The "little people," who had voted heavily for populist candidates in 1912, stood by Lane, but many of his middle class supporters either shied away or turned against him. CES Wood urged Lane to be a good party man and stand by Wilson. Lane's family, too, begged him to leave the battle before it took his life. But Lane would not be moved, though he grew sicker and weaker.

"When his motives and his patriotism were questioned, especially by those whom he loved and in whom he had unbounded confidence, the despair of his honest heart was so great and the agony of his blighted hope so severe that he never recovered his former self," George Norris sadly told a Senate Memorial Service in September, 1917.

"Within a few weeks he was a physical wreck," Norris continued. "Those who knew him became alarmed at his condition. He alone remained tranquil and serene. Before he came to the Senate he had been a physician for many years and had reached an eminent position among his associates in that profession. His trained mind told him that death was near, but during those few weeks that followed he never once expressed a fear or showed any hesitancy to meet the end that he knew was but a few steps in advance. During those days, after he had become so weak that he could scarcely walk, and when it was not safe for him to ride in a street car, I often rode with him in a taxicab from his office to his home."

"Lane's role in the futile opposition to preparedness had become increasingly difficult," Neuburger wrote. "He was subject to spells of nausea . . . and he suspected he had Bright's disease . . . Norris watched anxiously when Lane grasped the edges of his desk with trembling hands and called on the Senate to halt the 'nefarious traffic in death-dealing devices'."

When Wilson realized he had the authority to arm the merchant ships without congressional approval he promptly did so, bringing sheer joy to the vested interests, particularly the traders and financiers whose fortunes were tied to those of the Allies. Thomas W. Lamont, a partner of Morgan and Company, later stated that a half-million US citizens, almost all of them greatly affluent and influential, had loaned money to the Allies. Patriotism was a fine rationale for their investments, handsome profits made patriotism glow.

Predictably, American cargo ships bound for Europe were sunk and the pressure upon Wilson intensified. On April 2 Wilson appeared before Congress to argue that, since Germany was now waging war against the United States, the United States should declare war upon Germany. "The right," he solemnly declared, "is more precious than peace." The response was frenzied applause which, his secretary said later, prompted a shaken Wilson to confide to his secretary: "My message today was a message of death for our young men. How strange it seems to applaud that."

The debate in both chambers of Congress was spirited. The most memorable argument was made by Senator Robert M. La Follette, who thereby earned the title, "Champion of Peace."

Why, La Follette asked, if the United States pretended to be neutral, did it not also criticize the English, who had done no less than the Germans, and sometimes first, in curtailing freedom on the high seas.

And why, he continued, if the United States was to make the world safe for democracy against Imperial Prussia, did it not lift a finger against England for its exploitation of Ireland, Egypt, and India? If Russia was still ruled by a Tsar, would this nation refuse to become a belligerent? And what about the anti-democratic nations which were aligned with England and France?

La Follette reserved his most acid scorn for the assertion that the American people were clamoring for war. "Put to the voters," he asserted, "a war resolution would be shot down by a vote of ten to one." Denouncing the contrived efforts to herd the nation into combat, he told his colleagues and the nation: "The espionage bills, the conscription bills, and other forcible military measures which we understand are being ground out of the war machinery in this country are complete proof that those responsible for this war fear that it has no popular support and that armies sufficient to satisfy the demands of the entente allies cannot be recruited by voluntary enlistments."

In his address to the Senate, Norris read a confidential letter sent by a member of the New York Stock Exchange to his customers:

"Regarding war is inevitable, Wall Street believes that it would be preferable to this uncertainty about the actual date of its commencement. Canada and Japan are at war and are more prosperous than ever. The popular view is that stocks would have a quick, clear, sharp reaction immediately upon the outbreak of hostilities, and that they would enjoy an old-fashioned bull market such as followed the outbreak of war with Spain in 1898 . . ."

The letter from the New York stockbroker had been given to Norris by Senator William S. Kenyon of Iowa, who was anti-war but afraid to say so because he feared a rise of pro-war fever in his state.

On the eve of the war resolution vote, Lane told Norris that Bright's disease had taken its toll and he had only a few months to live. As La Follette guided Lane through the Senate Office Building, Lane whispered, "I guess this is sundown patrol for me, Bob, and for the peace hopes, too." Lane's friends knew that he had been hemorrhaging and that increasingly he experienced spells of blindness, and their hearts went out to him.

Lane had prepared a speech but he was too sick to deliver it. The manuscript lay on his desk as he coughed blood into his handkerchief, and several specks escaped to the pages and splotched them. When Norris, who had been tensely observing Lane, crossed the aisle to ask if he could do anything to help, Lane at first did not recognize him.

U.S. SENATE ADOPTS WAR RESOLUTION

Declaration Made That State of War Exists With Germany by 82 to 6.

LANE AGAIN VOTES "NO"

House Will Act Today—Capitol
Silent When Momentous Question Is Carried—Stirring
Debate Lasts All Day.

(Continued From First Page.)

of German interests in this country,
had been present.

Secretary McAdoo was on the floor
during the last few hours of the debate.

Applause Is Lacking.

As the last name was called and
the clerk answered the vote, 82 to
6, there was hardly a murmur of applause.

The great crowd was awed by the
solemnity of the occasion and sobered
by the speeches they had heard.

After the vote was announced the
Senate remained in session only a few
minutes. The galleries began to
empty at once, and the Senators
themselves, tired out by the long day,
left quickly. The Senate adjourned
until noon Friday to await action by
the House.

Six Opponents All of "Doxes."

All six of the Senators who voted
against the resolution were members
of the group of 12 which defeated the
armed neutrality bill at the last session. There was no attempt to filibuster this time, however, and most of the
11 hours of debate was consumed by
champions of the resolution.

Of the other six opponents of armed
neutrality, Senators Cummins, Kenyon
and Kirby voted for the resolution tonight. Senators O'Gorman, Clapp and
Works, the remaining three, retired to
private life at the end of the last session.

"Lane Again Votes 'No'."

The *Oregonian*

Tenaciously, though crushed in body and spirit, Lane clung to his seat during the day and night of debate so that, in the words of Alfred Lief, "he might register his eternal nay."

It was past eleven o'clock on the night of April 4, 1917, when Wilson's request for a declaration of war was passed by a vote of eighty-two to six. The six were: William J. Stone of Missouri, chairman of the Senate Foreign Relations Committee and a man who once prized his close association with Woodrow Wilson; Robert M. La Follette of Wisconsin; the courtly James K. Vardaman of Mississippi; George Norris of Nebraska; Asle J. Gronna, the solid, walrus-mustached prairie populist of North Dakota; and Harry Lane of Oregon.

("It is probably true that if the ballot had been a secret one, and it had been known that America was to send a conscript army overseas, the vote would have been closer," noted Stanford professor Thomas A. Bailey in his *Diplomatic History of the American People*.)

The six senators swiftly found themselves ostracized and shadowed. Norris said: "All manner of things were attempted to bring about [our] downfall and ruin. . . . I have had my office searched, my life traced since I left the cradle. My home in my absence has been hounded by secret sleuths, sometimes of the government, trying to find something that might be used to break me down."

All six suffered terribly, politically and personally, for their conviction, but their honor was redeemed by history and, in the case of La Follette and Gronna, by sympathetic sons, one of whom was to follow his father's footsteps into the Senate and the other to be elected to one of the highest offices in his state.

The House debate made a footnote in history when Jeanette Rankin of Montana, the first woman to sit in Congress, declared in her debut speech, "I want to stand by my country but I cannot vote for war."

The House approved the war resolution 373 to 50. Only one of the Congressional opponents of war represented an industrial state in the East, where the industrial and banking interests were strongest.

La Follette and several other anti-war legislators predicted what was already happening, that the war, in the words of the Beards, made "several thousand millionaires in the course of two years." The war also "[poured] out billions in extra dividends frequently in the form of stock, thereby enabling holders in effect to escape taxes on income."

Anti-war sentiment had early on been very firm but as the skillfully-crafted federal propaganda machine and the uninhibited media rolled into high gear, capitalizing on the merchant ship sinkings, the flags flew higher and the drums beat louder. Jingoism swept the nation, engulfing Oregon in the frenzy. The playing of German music, including Beethoven, became suspect; teaching German in high schools and colleges came to an end, either through edict or self-preservation; the vocabulary was altered: a Hamburger steak now appeared on the menu as Liberty steak; instead of calling for sauerkraut, people asked for Liberty cabbage; those stricken with German measles now found they had Liberty measles; a dachsund was renamed a Liberty pup.

Although German-Americans thundered their loyalty to the flag they were looked upon as alien to American patriotism and subjected to various forms of harrassment, including loss of jobs, a break in friendships, and surveillance by neighbors and civic authorities. The incarceration of Japanese-Americans in World War II reminded those who recalled history of the earlier persecution of the home-bred "krauts."

Despite the calumny and hatred heaped upon Lane after the war vote of April 4—far more vicious than the lashing he took for his opposition to "armed neutrality"—many small farmers and working people throughout the state stood

BANKERS RAP LANE

Oregonians in San Francisco Talk of Plans for Recall.

STATE NOT REPRESENTED

J. C. Ainsworth and Mr. Olmstead Say Vote Against War Does Not Show Feelings of Any Number of People of State.

SAN FRANCISCO, April 5.—(Special.)—Indignant at the action of United States Senator Harry Lane, of Oregon, in voting as one of the six "wilful men" against the war resolution at Washington last night, a group of Oregon bankers, who are here to plead for a branch of the Federal Reserve Bank at Portland, prepared tonight to take action to repudiate, if not recall Senator Lane.

Headed by Emery Olmstead, vice-president of the Northwestern National Bank, of Portland, and J. C. Ainsworth, president of the United States National Bank, of the same city, the Oregonians held an indignation meeting at the Palace Hotel.

"We want it made plain that Senator Lane does not by his vote represent any part of his constituency," said Mr. Olmstead.

"We are absolutely disgusted with him and will resent his disgraceful action with considerable force. If the legal machinery makes it feasible, you can be assured that Lane will be speedily recalled."

Mr. Ainsworth added his protest to that of Mr. Olmstead.

Both men are directors of the Portland Chamber of Commerce.

"Lane's vote represents his personal whim," said Mr. Ainsworth. "It represents no part of the public sentiment in Oregon, and we will leave no stone unturned to vindicate our loyalty and patriotism before the country."

"Bankers Rap Lane"

The *Oregonian*

with Lane, though unyielding attempts to silence them were waged by the captains of power.

"The bankers and utility company presidents voiced bitter denunciation of Oregon's junior senator," wrote historian E. Kimbark MacColl. One of the bankers took the lead in launching a campaign to recall Lane. The *Oregonian*, gratuitously donning the mantle of spokesman for the state, derisively commented that not only were the people of Oregon "ashamed of Harry Lane for what he has done" but that "the people of Oregon are ashamed of themselves for having sent Harry Lane to the United States Senate." Lane received in the mail threats of violence and German medals collected at Oregon Agricultural College in Corvallis, Lane's birthplace.

"Never since or afterward has an Oregonian been so crucified," observed MacColl. "The hatred fomented against Lane was without parallel in the history of the far West," wrote Neuburger.

The bitterness sweeping onto Washington from Oregon played havoc upon Lane. "The emotional strain of that wave of calumny added to his illness was too much for Lane," reported Neuburger. "Norris and La Follette urged his family and office staff to withhold the defamatory letters from him. One morning Lane called for his own mail, and after reading several letters from former friends denouncing him as a 'villain' and 'scoundrel,' he collapsed and had to be taken home . . . In the evenings Norris sat for hours at Lane's bedside, sadly describing the ceaseless march of the nation into war."

Two days after the war resolution passed, Lane engaged in a colloquy with Senator Reed of Missouri over a bill to utilize town lots for food. To Reed's remarks that food produced by town lots was "only a drop in the bucket," Lane replied with all his feeble strength that "Hundreds of thousands of acres of unused lands all over the country are not being cultivated. That is the fortification that in the long run will save this country."

He was never again to speak in the Senate. He came to the chamber only once or twice afterward, sat down, stayed a short while, and left, but he continued his work at his office up to the day he left Washington.

"He had only a few weeks to live, and he told Norris he wanted to see the snow-topped mountains of his State before he died," wrote Neuburger.

"Norris was at the Washington railroad station at midnight to say good-bye for the last time . . . Lane, pale and gasping, leaned on the shoulder of one of his daughters. He took Norris's hand between both of his own and managed a final smile. 'Good-bye, George! We will meet again,' he said."

As the mournful train sped toward the sunset rim of the continent, Lane continued to weaken. At the train's last stop he was carried from his coach and hurried to St. Francis Hospital in San Francisco. Several days later, at 11:45 P.M., Wednesday, May 23, 1917, seven weeks after he had cast his fateful vote, he died. The next night his body was shipped to Portland aboard the Oregon Express.

Overnight the newspapers changed their tune, though most remembered him gently only as mayor. The *Evening Telegram* was tenderest in tribute: "Not an old man as the world counts the years that come to those who reach manhood's golden time, he had to fight against a weakened constitution nearly his whole life. There passed away last night a kind and fearless Oregonian."

As the draped caisson rolled on through the heart of Portland, bearing the body of the sixty-two-year-old Harry Lane, the numbers on the sidewalk increased, with people hastening to the route from every street. A dusty, overalled man, pushing himself to see the procession not yet passing his point, gasped, "Am I late? Come down from Wallowa County. No time to change clothes. God bless you, Harry."

SENATOR LANE, ILL, ORDERED TO REST

EFFECT OF RECENT STRAIN ARE SERIOUS.

Oregon Man Loses 15 Pounds in Few Weeks and Seems to Be in General Breakdown.

OREGONIAN NEWS BUREAU, Washington, April 7.—Senator Harry Lane, of Oregon, is seriously ill. Today, on advice of physicians, he went to Takoma Sanitarium, in the suburbs of Washington, for a complete rest.

He was advised to give up his duties in the Senate a week ago, but refused to absent himself until the war resolution had been disposed of and he had opportunity to register his vote. He remained in the Senate throughout the long session Wednesday against the advice of his physicians, as he had determined to go on record against the declaration of war.

Senator Lane has been under considerable strain of late and shows the effects of it. He has lost 15 pounds in the past few weeks and is in a much weakened condition. His physicians have insisted that he must have complete rest.

The immediate nature of the Senator's ailment is not known. It appears to be a general breakdown.

Lane reported seriously ill in the *Oregonian,* April 8, 1917

"CITY ALL HERE
and
IT'S ALL TRUE" 6 O'CLOCK EDITION

Oregon

VOL. XVI. NO. 10. PORTLAND, OREGON, THURSDAY EV

SENATOR LANE SUCCUMBS IN SAN FRANCISCO

End Came Last Night as Result of Complete Nervous Breakdown Suffered While on Duty in Washington.

HAD LONG RECORD OF HIGH PUBLIC SERVICE

Was Honest, Uncompromising Fighter for Ideals He Considered Right.

***

Funeral to Be Tuesday.

San Francisco, Cal., May 24. —(U. P.) Accompanied by Mrs. Lane, the body of Senator Harry Lane of Oregon, who died in San Francisco last night, will be shipped to the family home in Portland aboard the Oregon express, leaving here this evening. A delegation from the United States senate leaves Washington tonight for Portland, arriving there Monday, and on Tuesday the funeral will be held. None of the details for the services in Portland will be arranged until Mrs. Lane reaches Portland.

***

San Francisco, May 24 — United States Senator Harry Lane of Oregon died at St. Francis hospital here at 11:45 o'clock Wednesday night.

The senator's death came after several months of suffering from a general nervous breakdown, complicated by high blood pressure.

Senator Lane arrived in San Francisco several days ago a very sick man, and went almost immediately to the hospital, where he was attended by Dr. H. A. L. Ryfkogel.

The senator's wife was at his bedside at the end.

Dr. Harry Lane, junior United States Senator from Oregon, former mayor of Portland, former superintendent of the Oregon State hospital and lifelong Democrat, was born at Corvallis, Or., August 28, 1855. He was the son of Nat H. Lane, a pioneer merchant, and grandson of General Joseph Lane, the first territorial governor of Oregon. He was graduated from the Willamette university in 1876. Completing a course in the medical school of the university he took a post graduate course at the College of Physicians and Surgeons of New York.

Of his immediate family Dr. Lane is

(Concluded on Page Ten, Column One)

LIBERTY LOAN PLANS FOR CAMPAIGN WILL BE ANNOUNCED SOON

D R. HARRY LANE, junior United States senator from Oregon, who died in a hospital in San Francisco, where he had been taken while on the way home from the national capital, as result of nervous breakdown caused by overwork in behalf of his constituents.

HIGH TRIBUTE PAID LANE B CHAMBERLA

Colleague of Late Se Praises His Innate Hor and Integrity of Purpo Every Capacity.

OREGON CONGRESSME SAY LOSS IS PEOP

Always the Friend of Ma and Ready to Help O gon Interests.

Washington, May 24.—(WAS) TON BUREAU OF THE JOURN General expressions of regret ov death of Senator Lane were hea the capitol today. His likeable were commented upon, and those have been most strongly oppos his views in the late struggle h senate joined with those who with him in a tribute to his sin of purpose and conscientious disc of duty.

United States Senator Chamb paid tribute to his late colleag follows:

"My acquaintance with Harry began when I was attorney ge of Oregon and he was superinte of the insane asylum. We were appointed of Governor Pennoyer though I cannot say that our rela have been intimate, they have cordial and friendly.

"Knowing his innate honesty integrity of purpose, I supported when he was a candidate for of Portland, publicly and priv and again when he became a cand for United States senate.

Integrity Never Questioned.

"I came in closer contact with in Washington than ever before while I have differed from him radically on many great questio have not at any time believe was actuated by any other than highest patriotic motives. His d ences with his friends in wh official capacity he has served never made any of them questio integrity.

"I thought it unfortunate that differed from the president and great majority of his colleague the senate at the time of the ship controversy. But even in controversy, no one questioned honesty of his views or his pu but felt that in a great national he only erred in judgment.

Acted on Conscience.

"The charge made against him some of those who agreed with at that time, that he engaged filibuster, I think, did him injust

(Concluded on Page Ten, Column Fiv

EIGHT SENATORS WILL LEAVE WASHINGTON FOR OREGON TONIGHT

Senate Adjourns Out of Respect for Lane; House to Send Committee, Too.

Washington, May 24.—(I. N. S.)— Out of respect to Senator Harry Lane of Oregon, who died last night in San Francisco, the senate adjourned immediately after convening today. A committee of eight senators was appointed to attend the funeral.

Senator Chamberlain of Oregon announced the death of his colleague to the senate.

"There was no citizen more

GOVERNOR HAS MIND MADE UP AS TO HIS CHOICE FOR SENATOR

Feeling at State Capital Is That Charles L. McNary Will Succeed Lane.

Salem, Or., May 24.— Governor Withycombe, in a statement given out today, announced that he has definitely determined upon his choice for the United States senatorship to fill the vacancy caused by the death last night of Senator Harry Lane, and he requests all other aspirants for the place and their friends to refrain from dis-

AUSTRIAN LINES ARE BROKEN BY ITALIAN BY TERRIFIC ATTA

Oregon Journal announces death of Harry Lane.

A suffragist turned to her husband. "He appointed the first woman health officer in Portland when he was mayor." A few yards away another woman called to the coffin, "The animals will pray for you, Doc." "Why?" she asked. "Because he was against caging animals," she replied.

A bricklayer overheard the owner of a gambling house mutter, "Should've happened sooner," and turned angrily, his face flushed. The gambler slid into the crowd.

A stumpy bow-legged man from Lake County sniffled and brushed a tear away with the sleeve of his denim shirt. "You were all we had, Harry." He turned to his partner. "Come on, Cowboy. We paid our respects. It's a long drive back to the ranch."

In an ornate downtown office building two immaculately-dressed men in a wainscoted suite looked out of their fifth floor window. "I don't see what they saw in him," one sneered. "A bunch of idiots," the other agreed.

A pair of Wobblies watched the procession from a street corner. "He was no radical," said one. "He was a radical to the war profiteers," said the other.

Charles Erskine Scott Wood, fingering his gray beard, wondered to himself, "Was he right?" Had he lived a few more years beyond his death in 1944 he would have read that Bob La Follette's son, Phil, had declared on the Senate floor that his father—and the other five—had been proven right. No senator arose to object.

At Grand Avenue and Stark Street, on the east side of the Willamette River, Lane's body was transferred to a hearse and taken to Lone Fir Cemetery, accompanied only by those invited to attend the private services at the grave.

"Beneath the spreading branches of the ancient cedar, in Lone Fir Cemetery, we laid to rest all that was mortal of Harry Lane," George Norris recalled. "Hundreds of his admirers whom he never knew visited this spot day after day for weeks after the funeral, and brought fragrant flowers to deposit upon the fresh mound."

Grave of Harry Lane in Lone Fir Cemetery, Portland
Ralph Friedman

Down in Jackson County, on a small farm near the California-Oregon border, which was lost during the Great Depression, John S. Byrne sat down at the kitchen table the night he heard of Lane's death, and by the light of a kerosene lamp composed a poem which he left with his children:

IN MEMORY OF HARRY LANE

All honor to that grand old man,
Our own true native son,
Far better that a hundred such
Did sit in Washington.

For those few names in future
Will be honored more by far
Than all that cringed the craven knee
And knuckled to the Czar.

The slimey "sheets" that branded you
A traitor to your State
Were forced to pay you homage
Though that homage came too late.

The greylings, who exempted,
Brought this war upon our land,
Bear the dollar marks of profit
Where their waist lines do expand.

Their patriotic mouthings
Are the merest kind of sham,
For they will charge in battle
As they charge our Uncle Sam.

They will never smell the powder smoke
Nor hear the dying groans,
Where the human flesh is rendered
And the vultures pick the bones.

All honor to you, Harry,
Though your sands of life have run,
You helped start a ball a rolling
And the fight is just begun.

As the stoutest hearts are needed now,
Our loss we ill afford,
For the mighty change is coming,
Whether peaceful or by sword.

Though you did not bear allegiance
To the course we're striving for,
Your actions coincided
With our views upon the war.

Though the Lord has called your spirit
And your clay to Mother Earth,
I am proud to call you Brother
From the state that gave you birth.

When Mothers' arms are folded
'Round some token of her son,
And an orphan's childish prattle
Mocks the laurels dearly won,

When brother kneels by brother
On the smoky blood-soaked plain,
Millions then will bow in anguish
And remember Harry Lane.

A Balanced View Of A Rocky Situation

A plea may be a strange way to start a story, but it is the only way I know how to write of the Balanced Rocks of the Metolius.

Hear me out, and you will understand.

Countless times I have said that I deliberately omitted from the last edition of *Oregon for the Curious* such remote precious places, nature-made or man-made, that for lack of protection were subject to vandalism.

I had a bitter experience to pull me to that conclusion. In the first and second editions I listed a site of ancient Indian drawings. By the time I began work on the third edition this priceless primitive art, this mark of history, had been completely effaced.

The Balanced Rocks of the Metolius were not new to me. I first saw them many years ago. A forest ranger at Bend had talked me out of putting them into the first and second editions of *Oregon for the Curious*, and of course I kept them out of the third edition. "They're impossible to protect unless you have guards around them twenty-four hours a day," he said. "Vandals come out here and shoot at the rocks with their rifles, and a bunch of rocks have been knocked off. If publicity gets out, the place is doomed. You won't find it on any map, and that's the way we like it."

When my friend Norman Oyler tracked down the Balanced Rocks I persuaded him to keep the area a secret. He agreed, as I knew he would, for Norman is as much a preservationist of the unusual and the memorable as anyone I know.

Balanced Rocks of the Metolius
Ralph Friedman

Then one day I saw in a Portland book store a photo of the Balanced Rocks on the cover of a travel text. Inside were more photos and some text. I was sick to my stomach. "My God," Norman gasped when I phoned. "Now comes desecration."

So the word was out and, as expected, newspaper articles followed. And down came more of the treasures.

My plea is not to keep away from the area—that would be fruitless—but to lend yourself to its survival.

The first white to report on the eroded slabs of volcanic debris wrote that they were "perched on pinnacles of twenty to thirty feet in height, and having a less diameter at the summit than the rock they sustain." He was physician-naturalist-geologist John Strong Newberry, on an exploration of the upper Deschutes country in the late summer of 1855.

There is plentiful suggestion in his account that Newberry was fascinated by the discovery, but it is as important to note that he did not include this find as one of the sketches of prominent landmarks in his classic 1855 railroad survey volume. Perhaps by omission he was trying to tell us something.

Probably the next white people to come upon the large, flat, slightly tilted, pinnacles-perched rocks on the north-facing slope of the Metolius River Canyon were homesteaders who founded the village of Grandview, eight miles eastward.

Now the formation has a new set of neighbors. Here on this high and otherwise silent desert is a housing development, as out of place as the rocks only a few minutes drive away. The few people I talked to there hoped I wouldn't spread the news. "We keep it quiet," said a man in retirement. "You know what people can do to places." He should know.

Obscured from the road in a shaley cavity, the Balanced Rocks of the Metolius make up one of the most intriguing geological settings in the state. Incongruous with the landscape in all directions, the rocks seem a trick of nature, as puzzling as Elisha's seven miracles of assistance. In general, the image is that of large toads sunning upon gray stumps, or of overgrown, tilted mushrooms, or of Stonehenge pillars capped by some rowdy giant. Take what imagery you wish, or come up with your own.

I have no inclination to go into further geologic detail, which I would borrow from persons far more learned in that field that I will ever be. Beauty has its own rationale—and for me the rocks are beautiful.

Balanced Rocks

Ralph Friedman Collection

Rather, I would leave you with this supplication: Give to the Balanced Rocks the reverence for life you give to yourself. This land needs both.

A View Not So Grand

The homesteaders came to a plateau of stubborn sage strewn with lava rocks that looked up to the ochre contours of the eastern slope of the misty Cascade Mountains.

As the newcomers toiled, breaking their backs and their hearts to clear the land, the sagebrush and the rocks became wicked and evil to them and, like Jezebel and Ahab, deserved each other, but the homesteaders deserved neither, they thought, and cursed both.

Below them was a river, running stealthily as a sinner fearful of stoning, and guarded from intrusion by volcanic walls and steep embankments. The water was the giver of life, but they did not have the means to capture it, and the river remained a taunt to their hopes. They left in defeat, one at a time and two at a time, scarcely turning back for a last glimpse of the homes they had built of the wood they had hauled from miles away or erected, uneven layer upon layer, with the boulders that covered their fields, or to see the simple frame schoolhouse that had bound them into a community. Those who left bitter would, in their scornful last looks, have turned the houses into pillars of salt.

Some of the wooden homes, and the schoolhouse, too, were torn down by remaining homesteaders for wood to feed their stoves or for cellar roofs and sides. It was the cannibalism of the high desert: Those who stayed took from those who departed; and when the next wave of homesteaders called it quits, those who hung on appropriated the belongings of the earlier pirates. And so it

A remnant of Grandview

Ralph Friedman

went until the last of the homesteaders moved away, leaving behind only their own homes, barns, and cellars.

The wind came like a hawk, wrenching loose in hungry searching or patient play, one plank after another, and dropping each to the ground, where the sun and the snow gnawed like vultures at the boards. The rain and the snow and the wind loosened a rock that was part of a roof, and after a while it thumped down onto what had been a floor. The adjoining rocks, with less to hold on to, also fell, and in due time the entire roof was gone.

So that is Grandview today—the roofless outline of a stone house, a scarecrow flap of boards that had been a home built of wood, a hollow cellar with dry throat, and some rock formations to indicate where other dwellings stood, upon the dead sea of a pilgrim dream.

Once a part of Grandview

Ralph Friedman

Grave Trail From Ladd Hill

Away, I'm bound away
Across the wide Missouri.
          Popular Emigrant Folk Song

A gravestone in a long-unused family plot on a hill west
of Wilsonville opened for me another page of Oregon lore.
It was through Elmer Kruse, a descendant of a pioneer who
fits only vaguely in the mainstream of this story, that I
found the flat, deeply weathered marker, sculpted in the
flowery style of the mid-nineteenth century.

A postal card from a man I did not know suggested I see
Elmer Kruse if I wanted a good yarn on Oregon history.
Mrs. Kruse, who answered the phone, gave me specific
directions, otherwise I might still be looking for their home.
Elmer Kruse and his wife told me of the tiny burial
ground—and that, when I found it, started me off on a
research trail leading to this brief account of one of Oregon's
most illustrious extended families.

Start in 1630 with George Geer coming to America and
establishing a home in Connecticut among the earliest
settlers of New England. Five generations later, in 1795,
Joseph Carey Geer was born, also in Connecticut. Without
his venturing West there might not have been a Geer clan in
Oregon. It was his grave I was seeking on the bluff out of
Wilsonville.

At seventeen Geer served in the War of 1812. Six years
later, a husband and father, he moved to Ohio. He liked

being a farmer there; the fruitful loam of Ohio felt good to him. But in 1840 he was once again caught up in the westering surge and took off for Knox County, Illinois. In 1847, when he was fifty-two and long past the time when most men dare, Geer set out on one more journey—across the wide Missouri for Oregon. Now he and his wife Mary had ten children. On the Willamette he said, "We go no further," and staked a claim on Ladd Hill, his property extending to the river. Most of the children, full-grown, went off on their own.

Ralph Carey Geer, one of Joe's sons, was thirty-one years old and ten years married when he reached Oregon. Settling in the Waldo Hills, south of Silverton, he started a nursery business with apple and pear seedlings carried across the plains. Later he became a schoolteacher, captain of a voluntary military company, member of the territorial legislature, a sheep grower (importing his stock from England), and a Willamette Valley pioneer in flax growing. But he and his wife, the former Mary Catherine Willard, are best remembered as the grandparents of Homer Davenport, the celebrated cartoonist.

One of Ralph and Mary's four daughters, Florinda, married Timothy Davenport, and in 1867 Homer was born, in a house which stood solid for more than a hundred years before burning to the ground. The Geer home, less than a mile away, where Homer spent much of his youth, is still intact and as graceful of line as ever.

More fame, however obliquely, was to reflect upon the founding Geers when a daughter, Ianthe, married John Kruse, the first man to put a steam-driven vessel on the river above Willamette Falls. His first abode was a log cabin, which can only be placed now by a giant fir looking down upon the Willamette. Eventually the fir became known as a "Witness Tree," because it bore the initials of the first surveyors. A few feet from where the cabin arose, John

Kruse completed a home in 1857. It had been remodeled when we saw it but on both sides and in the cellar the brick foundations of the original dwelling remained. Standing in the cellar I had a feeling I was at least a century back in time, but facing the 1857 Kruse house shone the very modern suburban home of John's grandson, Elmer Kruse.

Herman Johnson Geer, another of Joe's sons, was nineteen when he crossed to Oregon with the family. A year later, in 1848, he married Cynthia Ann Eoff, who in 1851 gave birth to Theodore Thurston Geer.

Herman was a farmer, too, and made it well in Marion County, especially in fruit raising, but he had his father's wanderlust. After parting from his wife, he moved way beyond the Cascades to Union County, living there until his death in 1903.

Theodore Thurston is the Geer most familiar to historians. Born in the Waldo Hills, he was the first native Oregonian elected governor of the state. Like most youngsters of his time, he took on adult work and responsibilities as soon as he became a teenager. At fourteen he put aside his school books to become a farmhand for his Uncle Ralph and then followed his father to Union County, where he helped Herman establish a successful nursery.

Theodore was twenty-five and with no more formal schooling than he had had ten years before, he returned to Marion County and took up farming on a half section of fertile land. Like Abraham Lincoln whom he vastly admired, Theodore read books by firelight and lamplight, argued politics with his neighbors, and lent a shoulder to every community enterprise. If there was a man needed to speak up for a new school or to organize the farmers in improving a road or to get a social evening started, the finger always seemed to point to T T Geer.

He had all the characteristics to put him in good stead with the rural folks. He was simple of word and fluent of tongue, honest and judicious, and he could change the directions of sentiment with an anecdote whose truth struck to the heart while tickling the ribs. In 1880 his neighbors rewarded Geer by sending him to the state legislature.

On the floor of the Oregon House of Representatives, Theodore Thurston Geer was a champion of his people, the farmers, and a knight of the small towns. He represented the strongest traditions of country life, and before his first term was up he was virtually assured of a second. He served four terms, all told, the last as speaker of the house. In 1889 he was elected governor on the Republican ticket and was popular with the citizenry, but he declined to run for a second term.

His service to the state, however, did not end with the close of his political career. For two years following his gubernatorial term he was editor of the *Oregon Statesman* in Salem; then he moved to Pendleton to edit the *Tribune* for three years.

In 1908 Geer crossed the state again, this time to Portland, where he spent the rest of his days writing. His *Fifty Years in Oregon*, published in 1911, is still regarded as one of the great books on the settling of the state.

As for Joseph Carey Geer, whom we left behind while we pursued his offspring, tragedy befell him soon after reaching his destination. *Transactions*, the journal of the Oregon Pioneer Association, recalled of Geer: "He had a very hard trip across the plains. His wife had been very sick with winter fever in Illinois, and on the plains she had a severe shock of palsy which made her nearly helpless, and being a very large woman, it would have worn out an ordinary man to lift her in and out of the wagon." She died a few weeks after arriving in Oregon.

Almost two years later Geer married Mrs. Elizabeth Smith, a widow. She bore him three children and died less than six years after she wed.

Gravestone of Mary Geer before erosion took its toll.
Phoebe L Friedman

Geer Cemetery. Joseph Geer lies under circled star. Mary Geer's grave is to the left.

Marcia Workentine

Within fifteen months Geer was at the altar again, this time with Mrs. Mary Strong, another widow. As his first wife had been a burden of love in her last months, so was Geer at the care and mercy of his third wife. The year they were married he had his eyes operated on for cataracts. The "surgeon" was a quack posing as an occulist, and Geer was totally blind for his remaining twenty-five years. He died August 28, 1881, at the age of eighty-six years, six months, and twenty-three days. A meticulous man, he would liked to have the exact span of his life measured.

We found Joseph Carey Geer on the bluff about five miles down from Wilsonville, above the juncture of the Wilsonville and Ladd Hill Roads. At the end of a stiff hike up the steep slope that was a ladder of underbrush traps, we reached the cemetery. In a corner of the shrouded burial ground a pile of broken stones weighed down the marker of Mary Weeks, another Oregon overlander. She was one of the three dead locatable—and perhaps all there was here. Joseph lay under a huge stone slab whose lettering had been effaced by more than a hundred years of wind, rain, sun, and snow. Only a veteran's symbol—War of 1812— identified his grave. Next to him, under a ponderous rock sheet whose lettering we could still decipher, was the grave of Joe's first wife, Mary. She had crossed many a difficult and lonesome river on the long and painful western journey, and now the eyes of the stone that lay across her mound were fixed upon the last of the rivers, the Willamette.

The Cosmopolitan Oregon

Welcome to cosmopolitan Oregon.

We have within our borders Lebanon, Holland, Norway, Palestine, and Jordan.

We also have—or have had—Nice, Berlin, Waterloo, London, Paris, Pompeii, Rome, Madras, Florence, Dundee, Glasgow, Toledo, Athena, and Joppa, giving us French, German, British, Italian, Indian, Scottish, Spanish, Greek, and Holy Land flavors.

Everybody knows Lebanon, the biggest town in eastern Linn County, but the other country places aren't as familiar.

Holland, in Josephine County two miles off the state road between Cave Junction and Oregon Caves National Monument, is just a rural outpost now, a long way from when it was connected with mining on the Althouse River. (Actually, alas, Holland was named for postmaster James E. Holland.)

Norway, six miles south of Coquille on Oregon 42, is for real. It was settled by Norwegians and as early as 1876 had a post office. There are far fewer people in the village now than there were in 1915, when the population numbered 125 and Norway had a creamery, school, and private electric lighting plant.

Palestine is a pastoral serenity encircling a church a few miles west of the road from West Albany to Buena Vista. Unlike the Holy Land of today, Oregon's Palestine has no Arabs, no Jews, no tourists, and no violence.

There was another Palestine in present Portland, not far

from Mount Tabor, named for a biblical landmark. It had a post office from 1891 to 1903 and was so far removed from downtown Portland at the time that newcomers to the big city were advised by local jokesters that they could see camels if they hied themselves out to Palestine.

All of the places in the state called Jordan, except in Linn County, were named after people. In Linn County a glorious vale south of the North Santiam River inspired the legendary circuit rider, Joab Powell, to name this dazzling scene for the Valley of the Jordan in the Holy Land.

Nice, across Alsea Bay from Waldport, honors jetty builder and salmon packer Harry Nice, not the sunny beach resort in southern France—but, we can dream.

Berlin is a telescoping of Burrell's Inn, done by the post office people in Washington, DC. During World War II some residents wanted to change the name but cooler heads prevailed. All that remains of Berlin now, a few miles east of Waterloo, is a country church, unless you count the cemetery out in the brush.

Waterloo was called Harris Ranch when the post office was established in 1874. A year later, after a whopping victory in a court case over land ownership, a local pundit hailed the verdict a "Waterloo" and so Harris Ranch became Waterloo. (At least there's a faint reference to history here.)

There's a London peak in Josephine County but it was named for Jack London. The hamlet of London, a few miles south of Cottage Grove Reservoir, started life as Amos in 1898. Four years later the post office was moved two miles and became London. No one seems to know why, but let's presume it was a salute to Great Britain's major metropolis.

Don't go looking for Paris, which was between Minnie and Horton and north of Alpha in northwestern Lane County. I spent half a day trying to track it down and I'm not sure if I found the right place. The post office, in a farmer's house, was named for George E. Parris; when the folks in Washington, DC, removed an "r" they came up with Paris, Oregon. Very enchanting—but nothing more.

Pompeii, near the present site of Government Camp, had a little more authenticity to it. It was named by a veteran Mount Hood guide because of the volcanic soil in the area.

Rome, in the southeast corner of the state, was so-called because the hills a few miles north reminded an early cattleman of the ruined temples of ancient Rome.

Madras, the seat of Jefferson County, is the real thing. No one is sure what inspired the name but it is obvious it had a distinct reference to the city in India.

I regret to report that Florence, on the coast, was named not for the beautiful Italian city but for an early Lane County state senator, AB Florence. (Now that you know the truth, hold the secret tight lest our sophistication melt away, showing us up as strictly provincial types.)

We have better luck with Dundee, the nut and wine town in Yamhill County. It was named by the 1874 arrival of William Reid, who hailed from Dundee, Scotland. (I was in that Dundee some years ago and can rightly tell you there is a big difference between the two places—but both have that fresh splash of greenness.)

Glasgow Point, on the east side of Coos Bay, was originally Jordan Point. Who came up with the latter name is a mystery to me but I like to think the person was thinking of Glasgow, Scotland, to which I also have been and which didn't at all remind me of anything around Coos Bay, except maybe the working class ambiance.

Toledo, just east of Newport, was named not for Toledo, Spain, but for Toledo, Ohio. Still, Toledo, Ohio derived its name from Toledo, Spain—so that's good enough.

Athena, north of Pendleton, was not named for Athens, Greece, but it is still Greek in name origin. A local school principal suggested it be called after a great goddess of

Sunday in Nashville

Ralph Friedman

Greek mythology. That seemed—and seems now—strange for a prairie town that still looks like it's out of an Edna Ferber novel—but nobody has ever objected.

Then, there's Joppa, once a post office about eight miles northwest of Forest Grove, probably somewhere near Gales Creek. Now, that was named for an ancient seaport in the Holy Land—and if it's long gone, at least Oregon did its best to be worldly.

For US big cities, the towns of Oregon have—or had—

Kansas City

Phoebe L Friedman

among other names, St. Paul, Boston Mills, St. Louis, Nashville, and Kansas City.

St. Paul is by far the largest, with a thundering 400 population. Boston Mills, east of Shedd, isn't any more. (The rocky mound once called Bunker Hill still stands.) St. Louis, a lively burg back in the 1860s, is down to a church. Nashville, between Logsden and Eddyville, barely casts a shadow in the vacancy of a county road. And if you know you're in Kansas City you've hit it lucky. Every time a road marker is put up it's ripped off. Which means, of course, that everything is up to date in Kansas City.

Unreal Encounters

After some troublesome surgery I was given a drug to check my pain. The medicine proved so potent that I was launched upon a series of hallucinatory episodes.

Before reading on you must know this much about hallucinations: They are amorphous, free-spirited, unpredictable; dreams that have gone beyond the boundaries of dreams; fantasy torn from its terrestrial mooring; phantasmagoria unloosed.

Hallucinations are not observable of time. They move in and out of centuries with ease. They are above and apart from geographical alignments and natural configurations. They wave an invisible wand and whoever is summoned to appear steps forth with alacrity.

Hallucinations insinuate themselves so convincingly in the psyches of the actors that truth is revealed as openly as the garments appear to the eye.

The narrator is seen only by the other figure; otherwise he or she (or it) is only a spirit voice. If you turn to look for the narrator your only sensation will be that of the wind upon the back of your neck.

Someone once asked me to define folklore. "Folklore," I replied, hoping to sound wise, "is the soul of history."

Still hoping to sound wise, I will define historical hallucination as the soul of folklore. And now:

Mural in Oregon's state capitol rotunda at Salem shows the Lewis and Clark expedition at Celilo Falls, on the Columbia River.

Courtesy State of Oregon

1

At the water's edge the deerskin party had halted, their canoes sighing in the hush-lap of the river after a stiff run upstream.

"Captain Lewis," I said. "You are a man of vision. What do you see here in two centuries?"

The red-haired Meriwether Lewis squatted on the bank and looked long at the river. "I'm glad I came when I did," he replied, and returned to silence.

A moment later there was a shout from the shore. "We eat well tonight!" cried Patrick Gass, holding aloft two large salmon. "An' there'll be more soon!"

Lewis swiveled to look up at me. "You asked me what I see. I see a river without salmon."

Sacagawea, hearing the translation, turned in fright to Clark. "What will my people eat?" she asked tremulously. "How will they live?"

William Clark looked beyond her. "How?" he asked bitterly.

Lewis arose, his face sad. "Gaze about you," he directed. "The river will be crowded. The people will come and they will break the river to their short-sighted will. They will build a Saint Louis here and the river will become prisoner to it."

For a moment Lewis said nothing further, then went on: "The skies will flash with great metal birds. The tall buildings will not be happy. There will be more guns in an acre of street than we have in our entire company. There will be afflictions here of a hundred kinds, and every cry of anguish. Look beyond the banks, the hills. There is room for a million people to pitch their tents, each affording privacy. But men and women and children such as we will break the law if they sleep nights on the grass."

"The grass belongs to the Great Spirit!" Sacagawea cried. "Who denies to the people what the Great Spirit has given?"

"The Great Spirit will be a fur pelt, to be fought over and merchandised," Lewis said grimly.

There was a long pause. Then Clark suggested, "This place does not bring joy to my heart. Let us find a further place."

"There is no further place," Lewis said simply.

2

There stood upon my porch a squat man with deep chest, a grizzled beard, powerful-looking arms, and bright dark eyes.

"Mornin' scout," the man bellowed. "Hear ye been scribblin' 'bout me. I'm Joe Meek."

I gestured him into the house and he seated himself cross-legged on the carpet.

"So!" he began, with bountiful timbre. "You have been tellin' tales 'bout old Joe." And his laughter warmed the room on that chill autumn morning.

Joe Meek
Courtesy Oregon Historical Society

"You told an awful lot of tales yourself," I responded amiably.

"An' now you're back to repeatin' 'em," he teased, his voice softer.

"I could never write as many as you told to Frances Fuller Victor," I said.

He threw back his head and laughed. "That pore sweet lady," he clucked, "I didn' ponder she took 'em serious-like. I got to storyin' an' she got to writin' an' we jest kept goin'. Didn' reckon she'd turn it all into a book. Big fat book, too. You read it?"

"Every word," I said, "and she made you a knight in shining armor."

"That pore sweet woman," he sighed.

"No more tall stories, Joe," I said firmly. "Come straight with me. You were a Mountain Man."

He nodded soberly. "I was."

"Was it an adventurous life? Was it romantic? Was it really that glamorous? Square with me," I implored.

Joe fixed his coal eyes upon me. "I tell you," he said, "it was a hongry life. Times when I woud've eatin' grasshoppers and dead snakes if they was any around. Times when I was down to rags. Times the Injuns came an inch from takin' my topknot. Times I was so by myself I could'a took up with a porcupine."

"But there were good times, good friends," I insisted.

"There be," he conceded factly. "The shootin' an' the dancin' an' drinkin' and the racin' an' the games at rendeevoo. An' the friends. Most gone. Killed, drowned, or the mountin' fever got 'em, or starved out. Took to guidin' all these pilgrims out here, took to farmin', runnin' stores, blacksmithin', that kind o' thing."

"But not you," I said. "Why not blacksmithing or running a store or really running a farm?"

"Work an' me never made it right," he chuckled. "Jest

couldn' git along. Had a farm but jist never could git aroun'
to farmin'. The chillun done that. As a young buck I couldn'
stay put. Had to be on the move, always on the move."

"But wasn't trapping work? In the cold streams? In the
winter blizzards?"

"Waren't work then." Joe replied quietly, "Or maybe a
kind o' work that suited my temper. Waren't the daily grind,
with some booshway lookin' over your shoulder."

"What was the best thing that ever happened to you?" I
asked.

Joe's face lit up, as though the incadescence of his soul
had awakened. "Virginia," he grinned proudly. "Named her
after my state. Left thar when I was'n more'n a boy, lookin'
at it now. Don' care what the preachers say, she's my wife.
Whar we met, in mountain country, I married her, good an'
true. She's all Nez Perce. Bunch a kids, fine as good cider.
Virginia raised 'em proper. Would fight a bar fer that fam'ly.

"These bible-poundin' settlers say I'm too Christian fer
Virginia, me bein' white an' all that," Joe continued. "Truth
is, Virginia's the good un. Never know'd a woman like her.
I'm the lucky un."

"What's life been all about, Joe?" I asked. "Why these
fancy stories and all that put-on stuff?"

Joe stared at his ankles. "I jest had a hankerin' to be
somebody," he said in his still soft southern tongue.

3

Even though he leaned on his cane he towered above me,
as his spirit seemed to tower over all the land. Beneath the
mass of white hair laying as snow atop a craggy granite
monolith, his deep-set eyes burned fiercely, though no rising
emotion fueled it.

"It was all business!" John McLoughlin boomed in his
rich Irish-Scottish speech. "Are you looking for tales of

Dr. John McLoughlin (October 19, 1784-September 3, 1857) from a tintype probably taken by D H Hendee or Joseph Buchtel in 1853 or 1854.

romance, of adventure, of patriotism? Bah! It was follow the dollar all down the line."

The Chief Factor of Hudson's Bay Company stood where the gate to Fort Vancouver had been. "Business," he repeated. "That's what started the Company. That's why it battled the Norwesters. That's why Parliament joined the Norwesters to the Company. Business. Profits."

"What about your dealings with the Indians?" I asked. "Wasn't that being humanitarian?"

McLoughlin humphed, "Why kill off people when it's profitable to co-opt them? Anyway, I had a bond with the Indians. My first wife was Chippewa. Margaret, my wife of forty-six years, was part Red River Cree. The Indians were people. I knew my place and they knew theirs. They profited, the Company profited. It was good business."

"Your kindness to the settlers," I said. "Was that all business?"

McLoughlin's cape fluttered in the Columbia breeze. "Of course," he replied with a tinge of irritation. Inwardly I retreated, fearing a cloudburst of his well-known "Irish temper," but he caught himself and proceeded slowly.

"I must confess," he said, "I did not believe the Yankees could cross the mountains in wagons. When I heard the report that they were on their way to the Pacific Coast I promptly advised my officers at the fort to disregard the rumors. When I was told that a wagon party had actually crossed the last range of mountains, I went out to visit them. I wanted to see what these daring, exceptional people looked like. When I had convinced myself that they were ordinary people and that millions like them were beyond the Mississippi and that a good number of them would move West, I knew it was only a matter of time before the reign of Hudson's Bay Company here was ended. So it was. Two decades. So many newcomers in so short a time."

"And your kindness?" I urged.

"Some of the Yankees came here penniless," he explained. "No food, no supplies. Starving people make poor customers. I put them on their feet and they, in turn, traded with Hudson's Bay Company. That is, until the Yankees set up their own enterprises. Some of the people never paid me back, not as much as a cent. Well, that's business, too, I suppose.

"I could see that the range of business had to be extended to keep a step ahead of the Yankees," McLoughlin went on, "so I betook myself to the falls at Oregon City and acquired land and built a mill. I invested in a Yankee scheme to bring cattle to this country. Then, realizing I could not beat the Yankees, I joined them, leaving Fort Vancouver and building a house in Oregon City."

"So you came out well," I concluded.

"Not so, not so," the great man continued, his voice now rueful. "Property was taken from me, by force, and the courts, and legislation. I was called greedy by those I had put on their feet and my faith was maligned. What in thunder has Catholicism to do with business? Business knows no religion; it is its own religion; that should be a first lesson of history."

"You had a mighty adversary in Jason Lee," I suggested.

McLoughlin sighed. "Ah, Lee, Lee. I won the battle and he won the war. My differences with Lee weren't because he was a Methodist missionary. I couldn't have cared less. It was a business quarrel. Lee wanted to drive Hudson's Bay Company out of the region, to take away our business. Strange, isn't it," McLoughlin said through tight lips, "that he should die in Canada. But in the end I won, too—a citizen of Oregon City, an American."

"And now," I said, "the old enemies are united in the Statuary Hall of Fame of the Capitol in Washington, DC: McLoughlin and Lee—the two representatives of the State of Oregon."

The probable home of Dr. John McLoughlin. The original of this
photo, taken about 1860, long after Dr. McLoughlin had left the post,
is in the Royal Engineer Archives, Brampton Barracks, England.

Courtesy National Parks Service

McLoughlin roared in laughter. "The businessman and the
preacher! Well, that tells you something about history."

4

Draped in black, her face a mask of age set in its final
mold, she sat in a rocking chair, her bony hands plaited.

"You must talk louder," said Abigail Scott Duniway. "My
hearing isn't as sharp as it was."

"I have come to ask you a question," I began.

Abigail Scott Duniway
Courtesy Oregon Historical Society

She fixed her heavily lidded eyes upon me, eyes that did not interpret feeling.

"You are the great woman who is hailed as the champion of women's suffrage in Oregon. Did the vote fulfill your dreams?"

She drew a lace handkerchief from her sleeve and touched it to her nose. "It is a difficult question," she replied tiredly. "You know," and her voice rose, "it was my husband who encouraged me to go after the vote. He convinced me that if women had the vote a lot of social and economic problems would be solved. I don't know . . ." and her voice trailed off.

I waited until she was ready to speak again. Eventually she did.

"The vote for women was necessary. It was long overdue. I would have done the same thing over again. But then . . ." and her head swayed sadly.

"It was ridiculous to think that all women act for good. No, the vote for women didn't make a better world. The vote didn't moralize women. I dread what I see and hear."

Her face tightened until the blood ran out and her fingers were the hue of ivory. "Love treated as cheap as dime store merchandise, children abandoned, divorce on every block, dope, drunkedness, are these the fruits of my struggle for women?"

"Abigail," I ventured, "have women in politics satisfied you?"

"Not all," she replied tersely. "Not all at all." And she bit out bitterly, "When I see what some of these women politicians are doing, I know that women are their own worst enemies."

I touched her hand, cold at the knuckles. "So wise a woman, history remembers you," I said.

"Not so wise," she interrupted.

"What have you learned?" I asked.

A tight smile squeezed between her frozen lips. "That there is more to life than having the vote," she said.

5

At the foot of the Pueblo Mountains I, the wanderer without home, spread my gnawed tarp on the sere sage beneath a wildrose slope and curled up to sleep.

Morning came in a salmon filet sky. I laced my shoes, took some stale crackers from my pack, stretched my arms to start another day, and started south. But I had taken only a dozen steps when a boil of dust simmered to reveal the form of a man.

"Hello, stranger," he greeted cheerfully. I could tell at once that he was an Indian. His black locks and copper skin attested to that.

"Good morning," I replied.

He approached until we stood only a foot apart and when he stopped his eyes searched mine.

"I take it you have not had breakfast," he said. He appeared to be about forty though he might look that way at sixty.

"A few crackers," I answered dryly.

"Then we must eat," he said. "Come with me." And he led the way through the wasteland to a large cottonwood tree nourished by a clear brook. Along the way neither of us said a word but when we came to the brook I exclaimed, "I did not know there was water here."

He smiled and gestured to the earth. I sat and he squatted a few feet away.

"What is your name?" he invited, as he began removing food from his pack.

I told him.

"Ah," he mused, bearing my name on his tongue. "Are you by chance Jewish?"

"Yes," I replied, somewhat defiantly, suspicious of his consideration.

"Ah!" he cried, slapping his hands together sharply. "We

are lantsmen. My name is Four Feathers Perlstein. Sholom Aleichem."

"Aleichem Sholom," I replied, bewildered.

"Here," he said, "I have a treat for you. Matzahs."

Stunned for a moment I asked him to tell me how he, an Indian, was Jewish.

"Why not Jewish?" he fired back with a smile. "Indians are Catholics, Methodists, Baptists, so on. Why not Jewish? But you want to hear the story, so I will tell you.

"The story began a hundred years ago," he started, as he laid out for me an orange, a banana, a chunk of cheese, and two hard boiled eggs, and poured me a cup of milk.

A hot flash of pink arose above a gully to the east and jetted toward an icicle blue cloud retreating over the Pueblos. "It will be a warm day," said Four Feathers, "but here we will be cool. And now I will tell you the story."

Sitting cross-legged he began his tale:

"My people are the Chitigla, an offshoot of the Paiute. We have lived many generations in a land that had no name for long but is now called Abraham Valley. It is pleasant, abundant. Few people know of it. No roads enter. Only trails lead into it. Our commerce is by horse and mule.

"There came into our land one day a stranger out of nowhere. He was a big man, with broad shoulders, dressed in deerskin, and on his head he wore a yamulka. This he kept on every day the rest of his life, except in winter he put a beaverskin hat over it.

"Here, I have mine with me, but I use it only for prayer," and he drew the black skullcap from the breast pocket of his doeskin shirt.

"The stranger told us his name was Isadore Perlstein and that he was a Mountain Man and had ventured off the path while looking for beaver streams. He said he would stay only overnight but the next morning he announced that he had found the people of his dream, true Israelites, both gentle and fierce, and that he would remain if the people would accept him.

"The elders came together in council and agreed to let him be joined to us. So he stayed, building for himself a house made of trees on the Trout Creek Mountains, planting, hunting, learning our language, teaching us English and Hebrew. He married a Chitigla woman and she begot him five children. My great-grandmother was the sister of Rachel Soft Plum, Isadore's wife, so I am his great-grandnephew. But by the time he became a father he had a new name, Coyote Calls.

"Slowly the Chitigla adopted the Hebrew faith. Slowly, through Coyote Call's wisdom and force of conviction he arose in status. He persuaded the Chitigla to send those children whom he had taught to schools outside. But we all returned to Abraham Valley.

"Coyote Calls built a synagogue, with the roof being the branches of our largest tree. He taught us the holidays. He showed our women how to make gefilte fish and knadels. And matzohs, of course. Take some more. I am glad you like them.

"Isadore Coyote Calls lived a long and beautiful life," Four Feathers continued. "He was almost a hundred when the Great Spirit took him. He was carried to the top of Sholomo Peak, where a Star of David was placed over his grave."

We talked all day. Late in the afternoon Four Feathers arose. "You must join us for the evening prayer. I will go now and bring eight of our brothers, so we will have a minyen."

I waited until nightfall but he did not return. I slept there, by the brook. In the morning I moved on.

6

She waltzed gingerly off the dance floor and into the velvet summer night, the train of music pinned to her calico skirt. I followed her compact figure, generating energy with every movement. Outside the Grange hall she straddled carefree one end of a teeter-totter. Following her lead, I took the other end.

"I came across the Oregon Trail in the early years," said Nettie Huddleston as the moon found an opening in the branches of the oak tree that covered us and revealed the brown glint of her eyes. "I was a girl but three-quarters of the journey yet to go my mother died and I became the woman of the family, with two little brothers and two baby sisters to care for, and I only ten.

"When we reached Oregon I helped build the cabin and I did all the cooking and the washing and the hauling of water and firewood and the mending and the planting of a garden and the feeding of chickens and the pigs and the milking of the goat and the mothering of the children.

"I've read a lot of stories about how romantic the travel to Oregon was. Hogwash! It was hot and cold, disease, death, boredom. And Lord, the mean things and the selfishness, as much those as the kind and giving. You have to understand this: the emigrants were people just like you see on the sidewalks of any city, all kinds. Driving a team of oxen didn't make them better or worse. If they were saints or sinners at home they were the same on the trail. And when they landed in Oregon they hadn't changed."

Nettie Huddleston paused and smiled impishly. "I did learn a pretty song or two on the Oregon Trail and one, sung to me by our guide, a tobacco-chewing Mountain Man, that was awfully wicked. Would you like to hear it?"

"Please," I said.

"Later," she said pungently. "I want to tell you first how it was here.

"I was thirteen when Pa remarried, to the widow Fellows. A month after I started to menstruate a distant neighbor came to the door and introduced himself. He was three times as old as I was and I didn't know him but when he asked Pa's permission to marry me, Pa agreed, and that's the way it was. Pa had replaced me with a wife and Harrison, the neighbor, had got himself a bride and doubled his land claim at the same time.

"I didn't change jobs. I changed locations, that was all. And at fifteen I became a mother. By the time I was twenty I had three children. Then Harrison took ill and died."

She frowned into the moonlight. "A widow at twenty," she said ruefully. "Deep into life when I should have been starting it.

"A year later I married Ogden. It was his third marriage. His first two wives had died, one on the trail, one drowned at home. I sometimes wonder if she drowned herself.

"Ogden was twice my age—and he was cruel. I should never have married him but I needed a man. A woman alone in that lonely country, with three little ones. I should have left him after I saw how cruel he was, but where was I to go? Pa couldn't take me in; he had the four young ones and three of his wife's children, and struggling to squeeze out a livelihood.

"I started my second marriage with seven children, three of my own and four of Ogden's. In the next six years I had five children by Ogden. I begged him to stop. He wouldn't hear of it. I was tired of child bearing. I would have done anything to prevent more children. God knows what my fate would have been if Ogden hadn't fallen off a horse and got himself killed. I wept the day he died, but they were tears of joy.

"Ogden's children went to his sister, his family wanted it that way though we all got along fine. I was thirty when I married for the third time. Thirty—and eight children.

Huddleston was a merchant of forty and lived in town, and for the first time I had some comfort. Huddleston married me to mother his six children by his first wife, who had died two years before. He was a good man and kind to me, and I made him a good home. I always earned my keep. I bore two children until I told him I would kill myself if I became pregnant again. I understand, he said, and that was that. It broke my heart when he died at sixty.

"I had a good many chances to marry again, but why should I? Huddleston had left me his business, the children were grown up. I was at fifty what I should have been at thirty, an independent woman. I didn't begin to live until I was middle-aged.

"If you believe the stories of pioneer days, it was the men who faced the greatest danger and were most at risk of death. Hogwash! Read the statistics, read the histories. You see a lot more widowers than widows. It was the woman who gave out first. I was an exception.

"So much hogwash!" blazed Nettie, gripping her end of the teeter-totter. "Life wasn't roses and cream. Not for the women. You bet! What romance was there in their life? Breeding machines, that's all they were for a lot of men. The men could have used a few books on sex. I wasn't fulfilled until my third husband."

I thought I heard her weeping but it could have been the wind, rubbing as a cat does, against the oak.

"There were some good times," said Nettie suddenly, brightly. "A dance in the Waldo Hills, a picnic at Silverton, a barnraising at Lewisburg, splashing barefoot in the creek, running with the children through the tall grass . . ." Her voice trailed into "a few good times."

We teeter-tottered to the creak of the wood and the bagpipe of the wind until the strains of "After the Ball is Over" drifted from the Grange hall.

"Let's go back to the dance," chirped Nettie, bouncing up.

She stopped me at the door, so she could see me better in the light.

"You're not bad-looking," she said with a spark of her eye and a toss of her chin. "If I was eighty years younger I'd give you a tumble."

Has It Really Been That Long?

Tacked to a wall of my dining room, which I have not used for eating for many years, are, among Sierra Club posters, calendars from half a dozen nations, and miniaturized prints of Degas and Utrillo, snapshots of my three grandchildren, my daughter at various birthdays, the dogs I have had, and, midway between a polar bear nursing her cub and a Vietnamese boy riding a water buffalo, a snapshot of a neatly dressed, raven-haired, smiling young woman and a rumpled, blonde, grinning young man.

The young lady's name then was Phoebe Lopatin; the young man was me, Ralph Friedman. The date was August 5, 1948, and the picture was taken only a few minutes after we met.

The place was Washington, DC. The occasion for our being there was to protest an administration policy which both of us felt would jeopardize the civil liberties of our nation. Phoebe was then working for Consumers Union in New York and was shop chairperson of her group. I was a merchant seaman on the beach. My union was on strike and I was a picket-line captain and head of the speaker's bureau.

One day, down at the union hall, the port agent said to me, "One of the guys who was supposed to go to Washington tomorrow with the union delegation can't make it. Can you take his place?" "Sure," I said. "I think it's an important issue."

I did not see Phoebe on the train going down or at the demonstration in front of the White House. After we disbanded, a union buddy and I were walking down a street when I spotted this lovely, brown-eyed, raven-haired lady resting on a government lawn. Impulsively I said to my friend, "This is the girl I am going to marry. Take our picture." And I reached for the camera she was carrying.

I saw her home that night and thereafter we were together as often as possible, though I never took her to a picket line, which could get scary.

Endless responsibilities, nights in a freezing room at the Brooklyn YMCA, one small meal a day, and insufficient clothing in the chill autumn of Red Hook put me in a navy hospital for eleven weeks. Phoebe came often, bringing me chicken soup. (Penicillin hadn't worked.)

We were married a week after I came out of the hospital. The wedding took place at city hall. The ceremony lasted about two minutes. The clerk rattled off something I could not follow and asked for the fee. (I think it was two dollars.) Phoebe was wearing her best dress. I wore the suit I had on when the snapshot near the White House was taken. By now a big patch covered the bottom, where the pants had worn out.

That night I came down sick again. Phoebe cried. But this time penicillin worked and soon, with the strike settled, I found a job on a luxury liner for a four-month, round-the-world cruise. Phoebe wrote to every port, and I returned with enough wages to start us west.

We traveled by bus to Chicago, bought a 1942 Chevy, and drove to an old gold mining camp on the westward flank of the Sierra. There we began the difficult life of trying to survive through writing and photography.

We lived together, through sunshine and storm, for more than thirty-four years, until cancer took her August 12, 1983, a week after the thirty-fifth anniversary of our first meeting. She did not have the chance to see the book I dedicated to her or, more importantly, her first grandchild.

Phoebe and Ralph—the day they met.
Ralph Friedman Collection

This lovely girl with an arm full of notebooks and newspapers, this tousled boy with his uneasy audacity. Whatever happened to them? Was it really real? How young and beautiful they were.

Index